PRAISE FOR
OWN YOUR TIME

"Money is a tool for independence and partnership. In *Own Your Time*, Andy Hill offers families a modern framework for building wealth, sharing responsibility, and creating generational change."

—**Tori Dunlap**, author of the *New York Times* bestseller *Financial Feminist* and host of the Financial Feminist podcast

"Simple, evidence-based investing has the power to transform lives. In *Own Your Time*, Andy Hill delivers a practical and heartfelt roadmap for families to achieve financial independence—not just to grow wealth, but to reclaim their most precious asset: time."

—**Paul Merriman**, founder of Merriman Wealth Management and The Merriman Financial Education Foundation

"Most of us think of retirement as a cliff, one day you're working, the next day you're not. Andy Hill shows there's a middle path. *Own Your Time* is a practical framework for scaling back, finding balance, and enjoying life now."

—**Paula Pant**, host of the Afford Anything podcast

"Andy Hill's *Own Your Time* is a precious gift to all who seek clarity and meaning in their financial lives. The author identifies crucial priorities, then guides the reader gently toward satisfying solutions to their financial dilemmas. His advice is sound, sage, and timeless. A book which should be read and re-read for maximum impact."

—**William P. Bengen**, author of *A Richer Retirement: Supercharging the 4% Rule to Spend More and Enjoy More*

"We often mistake success at work for success in life, but Andy Hill's *Own Your Time* reminds us that money and professional accomplishments should be means to a greater purpose. This book is a practical guide for designing a life focused on what matters most."

—**Simone Stolzoff**, author of *The Good Enough Job* and *How to Not Know*

"Walking away from the corporate grind takes courage and planning. In *Own Your Time*, Andy Hill shows families how FU Money and Coast FIRE can open the door to a freer, more intentional life."

—**Jamila Souffrant**, author of *Your Journey to Financial Freedom* and host of the Journey to Launch podcast

"Success is not about titles or climbing the corporate ladder. Andy Hill's *Own Your Time* shows families how to step away from roles that don't serve them and embrace the freedom to live fully as parents and partners."

—**Julien & Kiersten Saunders**, authors of *Cashing Out*

OWN YOUR TIME

OWN
YOUR
TIME

**10 FINANCIAL STEPS TO PUT YOUR FAMILY FIRST
AND ESCAPE THE CORPORATE GRIND**

ANDY HILL

WILEY

The manufacturer's authorized representative according to the EU General Product Safety Regulation is Wiley-VCH GmbH, Boschstr. 12, 69469 Weinheim, Germany, e-mail: Product_Safety@wiley.com.

Trademarks: Wiley and the Wiley logo are trademarks or registered trademarks of John Wiley & Sons, Inc. and/or its affiliates in the United States and other countries and may not be used without written permission. All other trademarks are the property of their respective owners. John Wiley & Sons, Inc. is not associated with any product or vendor mentioned in this book.

For general information on our other products and services or for technical support, please contact our Customer Care Department within the United States at (800) 762-2974, outside the United States at (317) 572-3993 or fax (317) 572-4002.

Wiley also publishes its books in a variety of electronic formats. Some content that appears in print may not be available in electronic formats. For more information about Wiley products, visit our web site at www.wiley.com.

Library of Congress Cataloging-in-Publication Data has been applied for:

Print ISBN: 9781394342778
ePDF ISBN: 9781394342792
Epub ISBN: 9781394342785

Cover Design: Paul McCarthy Cover Art: By Shutterstock AI
Printed and bound by CPI Group (UK) Ltd, Croydon, CR0 4YY

C9781394342778_221125

To Nicole, Zoey, and Calvin.
Thank you for inspiring everything in this book.
Andy (aka Dad)

CONTENTS

CONTENTS

INTRODUCTION

" Is the jar full?" asked the teacher as she stood in front of her class displaying a glass container with rocks in it.

"Yes," replied the class in unison as the jar clearly looked chock full of rocks.

The teacher then poured dozens of pebbles into the same jar. Since these pebbles were smaller than the rocks, they found their way into different gaps in the glass jar. She continued to pour the pebbles and even shook the jar to be sure there was no free space left. The glass jar was now jam packed with rocks and pebbles all the way to the top. She then asked her class the same question: "Is the jar full?"

The class, starting to grow more interested, exclaimed, "Yes!"

She then took out another container with sand and began pouring that into the glass jar with the rocks and pebbles in it. Sand immediately filled the smallest spaces of the jar surrounding the rocks and pebbles.

One final time, the teacher inquired, "Is the jar full?"

Laughing and smiling, the students all agreed, "Yes!"

The teacher went on to explain, "The glass jar represents your life and the time you have on this planet. And the rocks represent the most important priorities of our lives. One rock represents your health, another might be your family, your spirituality and another represents your friends and community."

"The pebbles symbolize other priorities like work, school and hobbies."

"And finally the sand represents material possessions like clothes, cars or phones."

"By filling up the jar with rocks then pebbles then sand, we are ensuring our time is prioritized for the most important things in our lives."

"Now if we were to do this in reverse order, sand then pebbles then rocks, we would find that there isn't much space or time for your most important priorities."

"This is why it's so important to own your time and put the big rocks in first. Take care of your health and leave space for quality time with family and friends. The pebbles and sand will make their way into your life for sure, but they shouldn't be your top priority."

This story has been told dozens of times and in countless different ways. It is a parable that has resonated with me for years as I've navigated how I'm spending my time on this big blue marble.

While it has a beautiful message and can be easily understood, I believe it leaves out one key ingredient: money.

Many of us would love to spend more time focused on our health, family, and friends while working less, but we can't afford it. Our lifestyles are so expensive that making time for the most important things in life feels impossible.

Millions of Americans are living paycheck to paycheck, leaving little room for the prospect of financial freedom let alone financial security. And this isn't just those of us who aren't making enough money. Forty-nine percent of those surveyed making $100,000 or more are living paycheck to paycheck.[1] This financial situation turns small mishaps into big anxiety-inducing emergencies. Instead of moving toward the things that matter, we're pushing ourselves further away from them.

Anxiety and uneasiness have seeped into the lives of parents as well. The US surgeon general released an advisory that points out that "41% of parents say that most days they are so stressed they cannot function, and

48% say that most days their stress is completely overwhelming compared to other adults ..."[2] Two major stressors that stood out in the surgeon general's advisory report are financial strain and time demands. According to the parents surveyed, there just isn't enough time available and not enough money to go around.

The feelings that these parents surveyed are experiencing isn't fiction. Mothers worked an average of 20.9 hours per week in 1985 compared to 26.7 hours per week in 2022. And fathers worked an average of 39.8 hours per week in 1985 compared to 41.2 hours per week in 2022.

While things have definitely changed over those decades, one thing that has not changed is the amount of time in a week. We got 168 hours in 1985, and we get 168 hours today. Not only are parents working more, they are spending more as well.

Even though wages have outpaced inflation over that same period, our lifestyles have inflated. The average home is getting bigger. What once was "enough home" isn't enough anymore. The average size of a home in 1985 was 1,650 square feet[3] compared to 2,299 square feet in 2022.[4] Larger homes require more upkeep, maintenance, and updates. In other words, they require more time and money, two resources parents don't have a lot of lately.

While we were expanding our homes over the past few decades, we also expanded our idea of the "ideal" engagement ring, wedding party, honeymoon, vehicle, outfit, phone, baby shower, children's after school activity, and family vacation at the same time. As the desire for these possessions and things (ahem, pebbles and sand) grew, our time and space for the important things (the rocks) became more difficult to fit into our life (jar).

I'm sharing these statistics and details with you because I'm a living, breathing embodiment of these statistics. I know what it's like to fill the jar with too much sand and pebbles and not enough rocks.

Straight out of college, I pursued what I thought was the "American Dream." I jumped right into my 40- to 50-hour workweek, bought a house, and leased a luxury car at the ripe young age of 22 years old.

In the beginning, I thought I was doing the right thing and making strides in my adult life. Quickly I realized that I was not only working for my employer for 40–50 hours a week; I was "working" for the mortgage company and the luxury car company too. When I wasn't working for my employer, I tended to my 60-year-old house. Paying bills, fixing my roof, cutting grass, meeting with appliance repair technicians, and visiting Home Depot way too often took up a lot of my spare time. This home truly felt like it owned me instead of the other way around. With the little money I had left over, I would send it to the luxury car company for their monthly payment. Evidently, looking good trumped feeling good in my twenties. The debt began to pile up. This was a period in my life where I did not own my time.

As I approached my thirties, I found some opportunities to increase my salary substantially. I went from earning an average of $42,500 in my twenties to earning $180,000 in my thirties. These pay increases definitely increased my quality of life overall, but they did come with massive trade-offs of my time. My workweek went up to 50–60 hours per week, and my physical and mental health started to become impacted. I went on medication for stress-induced acne. My cholesterol increased to the point where my doctor recommended additional medication to reduce the risk of heart issues. With more money came more pressure to improve my wardrobe, car, home, and even the restaurants I ate at.

This was all around the same time I met my wife and became a father. My mind and heart desperately wanted to spend most of my waking hours with my beautiful new family, but the realities of my workweek demanded something very different. My career in event marketing required long hours away from home either at the office or at events across the country. And if I wasn't hitting my sales goals at work, I wouldn't be earning the money I needed to keep up the lifestyle we were accustomed to. At least, that's how I felt at the time. The pebbles and sand were taking over. This too was a period in my life where I did not own my time.

In this era of young fatherhood, I started to become more interested in personal finance. My wife and I were good at making money as employees, but honestly, we lacked the knowledge on how to make our money work for us. One night I was watching *The Suze Orman* show. She had a segment called "How Am I Doing?" where she analyzed people's financial situations and gave them a letter grade A through F. One term that kept coming up was "net worth." Honestly, I had no idea what it meant, but given our six-figure combined income as a couple, I was unfoundedly confident that our net worth was huge and we were rich.

My wife and I decided to write out our net worth on a big whiteboard in our guest room. Assets (all the stuff we owned) on one side and liabilities (all the stuff we owed) on the other. After totaling our assets and subtracting them from our liabilities, we found out we weren't rich. We actually had a negative net worth of −$50,000. We owed more than we owned.

This epiphany moment made me realize that we were spending a lot of our time and money making other people rich. We were working too many hours in careers we both didn't enjoy and earning too much money to have nothing left to show for it. Something had to change.

Through some "spirited marital compromise," we agreed to utilize more of our money to create time freedom in our lives—for both of us. If money had the ability to change our lives for the better, then we were ready to make it happen.

This time freedom mission required some difficult changes in the beginning. Going from spending most of what we earned to spending less was challenging. Money fights, embracing new, less expensive hobbies, and saying "no" more often to family and friends when we didn't have the time or money available was really hard. But we knew by saying "no" to one path in life, we were saying "yes" to another better path: a life that gives us more time with our kids, more time to take care of our health, and more quality time with each other.

Let's fast forward to today in our forties. My wife and I both work around 20–25 hours per week in careers that we actually enjoy. I'm a solopreneur serving as a family finance coach and financial educator. And my wife works as an aesthetician after returning to school for a full career reboot.

Our relationship with our two children (now 11 and 13 years old) is everything we would have dreamed. We're both present parents who get to spend time watching the important moments of their lives unfold. Throughout their childhood, I've had the space and margin to volunteer as a soccer coach and PTO (Parent Teacher-Organization) treasurer.

My health has never been better. I'm spending more time exercising, eating healthy, and leaving space for connection with my wife, my parents, and friends.

I have honestly never been happier in my entire life. We went from full-time working and to full-time living.

Today, I own my time.

In this book, I'm going to share the details of how our family bought more of our time back. Not only will I be sharing our family's experience, but I'll be sharing the knowledge I've gained from interviewing more than 500 families on this very subject. These are work optional millionaire couples, financially independent families, and part-time solopreneurs who have cracked the code on owning their time.

In part one, we'll discuss the important step of making the commitment to change. This can be the most difficult step in the process of owning your time. We'll review how to define the life you want to live and how you and your partner can make it happen.

In part two, we'll chart the path of family wealth building. Because with family wealth, you gain the ability to create more family options. We'll review investing, complete debt freedom, and the process of preparing for your departure from the 50- to 60-hour workweek.

And last but not least, in part three, we'll review the destination of time freedom. If you're like me, you've never experienced this amount of personal time and options in your adult life. We're going to discuss how to make the most of it and how to protect it for decades to come.

This is our chance to completely empty out that glass jar representing your available time and start fresh. With financial strength and security, we can say "yes" to more quality time with family and friends and "yes" to a healthy long-lasting life filled with purpose and happiness.

Carpe diem!

NOTES

1. Martin, E. J. and Gage, S. (2023). *72% of higher earners are in credit card debt for at least a year: What is the best way to attack your credit card debt?* [Online]. Bankrate. Available at: https://www.bankrate.com/credit-cards/news/highearners-in-debt/
2. Health and Human Services. (2024). *Parents under pressure.* Author. Available at: https://www.hhs.gov/sites/default/files/parents-under-pressure.pdf
3. Riggs, A. (2016). *Size of homes: 1980's was bigger is better & 2000–2010's is similar and steady* [Online]. Available at: https://www.nar.realtor/blogs/economists-outlook/size-of-homes-1980-s-was-bigger-is-better-2000-2010-s-is-similar-and-steady
4. Borrelli, L. (2024). *What's the average square footage of a house?* [Online]. Bankrate. Available at: https://www.bankrate.com/real-estate/average-square-feet-of-a-house/

PART 1

COMMIT TO A BETTER FAMILY LIFE

CHAPTER ONE

DEFINE THE LIFE YOU WANT TO LIVE

"Begin with the end in mind."

– Stephen Covey

emento mori.

*M*This Latin phrase has been adopted by many who adhere to the stoic lifestyle. It translates to "remember you must die."

When I first heard this saying, it creeped me out. I thought, "Who wants to think about dying? And I'm young-ish. I'm not dying any time soon!"

As I looked into it further, this saying isn't meant to scare you. It's meant to inspire you.

Memento mori reminds us about the inevitability of death. We're all going to die someday. And when we look back on our lives when we're old and gray, are we going to be happy with how we've spent our time? Or are we going to be full of regrets for not living our lives to the fullest?

The concept of *memento mori* lights a fire under us to seize the day and begin living a life of purpose and meaning, a life that is defined on our terms with our personal happiness and fulfillment at the core.

That then begs the question: What kind of life do we want to live?

A lot of us launched into our careers, marriages, and parenthood with a vague idea of where we were headed. We saw our parents and our peers doing the same dance of life and followed their lead.

If you've picked up this book, you may be burned out, uninspired, or simply looking for a change.

Let's dive into the most important step of owning your time: defining the life you want to live.

CARVE OUT TIME TO DREAM

Dreaming is not something that comes naturally to many adults. We're so focused on taking care of the important tasks on our daily to-do list that we forget to take the time to dream.

When I was a kid, I remember having loads of free time to dream. Wandering in my backyard, riding my bike around the neighborhood, or writing in my notebook, I would think about what my life would be like.

My ideas around my "dream life" changed frequently during childhood. When I was a young guy, I wanted to be an NFL quarterback like Randall Cunningham from the Philadelphia Eagles. He could run the ball better than most NFL quarterbacks at the time and I thought that was pretty cool as an 80s/90s kid.

My parents supported my NFL dreams by signing me up for football when I was 7 years old. (Yes, we started early in Georgia.) Through some luck, support from my parents, and effort on my part, I was able to become a quarterback for the next 9 years of my life in Georgia and eventually Michigan. I had so much fun in that position and learned so much about the importance of teamwork and camaraderie.

As I got into my later years of high school in Michigan, I got beat out by some other taller, faster, and smarter quarterbacks who were a better fit for the job. I continued to enjoy high school football as a free safety and the team captain, but reality started to sink in that becoming an NFL quarterback (or playing in the NFL at all) probably wasn't going to be a part of my future.

Honestly, I wasn't that upset about my NFL dreams fading because I had found a new passion. With a youthful heart and plenty of free time, I had now set my sights on becoming a famous movie director. This was my new dream.

Iconic films like *Forrest Gump, Pulp Fiction,* and *Shawshank Redemption* inspired me to create my own movies. (Fun fact: All three of these movies were all in the theater at the same time in October 1994.)

After high school and football practice, I would spend hours in the video editing suite creating my own masterpieces. Our high school had an incredible video production department headed up by one of my favorite teachers, Steve Geresy. Movies, music videos, football highlight reels, and so much more were born in that edit suite.

I was so proud of all these video creations, and I made sure to give myself credit for each of the multiple roles I served in the video creation process. One video showcased my name in seven different roles as the writer, director, producer, editor, as well as several other important designations. Let's just say I was enjoying this new passion immensely, and my teenage self thought I deserved the credit!

My video production dream followed me into college at Michigan State where I got my bachelor's degree in media and communications. I learned from my professors about different ways to use my skills and passion for video production in the marketplace. My father worked in the automotive industry at the time, and he helped me get an internship at one of his video production partners when I was 19 years old. This experience helped me learn the type of video production I could do living in Michigan—not movies, not music videos, and not sports highlight films, but corporate automotive marketing videos.

The problem was I really wasn't interested in cars. Horsepower, torque, and zero-to-sixty speed were some of the most boring topics imaginable to me. But living in the Motor City, this is the type of video production business that was available. If I wanted to get a job, make money, and live near my family, then the corporate automotive life was the closest thing I could get to my dream life. So, I went for it.

All in all, my corporate automotive marketing career choice wasn't all that bad. It just wasn't all that good either. Working in marketing allowed me to pursue a lucrative career where I received progressive raises and promotions over the years. That helped me build wealth and security for myself and eventually for my wife and kids.

But pursuing money over meaning slowly started to drain my soul.

I felt like an empty shell showing up at the office every single day for years wondering if life was really supposed to feel like this forever.

My home life was wonderful. I found an amazing wife who always had my back. We created two incredible kids together. And we had a home where we all felt safe and happy.

My work life did not feel the same. I worked long hours doing work I didn't care about for people who didn't seem to respect themselves or their colleagues' well-being. This definitely was not the case for everyone I worked with. My life is blessed beyond belief based on many of the relationships I built during my corporate career. But the fact that this unignorable toxicity kept repeating itself over the years made it difficult to want to continue showing up for work every day.

Older executives bragged to me about cheating on their wives and the number of "side women" they had.

Managers would gauge their success (and mine) by how late we could stay at the office and how little sleep they got the night before. This meant working through illnesses and, in one unforgettable instance from a former colleague, ignoring the signs of a heart attack.

Working in client services, there were countless times where we were belittled and treated poorly, oftentimes for things that were completely out of our control. A client of mine berated me in front of my team for not quieting down a tropical bird who was audibly squawking during an important presentation by her CEO. The problem with her request was that the event, approved by the same CEO, was taking place at an actual bird sanctuary! I'm laughing now as I share this, but it was not funny at the time.

I felt lost, sad, and trapped. Lost on a path to nowhere. Sad to give most of my time to work and not enough of my time to family and friends. And trapped because I needed this job to pay for the life I had created for myself and my family.

The positive side to feeling this way was that I became motivated to find a way out. When you're down for so long, the only direction you can go is up.

I began seeking out sources of motivation so I could remember how to dream again. My dreaming muscle had atrophied due to lack of use after a decade plus in the corporate world.

At the recommendation of my brother-in-law, David, podcasts became my go-to source for motivation and inspiration. It was a fresh medium, and the space was filled with advice, stories, and guidance for people just like me.

I listened to countless stories of people who carved their own path, followed their passion, and created better lives for themselves. Those stories lit a fire inside me, and I started to feel alive again.

After finishing different episodes, I would take time to reflect on what I learned and observe which ideas resonated with me most.

Time was a rare resource at this point in my life so I had to find pockets where I could. Ten minutes here and there began accumulating into hours of dedicated time to dreaming and planning a better life.

I felt like a kid again. That same kid who dreamed of being an NFL player and a famous movie director was now planning the next stage of his life. I was feeling hopeful.

Hope is the spark that many of us need who feel lost, sad, and trapped in our careers. It's important to recognize that while this may be our current stage in life, it doesn't have to be our entire existence. We can make a change because we are in control.

Once we recognize change is possible, it's time to start dreaming about what is possible. Start by asking yourself some thought-provoking questions:

Scenario 1: You open up your mailbox and find a check for $5,000,000 with your name on it. No taxes, no fees, and no strings attached. This money is yours. What would you do? What would your day look like? How would you spend your time?

Scenario 2: A doctor tells you are going to die 1 month from now. How will you spend the next month? What do you do with your time? And who would you spend your remaining days with?

Scenario 3: You recently died, and someone is reading your obituary. What is written in that obituary that you feel proud of? What challenges did you have to overcome to make your best life possible?

Pause and take some time to read and answer these questions. This can be your moment of introspection. It can open up your eyes and heart to what is possible for your future.

For example, I'm going to jump into the way back machine and answer the questions from the first scenario as if I'm right in the midst of my hectic corporate career again. Taking a deep breath and here I go …

Scenario 1:	You open up your mailbox and find a check for $5,000,000 with your name on it. No taxes, no fees, and no strings attached. This money is yours. What would you do? What would your day look like? How would you spend your time?
Andy Hill:	I would immediately quit my job and thank my clients, colleagues, and supervisors for the opportunities they've provided me over the years. In all honesty, I was there for the money and not for the work. Since I don't need the money anymore, I'm out. Peace and best wishes.

After getting back 50–60 hours in my week, I would spend more of it with my young family. With two young kids at home, I'm missing a big part of their childhood, and it's eating me up inside knowing how quickly these years will fly by. My wife and I have grown further apart as my distaste for my corporate life expanded. I want to spend more quality time with her having fun, laughing, and making new memories … like it was when we first met.

I'd also focus more of my time on my health. As my career grew, my fitness routine tanked. Exercising, sleeping through the night, and cooking heart healthy food would earn more of my time.

I haven't hung out with my good friends in a long time. That would change right away. I would host more get-togethers and plan vacations with my friends and their families whenever possible.

For a portion of my week, I would give and serve others in my community through volunteer work or the development of a solopreneur business. Of course, my hours "working" would need to be limited because I have so many other incredible things going on in my life.

That sounds like a great life to me.

As you go through these scenarios, you may find a recurring theme. It's not a coincidence. It is who you are and what you feel you're missing.

This dreaming exercise should serve as a gentle reminder of what you value. These are your big rocks. And they need to find their way back into your jar of life. This becomes easier when you have a partner supporting you.

SHARE YOUR DREAMS WITH YOUR SPOUSE

Harvard has been conducting an incredible longitudinal study about happiness for the last 80 years. They follow, interview, and research people about their lives in hopes of answering questions about what makes for a happy life. Not only have they tracked the lives of individuals, but they've kept the study going with their children and their children's children.

Known as the *Harvard Study of Adult Development*, it is now considered the longest scientific study of happiness ever conducted.

I had the pleasure of interviewing Dr. Robert Waldinger, the director of the Harvard Study of Adult Development, on my podcast. As someone who has been pursuing a happier life, I cut right to the chase and asked him the conclusion of their 80-year study.

"Two things," shared Dr. Waldinger. "One won't be a surprise. If you take care of your health, it really matters. You'll live longer and feel better as you get older. The other thing we were surprised by was that the people who stayed the healthiest and lived the longest were the people who had the best relationships with other people."

The people with the happiest lives are those that have others to share their lives with. If you're reading this and you have a supportive spouse or partner, you are already winning. Nearly a century of research has shown that your relationship truly matters in terms of the quality of your life.

Achieving our goals and realizing our dreams can be difficult, but it can be easier with a supportive partner by your side. It can be more fun too.

After going through our thought-provoking scenarios, you now have a general idea of your personal dreams, goals, and values.

It's time to share those dreams with your partner. After all, your best life will be better if you're able to spend it with the love of your life. Harvard scientists say so.

These types of important discussions around life and money are best not to have in passing. Schedule a convenient time with your spouse where you are both able to relax, speak freely, and lack distractions. This can be really difficult with kids. As a father of two, I know this from experience.

Honor this get-together just as you would a doctor's appointment or an important work meeting. Put it on the calendar. Leave enough time for you to really open up and have a good conversation together.

If you're better at chatting with a beverage in your hand like I am, have this dream-sharing session over your morning coffee on a weekend. Or have the conversation with a glass of wine during a weekend happy hour.

Share your dreams, goals, and core values with your spouse. This may feel uncomfortable but lean into that discomfort. Doing something new and different with your life can feel radical, but the payoff can be radically life changing.

After you divulge your dreams to the love of your life, ask them to do the same to you. Prompt them by asking the same thought-provoking questions.

You may be surprised at what you learn. While you're seeking support from your partner, you will more than likely find ways to support them with their dreams in return.

Outside of the deeper thought-provoking questions, you can get more granular with your questions as well:

- Do you want to start your own business? If so, what type of business?
- Is there a desire to stay at home with the kids as they grow up?
- How are you enjoying your career? Do you see yourself there long term?
- Do you want to start a new career?
- Would working part-time feel more comfortable than working full-time?
- Is travel an important part of your future?
- What does your ideal retirement look like?

It's important that you stick to life enjoyment goals as opposed to numeric, money-focused goals. For some of us, the numeric goals like debt freedom, net worth milestones, or investment totals are motivating enough to move forward.

For others, they can sound like hollow destinations that require a lot of sacrifice with little payoff.

When I originally got excited about improving our family's financial situation, I latched onto our net worth number. That negative net worth just made me ache. Building a better life when we're in the hole financially was going to be tough. My first instinct to get out of that hole was to eliminate our debt. After all, it was easy to understand that eliminating our $50,000 of student loans and car debt would help us get to positive net worth territory.

In my amped up state, I proposed this idea to my wife after she returned from a busy day at work. It went a little something like this.

"Babe, I've got a great idea. Our net worth is −$50,000. If we eliminate our debt, we'll get into positive territory, and we'll be debt free (outside of our mortgage). To do this, we'll need to decrease our spending and save a lot more of our money each month in order to pay down the debt. It'll be a tough change, but it'll be worth it in the long run. What do you think?"

She stared at me in confusion like I had just delivered bad news in another language. Her face said, "That idea sounds horrible," but no words came out of her mouth. Before I knew it, she had retreated to our bedroom for some solace.

Shocked by her lack of interest in my brilliant financial plan, I wondered what I did wrong. Then it hit me. She just had a long day at work, and she's pregnant. The last thing she wants to hear about is enjoying her life less.

Also, my delivery was all wrong. I approached the conversation speaking from a numbers-focused mindset. The financial freedom I was trying to describe to her probably sounded more like financial deprivation.

It was time for a do-over. With my next attempt, I decided to approach the conversation from an emotional, dream-focused, and purposeful perspective.

Instead of cornering her at the door after getting home from a rough day at the office, I planned a more convenient time for both of us to talk, a moment where the stress of the workday wasn't ever present in our minds. We sat down on a relaxing weekend, enjoyed some pizza, and started to talk about our future together. We were newlyweds after all.

We started dreaming together. I asked her what her ideal working situation would be when our daughter arrived in the world. She told me that she'd eventually love to be a stay-at-home mom. Not being thrilled with her career choice and the pace and attention it requires, stepping away to focus on motherhood would be a dream scenario.

As we spoke about it further, her smile brightened up the room. She was picturing the luxury of not answering demanding client emails on the weekend, avoiding anxiety-inducing colleague drama, and spending her days focused on her new baby girl.

The conversation moved to our future home. I thought living in my bachelor pad with beer bottle decor was quite chic, but my wife was more interested in a better school district and more space for our growing family.

Eventually, I came around to her reasonable idea that upgrading our living situation could be a great idea in the coming years.

These types of open conversations continued over the following weeks, months, and years in our marriage. This dedicated time eventually inspired us both to ask another important question: How do we make these dreams of ours become a reality?

That's an exciting question to ask.

PLAN YOUR PATH TOGETHER

In my experience, the answer to this question is a combination of a few key resources: time, energy, and money:

- **Time** to dedicate to making a plan and seeing it through
- **Energy** and willpower to make the impossible possible
- **Money** needed to slowly but surely own your time

If we don't prioritize these resources and harness their power, we won't be able to realize the dreams we have. They will just remain as fantasies for the rest of our lives, and they will never become reality. We'll talk about them from time-to-time and say "wouldn't it be cool if … ," but they won't happen unless we're willing to make them happen.

The first and most important step is to schedule a money date. The goal of the money date is to set aside **time** as a couple to have important conversations about your financial future together. You review how you used your money from the previous month, what you want to do with your cash this month, and how you're tracking on your overall financial dream goals.

Outside of the obvious financial benefits of this activity, these meetings are great for your marriage too.

For me and my wife, we discuss what's important to us, how we're going to get there together, and how we see our relationship growing over the years to come. With two kids in the house, time for discussion can be limited. The money date gives us a little break and helps me feel closer to my wife.

This get-together shouldn't be something you do sometimes. It should happen regularly (preferably monthly or every other week, depending on your financial situation) and should be honored like any other important meeting. If you feel like living your dream life is worth it, then showing up for an hour once or twice per month with the love of your life is doable.

Conversations around money can be boring, annoying, or stressful for some partners. That's why it's important to make your money date fun. Order some pizza, drink a glass of wine together, or sit outside in the sunshine. Don't treat it like a business meeting. This should be enjoyable!

When our kids were young, we took our money date to a kids' play place. That way our kids could run around like crazy people while we planned out our financial lives. As they've gotten older and less dependent on us for constant entertainment, they see us meeting and discussing our lives together. I'm hopeful they are watching our example so they can see how to put their dream life into action in the future.

With the money date scheduled, it's time to take action.

Do your best to start with your "why" when these meetings begin. If your money date motivation is to ensure you and your spouse can eventually transition away from your soul-sucking careers and move toward part-time work you enjoy, don't forget to remind yourselves of that as you start planning. As you continue these regular get-togethers, your **energy and willpower** may fade. After all, changing your life for the better requires long-term effort. And effort is hard. Especially the long-term kind! It's important to remind yourself why you're doing the money dates. Without a "why," distraction and temptation will win.

You've committed your time and energy, now it's time to use the third powerful resource at your disposal, which is your **money**. I've interviewed hundreds of money experts, and I often like to ask the question, "Can money buy happiness?" Some are adamant that money cannot buy happiness while others declare 100% that it can. Like most things in life, the answer is personal and usually somewhere in the middle. If you're looking for true love and companionship, money can help, but I don't think it can buy you that type of happiness. When you're talking about owning more of your time, money can definitely buy happiness.

And the best way to plan your money in accordance with your family values, dreams, and goals is with a budget. If you're not familiar with a budget or have never created one before, the concept may feel foreign at first. After consistently using one to empower your life plan, you'll be inspired by what it can do for you.

A budget is simply a plan for your money. You and your partner earn income from your work, and the budget maps out how you'll use that income. For example, if your combined household income after taxes is $10,000 per month, your budget will break down how that $10,000 gets utilized.

Since we're talking about prioritizing our "rocks before the sand," it's important that your budget reflects that. Everyone will have different top priorities, so there's no one right way to do this. But all in all, allocating more money to family, your health, your marriage, spirituality, and creating community ("rocks") has a better long-term return on happiness than material possessions ("sand"). Let's look at a hyperbolic "Sand Before Rocks" monthly budget versus a "Rocks Before Sand" monthly budget to illustrate the difference.

Sand Before Rocks
INCOME

- Partner 1: $5,500
- Partner 2: $4,500

TOTAL INCOME: $10,000

EXPENSES

- Housing: $5,000
- Cars: $3,000
- Sports Betting: $1,000
- New Clothes: $450
- Alcohol/Cigarettes: $270
- Food: $250
- Saving and Investing: $20
- Family Entertainment: $5
- Giving: $5

TOTAL EXPENSES: $10,000
REMAINDER: $0

In the "Sand Before Rocks" scenario, we may feel momentary comfort living in a spacious house and driving luxury cars that take up 80% of our income, but long term, this will become a painful life situation.

Without saving, an emergency expense or getting laid off at work could drive us into high-interest debt that could last for years. The top causes of bankruptcies in the United States are due to medical debt and job loss.[1] Those pricey mortgages and luxury car lease payments become hard to pay when our income gets hit.

Without investing, we're setting ourselves up for a lifetime of work. Americans are working longer than previous generations,[2] and some aren't retiring at all. The average retirement age in 1991 was 57 years old. Fast forward to today, and that average retirement age has increased to 62 years old. Unfortunately, the average lifespan has only increased by 3 years during that time frame, going from 75 years old in 1991 to 78 years old today.[3] So on average, we're working longer and enjoying fewer years in retirement. That's why it's crucial to invest for our retirement (or early retirement). We are quite literally buying back years of our lives.

Without allotting time and money for family connections and entertainment, we're missing out on making core memories with the ones we love. Sure, we can enjoy family bonding without a bunch of money. There are countless free or frugal ways to have fun. But it's hard to deny that money helps to amplify that family fun. Money can buy us plane tickets to a sunny vacation during winter, pizza for movie night, and a basketball hoop for the driveway.

Without giving, we're missing out on one of the most natural forms of happiness. Studies have shown that the reward centers in our brains "light up" when we spend money on someone other than ourselves.[4] Since giving is a social activity, researchers found that there is a release of oxytocin, otherwise known as the "love hormone." Not only do we become happy, but the recipient of the gift (if it's a thoughtful and selfless gift) also becomes happy. And then you're happy because they are happy. Karma at its finest.

Rocks Before Sand
INCOME

- Partner 1: $5,500
- Partner 2: $4,500

TOTAL INCOME: $10,000
EXPENSES

- Saving and Investing: $3,000
- Housing: $2,000
- Family Entertainment: $1,500
- Vacation Savings: $1,000
- Food: $1,000
- Giving: $1,000

- Cars: $250
- Other: $250

TOTAL EXPENSES: $10,000
REMAINDER: $0

In this "Rocks Before Sand" approach to budgeting, the important family values (rocks) have been given more priority. Material possessions (sand) are nice, but they just aren't as important.

Our house may be smaller, but our time working in the corporate world will be shorter because we can save and invest more.

The vehicles we drive may not be brand new, but we have money to fend off emergencies or job loss if it comes our way.

Instead of spending the bulk of our money and time gambling, drinking, and smoking by ourselves, we trade that for family vacations, birthday parties, and giving back in our communities. (I admit this comparison is a bit hyperbolic to prove my point.)

Once we've decided on our most important values as a couple (and as a family), we need to ensure our budget reflects those priorities.

For years, I used a spreadsheet to craft our family's overall budget. It was simple to create and adjust. The only problem was that it took a lot of time to update. Since my wife wasn't thrilled by looking at the numbers as much as I was, I needed something that would help us use our money in accordance with our values and not take all day to do it. That's why the money nerd in me was thrilled when fintech (financial technology) revolutionized family budgeting over the last decade.

All of a sudden, manually updating spreadsheets gave way to automation. Instead of me updating our budget to show how much we spent on groceries, our budget was now telling me how much we spent.

Although the players have changed over the years, here are a few of the best budgeting apps for couples and families:

- **Monarch Money:** A couples focused money management system that helps you organize your family finances
- **YNAB (aka You Need a Budget):** A detailed budget-first system that ensures you're only spending money you have (and not the other way around)
- **Quicken Simplifi:** A simple budgeting solution from the creators of the classic budgeting software company, Quicken

Consistent use of any of these budgeting apps will significantly improve your family's financial life. I can say that with confidence because using budgeting apps like these over the last 15 years has helped us build millionaire family wealth and significantly improved the communication in my marriage. Do we still have money fights every once in a while? Sure. But they are at least informed money fights!

Since the landscape of fintech changes so rapidly, know that we always keep an up-to-date list of the best budget apps for families on our website, MarriageKidsandMoney.com.

Whether you're using the simple spreadsheet or an automated app, it's time to get started in creating your family budget. Your first pass at this process is going to be sloppy. Know that going in. It's like riding a bike, though. You might stumble at first, but every time you show up, you'll get a percentage better at it. And since we're talking about creating a better life for yourself, this is an exercise where you want to keep showing up and improving.

Start by detailing your monthly income. Include sources like your salary, your spouse's salary, rental property income, business income, or any other investment income.

Then move on to estimating your monthly expenses. Start with the "Big Three":

- **Housing** (rent, mortgage, etc.)
- **Transportation** (auto payments, etc.)
- **Food** (groceries, takeout, food delivery, etc.)

According to the Bureau of Labor Statistics, these three costs on average can take up 63% of household spending.[5] If you're not sure how to estimate these three big expenses, download your latest credit card statement or bank statement and see what your recent spending has been in these areas. Then move on to all the other expenses in your life, like saving, investing, giving, loan payments, utilities, daycare, entertainment, healthcare, education, clothing, and so on.

If you are more excited about this part than your spouse, that's okay. Take the lead in developing the budget. Just make sure your spouse agrees with the allocations you've set. This way, you're moving down this path of financial improvement together.

After you've crafted the budget, take a second look at it and ask yourself a few questions:

- Is this budget set up with our goals, values, and dreams in mind?
- Will this setup help us move in the right direction for our family?
- Does this budget feel too restrictive, like all work and no play?
- Are we being unrealistic with these numbers?

Make sure your partner provides feedback too. If either party feels like the other made most of the decisions on the budget, this could come back to haunt your marriage later. No one wants to feel powerless when it comes family decisions, especially when it comes to money. Historically, women have had less financial power and decision-making in society. This doesn't mean your relationship is like this, but it is worth recognizing historical facts. Women couldn't vote in the United States until 1920. If that seems like ages ago, then you might be shocked to know that women weren't able to open a bank account or get a credit card with their names on it without a male cosigner until 1974.[6] Of course, significant progress has been made over the last 50 years when it comes to gender equality. It is important to recognize our generational biases when it comes to discussions around money. If you grew up in a household where your father earned all the money and made all the financial decisions, you may unknowingly have a bias toward the man making all the decisions with money. It's important to discuss these topics together with your spouse and ensure your relationship feels right for both of you. The money date can help with this.

The money date can also be a time to check in on the dozens of other things going on in your family life. It doesn't just have to be about money. My wife and I take this time to review our calendar for the month, plan vacations, and discuss our children's (seemingly endless) activities. Since life can be busy with kids in the house, our money date allows us to catch up and ensure we're on the same page as a couple.

Weeks and months will pass, and this process will get smoother over time. Small disagreements may start to flare up in the beginning. Realize that is completely normal. It's important to continue the process and proceed with an empathetic heart. If your partner feels like the budget is too restrictive and you disagree, try stepping in their shoes for a moment. While your financial goals and dreams are important, remember that the journey should be enjoyable too. Think about things from your spouse's perspective and find a reasonable middle ground.

As you're finding that middle ground, commit to each other that your dream life is worth it. Meeting with each other for your money dates consistently will help you realize a life you never thought was possible. The great thing about this process is that your dream life starts to get closer with each meeting. As a runner, I liken this process to a half marathon.

In order to complete a 13.1-mile race, you need to first train by running your first mile. You build up to 2 miles, 5 miles, and all of a sudden you're running 10 miles at a time. Without even completing the half marathon, you've become healthier, more disciplined, and prepared to take on a tougher challenge.

Family financial fitness is the same thing! You start with your first money date. It was tough, confusing, and a little contentious, but you showed up and learned a lot. The next money date you're a little smarter about your money situation, you know some important things about your spouse's feelings around finances, and you found a budgeting tool that makes the process easy. Fast forward, 3 months later, you're financially fit and ready to complete your financial version of a half marathon.

In the next chapter, we'll review a "half marathon-like" financial milestone that will allow you to own more of your time. And that is eliminating debt from your family life forever.

But first, let's hear from another family about their path to own their time.

FROM THE PODCAST

Family: Joshua and Carly, 35 years old from Arizona
Money Milestone: $950,000 net worth

Andy:	*What was your motivation for building your family's wealth?*
Joshua:	I wanted to make sure I have enough money to support my family. My dad was a good role model for that. Also, I want to be able to go to my kid's activities when they have them and not be like "I have to go to work in order to get a paycheck to put food on the table." Overall, I wanted to have more freedom in my life as I got older.

Andy:	*Now that you are near millionaires, what dreams and goals do you have for your family?*
Joshua:	We typically don't like to buy a bunch of expensive things. We like travel, having a staycation for a day or two … that's more where we prioritize our money. As we've moved through the process it's allowed a lot more freedom. When we first took our daughter to Great Wolf Lodge there was a lot more like "Okay, well we have $5 to spend on the dessert. Here she gets one bowl." And now as we've gone through our journey it's like "Okay, we can relax the strings a little bit now. Let's just relax and enjoy the vacation." So, it's more continuing to build experiences that they can look back on versus giving them or having whatever I want.
Andy:	*What's one piece of advice you'd share with other families who want to build wealth and freedom like you have?*
Joshua:	Focus on "what's one hour of your time" or "what's 1% of your salary." Figure out in your budget where you can tighten a little bit to get that extra $20 a month. Maybe you're just saving one hour of your time a month. That's fine start. Maybe next month you can get two hours or an hour and a half. It just gives you a small line in the sand to try and step forward slowly but surely, and then you'll eventually get to the point where you have $1,000. You might be wanting to try to get to $1,000,000 but you're going to be crossing a whole bunch of milestones that a lot of people are trying to get to.

Carpe Diem Action Steps

- Set aside 30 minutes to dream this week. Ask yourself the thought-provoking questions we reviewed earlier in the chapter. Start jotting down ideas, goals, and dreams for the coming decades.

- Share your dreams with your spouse and ask them to do the same with you. This is an opportunity for connection and for fun in your relationship. Enjoy it.
- Schedule your first money date. Be the leader that gets this family ritual in motion. Time spent on these action steps could change the course of your family's life for generations to come.

NOTES

1. Debt.org. (2025). *Bankruptcy statistics.* Available at: https://www.debt.org/bankruptcy/statistics/
2. Garber, J. (2024). *What is the average retirement age?* [Online]. NerdWallet. Available at: https://www.nerdwallet.com/article/investing/social-security/average-retirement-age-us
3. Centers for Disease Control and Prevention. (2025). *Fast facts—life expectancy* [Online]. Available at: https://www.cdc.gov/nchs/fastats/life-expectancy.htm
4. Novotney, A. (2022). *What happens in your brain when you give a gift?* American Psychological Association. Available at: https://www.apa.org/topics/mental-health/brain-gift-giving
5. US Bureau of Labor Statistics. (2023). *Consumer expenditures* [Online]. Available at: https://www.bls.gov/news.release/cesan.nr0.htm
6. Smithsonian. (2024). *Voices of independence: Four oral histories about building women's economic power* [Online]. Available at: https://womenshistory.si.edu/blog/voices-independence-four-oral-histories-about-building-womens-economic-power

CHAPTER TWO

EMBRACE THE DEBT-FREE LIFE

"The world as we have created it is a process of our thinking. It cannot be changed without changing our thinking."

– Albert Einstein

R ich.

Wealthy.

Millionaire.

These words can conjure up dozens of images in our brains. Since we've been constantly bombarded with marketing messages for most of our lives, the image of rich might mean a luxury car, an expensive watch, or a mansion. They are usually associated with good-looking people who appear quite satisfied with their lives overall. If the luxury goods industry can convince us that ownership of these expensive things is the definition of a happy life, then we're more likely to subconsciously spend our lives pursuing them. And voila, we become lifelong customers.

It's worked very well for companies like Louis Vuitton Moet Hennessy (LVMH). Its owner, Bernard Arnault, is one of the richest people in the world, with a $178 billion net worth.[1] LVMH makes tens of billions per year selling luxury fashion, jewelry, and alcohol.

It's not just luxury goods that have caught our attention as the definition of rich. Cars, trucks, and SUVs are huge status symbols for the typical family. Depending on your preference and how you outfit the vehicle, new electric cars and pickup trucks can easily cost us $100,000 or more.

The latest technology can also be an alluring symbol of wealth as well. Smartphones, headphones, and laptops have all become important luxury staples over the last decade. This is especially true as updated tech comes out each year.

Education has also become a way to show we're the best of the best. Where we get our degrees from and how many degrees we earn can be an indication of our status in society.

The list goes on. As parents, we can get swept away in "doing what's best for our kids" by buying brand-new top-of-the-line strollers, signing them up for travel sports, and committing to private schools.

I'm not saying these things aren't important. In fact, I've used my time and money to buy some of these things listed.

I am saying that if you desire to truly own your time, these things are not worth going into debt for.

American household debt is at an all-time high, sitting at $18.04 trillion.[2] This includes credit card debt, which is also at a record high of $1.21 trillion. Auto loans are at an astonishing $1.7 trillion, and student loans are near $1.8 trillion.

For many families, these record-high debt numbers are due to having a lower income, increased interest rates, and the general rise in the cost of living. In other words, they are just trying to get by. Their use of debt is a lifeline to food, transportation, housing, education, and security.

Then there are many families making a healthy household income, who aren't saving anything. As noted previously, recent survey data found that 49% of families making $100,000 or more are living paycheck to paycheck.[3] And 22% of high-income households have said that the reason they are in debt is because of lifestyle choices like vacations and entertainment plans.

Our desires for that "rich life" are exceeding our income.

Not only is the math not working in our financial benefit, but carrying debt can be emotionally and psychologically damaging. Debt can lead to increased money fights in marriage and contribute to the increased risk of personal depression and anxiety.[4] That relationship uneasiness and mental health impact can become very apparent to our children, who in turn become depressed and anxious.[5]

Debt also locks us into jobs we don't enjoy. In a recent Gallup poll, 50% of US workers reported feeling daily stress at their jobs.[6] Globally, 19% of those surveyed reported being miserable at work.

We set out to own things that we thought would give us a rich life, but those things ended up owning us.

To own your time, you must commit to saying goodbye to debt forever.

UNDERSTAND THE LIFE-CHANGING BENEFITS OF DEBT FREEDOM

Telling people not to buy the shiniest of shiny things unless they have the money to do it is not a popular message. In our YOLO (You Only Live Once) society, not many people are interested in delaying purchases they feel will make them happy. But as my wife likes to say, "The difficult thing to do and the right thing to do are often one and the same."

Let's tick through the list:

- Eat more vegetables.
- Get more sleep.
- Exercise more.
- Drink less alcohol.
- Eat less dessert.

These are all bummers on the surface, but long term, we all know they are right. So, I'll add one more to the list: Don't buy things if you don't have actual money to pay for them.

It sounds obvious, but it is difficult to actually do.

When I was in my twenties, I wanted a lot of things because I wanted to feel and look successful. Vacations, a luxury car, a house, a lawn service, a carbon fiber road bike, and a master's degree topped my list of stuff to buy in order to feel like I made it in society. The only problem was my income couldn't actually afford those luxuries. Debt began to pile up, and those things started to own me.

My story is a common story. Many people experience desire for things they want but simply can't afford.

After having been owned by my debt, I'd like to propose a different way of thinking: Let's enjoy those luxuries of life when we have the money to pay for them.

I've lived with debt, and I've lived without it. And I've interviewed hundreds of people who have done the same. The following are just a few of the benefits of choosing a debt-free life.

Less Stress

The stress in my corporate career was real. I remember thinking if I performed poorly and lost my job, my family's happiness could be impacted drastically. But each time we paid off one of our debts, my stress level decreased. It was like a weight was slowly being lifted off my shoulders.

When you are debt free, you are alleviating a major stress point in your life. One source of annoyance and pain is now gone. You don't have to think about it anymore. If you choose to make debt freedom a commitment in your life, this stressor is eliminated forever.

Reduced Cost of Living

As our families grow, so do our living expenses. Kids cost money no matter how frugal we are. By some estimates, raising a child to 18 years old in the United States can cost a staggering $297,674.[7] My wife and I don't spend nearly that much on our kids, but we also live in Michigan, which is a lower cost of living state, but I understand how this is possible for many.

As parents, we can make room in our budgets to support our growing needs as a family without debt in our lives. This way you'll be in a strong position to provide a good life for your family and improve your financial future as well.

More Money to Save

When your debt is gone, you suddenly have a lot more money available in your budget. This is an excellent opportunity to begin saving more. Most financial professionals recommend a 3- to 6-month emergency fund to protect against the unexpected. Surprise moments like job loss, medical emergencies, vehicle breakdowns, home repairs, or your kid cracking the porcelain sink with a water glass (personal experience) can all happen. When you've got money set aside, these emergencies don't feel like emergencies as much.

Saving doesn't just have to be for emergencies either. Vacations, cars, phones, generous gifts, and home upgrades are all smart reasons to save. If we have the money set aside for these things ahead of time, we're less likely to go back into debt to pay for them.

More Money to Invest

Investing our money for long-term goals like college, retirement, or even early retirement can bring unattainable goals within reach. With debt gone from your life, investing becomes easier.

Instead of paying interest on your debts, you are now compounding interest as an investor. This is how generational wealth becomes a reality for many. Taking advantage of your workplace 401(k) is often an excellent place to start. As your wealth grows and you are on the right track for financial independence, you can choose to support your children with their financial futures as well with a 529 college savings account.

Reduce Weekly Hours Worked

After my wife and I eliminated our debt together, we felt confident that she could reduce her hours to part-time at work. She went from 50–60 hours per week to 20–30 hours. As the hours decreased, so did her pay. This income change was difficult in the beginning, but after a few months, we got used to it.

By trading a reduction in income for 20–30 hours back in my wife's week, she was able to take care of her health, spend more time with our newborn daughter, and create a priceless bond with her.

Retirement Becomes Easier

When you set a retirement investing goal, this is often projected based on your annual expenses. A common rule of thumb is to multiply your annual expenses by 20–25 to find your retirement goal number.

For example, if your annual expenses are $100,000, then your retirement target goal should be $2,000,000–$2,500,000.

Let's say you were spending $750 per month paying down your debts. Now that you are debt free, your annual expenses are only $91,000. This makes investing for retirement easier. Your target retirement number is now only $1,820,000–$2,275,000.

By eliminating debt from your life, you could shave hundreds of thousands of dollars off your target retirement number. Additionally, you're shaving years off your traditional working life.

Become More Generous

Holidays, birthdays, weddings, baby showers, graduation parties, religious celebrations, and charity events are all opportunities to be generous. The problem is when we're in debt or working to pay it off, it can be difficult to feel like giving. When the debt is gone, this is an opportunity to change that.

Tip the server at the restaurant a bit more. Be the generous aunt or uncle on your niece's birthday. Support your friend with a thoughtful wedding gift. Give a dollar to someone on the street who is down on their luck without thinking twice about it.

With more margin in our budget, we can be the generous person we've always wanted to be.

Show Our Kids the Benefits

When your kids see you working hard to eliminate debt from your life, they are watching you change your life for the better. That's a life lesson they aren't likely to forget. It's not the things we say to our kids but the things we model for them that help them become better adults.

By showing them that the "difficult choice is often the right choice," we are setting them up to comprehend that the good stuff is worth fighting for. They will grow up knowing that if they want something, they have to work for it. The important gifts of life are not simply handed to you. You need to put in the effort.

Outside of learning perseverance, your children will also realize that they can't buy something if they don't have the money for it. If they can harness this financial superpower knowledge at a young age, they will thrive as young adults, and eventually young parents themselves.

Beyond these eight benefits of a debt-free life, think for a second about other personal motivators. Ask yourself a few questions:

- If I didn't have a car payment anymore, what would I do with that extra money?
- When my student loans are gone, how will that change my life?
- By stopping my habit of overspending on my credit card and deciding to pay off my balance for good, how could I reallocate my budget to make my family's financial situation better?

As you're answering these questions, think in terms of those important priorities we discussed earlier (aka our "rocks"). If we value taking care of our health more or spending more time with our family, ensure that this debt freedom path will help you get there. You are in charge of your better tomorrow.

ASSESS YOUR DEBT SITUATION

After reviewing the benefits of a debt-free life, you may be ready to commit to this countercultural path. The best place to start is with reviewing your current debt.

I remember this moment well in the beginning of our net worth building journey. Our income was solid as we were bringing in north of $100,000 as a couple. Also, our assets were decent since we owned a home and a car. We even had some cash and retirement accounts.

The problem was our liabilities (also known as debt). Like many people, we had borrowed to get the home (a mortgage), the car (car loan), and my master's degree (student loans). The amount of money we borrowed was more than the money we had. We were broke as a joke as we started our marriage.

Assets		Liabilities		Net Worth	
Home	$140,000	Mortgage	$177,000	Assets	$176,000
Andy's Roth IRA	$8,000	Student Loans	$28,000	Liabilities	$226,000
Nicole's 401k	$8,000	Car Loan	$21,000		
Cash	$2,000				
Nicole's Car	$18,000				
Total Assets	$176,000	**Total Liabilities**	$226,000	**Total Net Worth**	−$50,000

The mortgage was higher than the value of our home due to the rapid drop in real estate prices during this time in metro Detroit. We were "underwater" by $37,000 on our home at the time.

Our car value was lower than our loan amount because that's the nature of vehicles. They are a depreciating asset as opposed to stocks and homes (well, typically).

And the student loans for my MBA program were an "investment" in my future career. I wish I would have analyzed the necessity of an MBA degree in my career field[8] before spending nearly 6 years in night school completing it, but that's a whole different story.

While it was depressing at the time, it became motivating to actually have the knowledge of the problem areas. This was a starting point for us. We knew what we needed to tackle.

Different Types of Debt

To help you familiarize yourself with the type of debt you might have, let's go over some common areas where people tend to borrow money. We'll start with the highest debt amounts in the typical American household and work our way down.[9]

Mortgage Debt

A mortgage is a loan people take out when they want to buy a home. You're probably well aware of this because mortgages are very common forms of debt.

Most of the time, this form of debt is an excellent way to become a first-time homeowner. With the average home price in the United States hovering around $500,000,[10] the majority of people are not able to buy a home outright without a loan.

However, I do find it chilling when you actually translate the word into its French origin. Mortgage actually breaks down into "death pledge." Evidently, we're supposed to have these things until we die? We'll save that discussion for a later chapter.

Total mortgage debt in the United States (Q4 2024): $12.605 trillion
Average mortgage debt per US household (Q4 2024): $263,180

Home Equity Line of Credit

Another form of housing debt is called a home equity line of credit (HELOC). This loan allows you to borrow based on the equity in your home.

For example, if you bought a home for $200,000 five years ago and now your home is worth $500,000, you have some built up equity. Some home-owners choose to borrow against their home's equity in order to pay for home repairs, upgrades, or really anything they want. Since a home equity line of credit typically comes in at a much lower interest rate than other unsecured debt like credit cards, some choose to use their HELOC to pay off other higher interest debts.

Total home equity line of credit in the United States (Q4 2024): $396 billion
Average home equity line of credit in the United States (2024): $45,157[11]

Student Debt

Just like homeownership, the price tag of college has become so out of reach for the majority of American students. Student loans are a debt instrument that allows students to borrow money to pay for tuition, fees, room and board, and much more.

While there are many other options to consider when it comes to post-secondary education with a better return on investment, student loans have become massively popular over the last couple of decades. In the last 15 years alone, student loan debt in the United States has increased by $1 trillion.[12]

Total student loan debt in the United States (Q4 2024): $1.777 trillion
Average student loan debt (federal) in the United States (2024): $38,375
Average student loan debt (private) in the United States (2024): $41,618

Auto Debt

If you live in state like me with little to no public transportation, having a car can be a necessity. Getting to your job, picking up groceries, and taking the kids to preschool would be really tough without a trusty automobile.

While borrowing money isn't required to get a car, it too has become a popular choice for many Americans. Auto debt is the third largest form of debt in the United States.[13]

Auto loans last anywhere from 12 to 96 months.

Total car debt in the United States (Q4 2024): $1.655 trillion
Average car debt (new vehicles) in the United States (Q4 2024): $41,572
Average car debt (used vehicles) in the United States (Q4 2024): $26,468

Credit Card Debt

As opposed to mortgages and auto debt, credit card debt is typically a type of unsecured debt. This means that it is not tied to a specific asset. With a mortgage, lenders have more trust that you'll pay back that loan because if you don't they can use your house as leverage. Same goes with an auto loan. Credit cards are different. Lenders allow you to borrow a certain amount of money each month based on your income. Because this is more of a risky bet for the lenders, the interest rate can be much higher than secured debt like mortgages and auto loans.

With high interest debt like credit cards, late payments and unpaid bills can add up fast. This can happen for many reasons including job loss, rising cost of living, or simply impulse shopping and purchasing those items on a credit card.

Total credit card debt in the United States (Q4 2024): $1.211 trillion
Average credit card debt in the United States (Q2 2024): $6,580[14]

Other Debt

Outside of the big debt players already mentioned, there are still a multitude of other ways people borrow money. Some of those could include the following:

- Personal loans
- Medical debt
- Business loans
- Tax debt
- Payday loans

However you slice it, if people are looking to buy something, there is likely someone out there who provides a loan to get it. It's good to recognize the type of debt out there so that you can begin assessing your true liabilities.

Why Interest Rates Are Important

Not all debt is created equal. Debts like mortgage and auto loans typically have lower interest rates depending on your credit score and history when compared to higher interest debt like credit cards. The average 30-year fixed mortgage rate is around 6%,[15] and the average credit card interest rate is hovering around 24%.[16]

There's a huge difference there when you're analyzing your current debt situation.

Let's say you are the average American household with $6,580 of credit card debt, and your interest rate is 24%. Your goal is to chip away at this credit card debt and pay it off in a reasonable time frame. You're able to pay the minimum payment plus a bit more so your total monthly payment is $215. Unfortunately, with a 24% interest rate, you're paying a lot of dough to your lender for a long time. In this scenario, you wouldn't pay off this credit card for 4 years, and you'd end up paying a total of $10,282 on your original $6,580 debt. That's because $3,702 went to interest.[17]

When you're trying to get ahead, high interest debt like this can be deflating. That's why it's important to know the interest rate you're committing to before taking on the debt.

Knowing Your Liabilities

We've discussed the different types of debt and why it's important to know the interest rates on that debt. It's time to get serious about your personal debt situation.

Start by listing out your debts, understanding your total balances and the interest rates. If you're unsure where to find this information, start by downloading your bank statement and see who you've been paying each month. Or you could take advantage of a free credit report at annualcreditreport.com to see how many outstanding loans you have. Despite the URL name, this service, enacted by law, allows you to receive free credit reports weekly.

As you start to uncover your current debts, write them down or put them in a spreadsheet so you know what you're dealing with. For example:

- Auto Loan
  - Lender: Audi Financial Services
  - Balance: $20,000
  - Interest Rate: 8%
- Student Loan
  - Lender: Aidvantage
  - Balance: $30,000
  - Interest Rate: 6%
- Credit Card Debt
  - Lender: Capital One
  - Balance: $5,000
  - Interest Rate: 20%
- Personal Loan
  - Lender: Your Mom
  - Balance: $500
  - Interest Rate: 0%
- Mortgage
  - Lender: Chase Bank
  - Balance: $250,000
  - Interest Rate: 6%

With this newfound knowledge, you know your starting point. This is good information to have as you begin your debt pay down journey.

CREATE A PLAN TO ELIMINATE YOUR DEBT

You've totaled up your debt situation (outside of your mortgage), and it's not looking so hot. It totals up to $55,500 of personal, student, car, and credit card debt.

At first glance, this feels completely overwhelming. It's enough to make you want to stop and give up.

I remember this moment well. My wife and I had just under $50,000 of debt at the start of our marriage. We had student loans, car loans, and a home equity line of credit. It was paralyzing.

But then I reminded myself why we were doing this. We wanted to control more of our time. Both my wife and I had a high desire to be present parents. With a lot of debt in our lives, we knew that we would have to work at jobs that required more of our time. The more debt we had, the more time we would need to spend at work paying it off.

That motivation was enough for us to start tackling the debt head on.

DEBT ELIMINATION STRATEGIES

You've got the knowledge and the motivation. Now you need to pick a strategy.

Here are three different debt destruction strategies that I've learned over the past 10 years that I've been podcasting and speaking with other financially free families. These strategies are tested and will help you crush your family debt situation.

Debt Snowball

People (including me) have a tendency to think of personal finance as a math problem. The reality is that money is more emotional than we realize.

That's why the Debt Snowball is an effective method for eliminating debt.

The Debt Snowball method suggests lining up all of your debts from smallest balance to largest balance. You then tackle the smallest one first. The reason behind paying off the smallest debt first is that psychologically you get a quicker win for eliminating that debt. You then feel motivated to continue your debt-free journey.

There's nothing worse than starting a big, complicated project, like paying off your debt, and then giving up just at the beginning. You gathered all the knowledge, and you had the initial motivation, but the big, complicated project made you want to give up immediately. The Debt Snowball recognizes this human tendency and suggests that you give yourself a little grace by making the first step the easiest.

To illustrate the Debt Snowball in action, let's revisit our debt totals, leaving off the mortgage for now.

Before Applying the Debt Snowball

- Auto Loan
  - Balance: $20,000
  - Interest Rate: 8%
- Student Loan
  - Balance: $30,000
  - Interest Rate: 6%
- Credit Card Debt
  - Balance: $5,000
  - Interest Rate: 20%

- Personal Loan
  - Balance: $500
  - Interest Rate: 0%

After Applying the Debt Snowball

- Personal Loan
  - Balance: $500
  - Interest Rate: 0%
- Credit Card Debt
  - Balance: $5,000
  - Interest Rate: 20%
- Auto Loan
  - Balance: $20,000
  - Interest Rate: 8%
- Student Loan
  - Balance: $30,000
  - Interest Rate: 6%

In this scenario, tackle your smallest debt first and then work your way up to eliminating your largest debt. While mathematically it doesn't make a whole lot of sense to pay off your 0% interest loan to your mom first, psychologically it makes a ton of sense. You'll get the quick win satisfaction of paying off a debt, and you'll get your mom off your back from the loan she gave you years ago. Double win!

Depending on your income and your ability to save, you could be experiencing these dopamine-spiking wins within the first month of your debt-free journey.

Debt Avalanche

As much as I'm convinced about the psychological wins associated with the Debt Snowball strategy, there are folks who are more convinced by math. They can't understand why you would let a 20% interest rate debt to your credit card company linger. To them, that seems like financial madness to pay off a 0% interest rate loan first.

Those individuals should use the Debt Avalanche method when considering how to pay off their family debt.

The Debt Avalanche method is focused on paying off the debts with the largest interest rate first and paying off the debts with the lowest interest rate last. With this thinking, you're paying off the debt to your mom at the very end of our debt-free journey, not first. (Sorry, Mom!)

Here's how the two methods differ.

Debt Snowball (Lowest Balance First)

- Personal Loan
  - Balance: $500
  - Interest Rate: 0%
- Credit Card Debt
  - Balance: $5,000
  - Interest Rate: 20%
- Auto Loan
  - Balance: $20,000
  - Interest Rate: 8%
- Student Loan
  - Balance: $30,000
  - Interest Rate: 6%

Debt Avalanche (Highest Interest Rate First)

- Credit Card Debt
  - Balance: $5,000
  - Interest Rate: 20%
- Auto Loan
  - Balance: $20,000
  - Interest Rate: 8%
- Student Loan
  - Balance: $30,000
  - Interest Rate: 6%
- Personal Loan
  - Balance: $500
  - Interest Rate: 0%

There is no right or wrong answer with these two methods. This is an absolute personal decision. It's important to ask yourself if you are more motivated by psychological quick wins or by financial savings. Whichever of these two keeps you going throughout your debt-free journey that is the one you should choose.

Debt Hatred

For fun let's add in one more. We accumulate debt in our lives based on decisions we made in the past. And as we look back, some of those decisions really bother us.

Maybe you financed the purchase of a couch you just had to have. And then after a few years, you realize that the couch wasn't put together well. Every time you sit on it lately, a spring painfully pokes you in the back.

All of a sudden, you despise this couch you used to love. But you still owe thousands of dollars for it. That is a type of debt that you would really hate.

Perhaps you went back to school to pursue a master's degree. But halfway through you found that you could not complete the coursework due to health challenges. Nevertheless, you still must pay back the student loans accumulated. This is another form of debt that you probably hate.

That's why we need the Debt Hatred method.

With this method, you would pay off the debt that you hate the most first. This one is similar to the Debt Snowball method in its psychological roots. If you can eliminate the debt that gives you the most heartache, you will be more likely to feel rewarded on your debt-free journey.

Debt Hatred (Highest Amount of Rage and Anger First)

- Student Loan
  - Balance: $30,000
  - Interest Rate: 6%
- Personal Loan
  - Balance: $500
  - Interest Rate: 0%
- Credit Card Debt
  - Balance: $5,000
  - Interest Rate: 20%
- Auto Loan
  - Balance: $20,000
  - Interest Rate: 8%

These three methods are different ways of planning your debt destruction path. Choose the best one that fits your personality and your family situation. There is no single right answer here.

My wife and I went with the Debt Avalanche method because our debts were similar in balance and one had a higher interest rate. We decided to go for that first.

If I had to recommend one method for the majority of people, I would suggest the Debt Snowball method. Getting quick wins early on in the debt-free process is a smart move.

IMPLEMENT YOUR DEBT ELIMINATION STRATEGY

You've analyzed the various strategies, and you've decided to go with the Debt Snowball.

It's time to begin tackling your $500 debt that you owe to your mama. Your sweet mother gave you $500 a few years ago to help you with a small bathroom upgrade at your house. You didn't have the money yourself, so you asked Mom if she could help you out, and you promised to pay her back. Unfortunately, you never got around to paying her back because life got in the way. What's even more unfortunate is that your mother brings up this loan at Thanksgiving dinner every year since. While there might not be interest on this loan, there is a definite annoyance factor that continues to compound annually. The time has come to pay back your mother and end this multiyear loan.

After reviewing your newly developed budget, you and your spouse find a problem. You are spending all the money that you are making. Between you and your partner, you're making $10,000 each month, and unfortunately, you're spending $10,000. This is when you realize that you need to grow the gap between your income and expenses.

By growing the gap between your income and your expenses, you will create options and strength for your family's future. There are two sides to the "growing the gap" coin: increasing your income and decreasing your expenses. Both methods require effort and partnership. This is where the real work begins.

Increasing Income

Finding ways to increase your income can feel daunting at first. If you go at it with a creative mindset and an openness to try new things, your debt-free journey will be so much easier. During your next money date, you and your spouse can discuss simple and easy ways for you to increase your income. With that increase in income, you could easily pay off your debt to your mom in a matter of weeks, if not days.

To get your brainstorming started, here's an idea that could easily land you $500 in a matter of days.

Turn Your Trash into Cash

As a society, it is amazing how much stuff we accumulate. We have clothing hanging in our closets that we never wear, toys that our kids never play with, and electronics that we don't use because they just aren't the latest and greatest. This buildup of wasted stuff can be quite disheartening because we are essentially working hard every day to buy things we don't really need.

Today, we're fixing this. We're going to create some freedom from this pile of stress and make money while doing it. Let's turn your trash into cash.

Here is a brief list of easily sellable items that could be sitting around your house right now:

- Clothing
- Designer handbags
- Jewelry
- Electronics
- Furniture

- Gift cards
- Kid's toys
- Instruments
- Bikes
- Appliances
- Baby supplies

Set aside some focused time to walk around to each room in your house and look for items like these. When you come across these items in your search, put your best Marie Kondo hat on and honestly ask yourself these questions:

1. **Do I need this?**
2. **Does this item make me happy?**
3. **Do I want it more than I want cash in my pocket today?**

Over the years, my wife and I have easily sold more than $10,000 worth of our "old stuff." This extra cash helped us to pay off debt, invest for the future, or simply have some extra cash for the babysitter.

Take inventory of 10 higher priced (more than $20) items in your house that you don't need or use. We could go higher than 10 items, but for the sake of getting through this exercise quickly and putting some fast cash in your pocket, let's stick with 10 for now.

If you're not sure how much your item will sell for, the magic of the internet is ready to help. For any larger items, like a treadmill, a couch, or a bike, use a local online marketplace like Craigslist, OfferUp, or Facebook Marketplace. Look up a description of your items in the search function to see how others have priced a similar item in your area.

Let's try a Graco Baby Swing as an example. Once you're on your area's online marketplace site, look up a description of the swing. I typed in "Graco Baby Swing." It came up with a lot of options.

Find a swing that looks similar to yours (quality, condition, etc.), and price it slightly less. This way you'll get contacted quickly as your price beats out the local competition. Using our example, there are a lot of Graco Baby Swings going for around $80. Price yours at $60, and it'll be sold in no time.

For smaller items like new clothes with tags or video games, sites like eBay can also be a good resource for checking out how much your items could sell for. AI tools like ChatGPT can make this process much easier too.

We do have one rule that works well for our family. We've coined it our *$20 Rule*. If you can't get $20 or more for your item, I would not suggest selling it. The amount of time you will waste in cleaning, staging, photographing, and selling is not worth it in my experience.

There are dozens of national and local charities that would love for you to donate your items to support their cause. We take all of our "below $20 items," box or bag them up, and give them away. After we give these items away, we feel a sense of relief and freedom that comes from ridding yourself of the stuff in your life that you really don't need. Also, you're supporting a cause that could truly use your unwanted goods.

Some organizations like Goodwill, Vietnam Veterans of America, Salvation Army, and Purple Heart even come to your house and pick up your items from your front doorstep.

Earn More Money Where You Work

Outside of selling stuff you don't use or need any more at your house, the next best place to go to earn more money on your debt payoff journey is where you're already being paid. Yes, I'm talking about your current employer!

While selling things around your house is more of an immediate-term money strategy, getting more money at work is more medium term.

This process will last longer than a weekend, but it could yield a lot more money too.

For those of us who have the ability to work overtime, this can be an easy way to earn extra money. I interviewed a police officer named Keith from California who used this strategy to become completely debt free. He picked up overtime hours and sometimes worked unusual schedules. With his extra money, he threw it at his debt. In short order, he was living debt free, including his mortgage, in California! It's a temporary sacrifice that affords a lot of freedom in the long run.

Outside of overtime or working odd hours for your employer, look for ways to increase your salary. This might mean pursuing additional certifications or other credentials. Other times, it might mean sitting down with management for a performance review or negotiating a raise. If you are exceeding expectations at work and you can prove it, this is a good basis for a conversation about a compensation increase.

If you see no sign of income increases where you currently work (no matter how much effort you're putting in), consider looking for a new place to work. You may see an increase in pay and a better work environment overall.

Lastly, if bonuses and commissions are a part of your potential workplace income, take advantage during this debt pay down time frame. This may be the motivation you need to crush your goals at work and be well rewarded for it.

Explore a Side Hustle

Selling your old stuff is a quick way to get cash. Earning more at work takes a bit longer but could be more lucrative. Depending on the route you choose, a side hustle is a smart third option for earning more money.

A side hustle is work you do outside of your 9-to-5 career. You could fit your side hustle before work, after work, or on the weekends. This isn't the most ideal option when it comes to owning your time, but remember these are short-term sacrifices for long-term peace and enjoyment.

If you decide to go the side hustle route to help pay off debt, I'd recommend putting a time frame on the side hustle. That time frame should be aligned with your debt-free journey. I interviewed Brandyn, a mother from Texas, about this very topic. She told me that she and her husband used a variety of side hustles over a period of 5 years. These included waiting tables, DoorDash, and working at Home Depot. They were able to eliminate more than $100,000 of student loans, car loans, credit cards, and medical bills. Once they eliminated that debt, they stopped the extra work and enjoyed life without this heavy debt burden.

Side hustles like Uber or DoorDash can be quick routes to cash in exchange for your time. On the other hand, starting a side hustle based on a skill you already have could be more lucrative. For example, if you are knowledgeable about a specific industry and you're a decent writer, you could try your hand at freelance writing. Similarly, if you have graphic design experience, you could offer this to the marketplace as a side hustle too. While these side hustles may take more time to ramp up, the opportunity for increased pay over time is higher.

Ultimately, your choice in your debt freedom side hustle could align with your long-term vision for your future work life. Catherine from Michigan described this to me during an interview together. She was looking for a way to help pay down student debt while taking care of her twin babies at home. Freelance writing became her side hustle of choice. Not only did she eliminate tens of thousands of dollars in debt, but she eventually grew a six-figure freelance writing business for herself. Today, this is her full-time business outside of being a mom to her two (now much older) twins.

Reduce Expenses (Not Your Happiness)

Spending less money is a difficult conversation to have. When we align spending money with fun, it can feel like a huge buzzkill to most people to think about spending less.

The great thing about increasing your income is that there is no ceiling to how much you can earn. Decreasing your expenses does have a floor though. Spending nothing at all would be horrible for your family's happiness level. But spending all the money that's coming in doesn't work if you want to eventually own your time. We need to find that happy medium.

Let's start by discussing some of the easiest and least painful ways to reduce expenses.

Eliminate Unused Subscriptions or Memberships

After crafting your budget, you'll start to see where you're spending money. Examine your monthly or annual memberships and decide if you are fully utilizing them. These can be things like the following:

- **Streaming services:** Which apps do you actually use for your favorite shows?
- **Meal kits:** Are you using all of your delivery meals? Or are you throwing out money?
- **Gym memberships:** When was the last time you went to the gym? Are there less costly ways you can stay fit?
- **Private clubs:** Do you actually use this club, or do you just like the prestige of being a member?

- **Amazon Prime:** Do you buy more than you need just because you have the same-day shipping convenience?
- **Software subscriptions:** Do you have recurring charges for software or apps you don't even use?

If you use these things and get joy out of them, great! Keep them and enjoy them. If you don't really use them and you can see the money going to better use, think it over and consider cancelling to free up some monthly dough. This cash could be used to accelerate your debt freedom.

Reduce Monthly Bills

Bills, bills, bills. They definitely add up each month. If you think of how much money we actually receive in our paychecks and then how much we get to keep for the activities we enjoy, it can make you ill.

Now is your opportunity to take some of your hard-earned money back! You work too hard to pay extra to the cable company, the cell phone provider, and your insurance carriers.

A smart place to start in tackling your bills is with the cable company. First, get a copy of your bill to understand what you have in your cable company package. Understand the details of what is in your subscription like what type of internet speed you have and what channel subscriptions you have.

Shop around to one or two other competitors in your area. Ask each of the competitors to provide you with their best offer (pricing/package) as you are considering leaving your current provider.

Write down the offer, ask them to send it over email, and get their contact information so you can reference whom you spoke to originally. Sometimes they have "offer amnesia."

I remember being so nervous to leave AT&T for Xfinity because they marketed to me so well about their super-duper internet speeds. I've been with Xfinity for more than 3 years now, and the internet speed is all I need. We were able to reduce our overall bill by $30 per month ($360 annually). It was worth the hour of research and a couple phone calls.

If you find yourself not watching cable but you have it just in case, consider cutting the cord altogether. We cancelled our cable more than 5 years ago, and we don't miss it. Netflix and a couple of other subscriptions are plenty of entertainment for our family.

Similar to the previous cable company exercise, shop around to competing cell phone providers. There is so much competition in the marketplace for lower monthly pricing with similar functionality. My wife and I switched from one of the big wireless carriers over to an MVNO plan 3 years ago and the reception and data experience is the same if not better. We've saved hundreds of dollars per year on the switch.

Lastly, talk with your current home and auto insurance provider(s) and review your current coverage together. Ask them the following questions:

- What discounts exist that I'm not taking advantage of?
- What would be my potential savings if I bundled my home and auto insurance together?
- What other savings opportunities can you provide to me today?

After this line of questioning, you will more than likely net some savings opportunities. If not, take a look at other home and auto insurance providers to compare rates and quotes. Similar to the cell phone and cable company examples, there is a lot of competition in the insurance business. I'm sure you've seen their countless mind-numbing (yet sometimes humorous) commercials. These companies are fighting for your business.

If you have a 3-month emergency fund set up for yourself and your family, consider going with a higher deductible plan so you can lower your insurance payments overall. This goes for home, auto, and health insurance. The more risk you take on with a higher deductible, the lower your insurance payments will be. Obviously, you'll want to ensure you have the right savings lined up, you're in good health (health insurance), you don't live near a flood zone (home insurance), and you have a good driving record (auto insurance) before making any changes like this to your deductibles.

I switched to a higher deductible healthcare plan and saved more than $1,300 per year. If an emergency happens, then I will have to shell out funds from our emergency savings to pay for our higher deductible, but I'll take the savings now and focus on keeping myself and my family healthy in the meantime.

Make the Credit Card or No Credit Card Decision

If you consistently find yourself spending more than you plan each month and accumulating credit card debt, it may be time to take a break. This isn't goodbye forever to your credit card, but it's goodbye until you get your spending under control.

My wife and I paid off and cancelled our credit cards for 5 years. We hated the feeling of losing out on those precious credit card points, miles, and rewards. But this short-term sacrifice helped us ensure we became debt free and stayed debt free.

During one month early on in our financial independence journey, we found that we overspent on our budget by around $500 while using credit cards. This was due to a planned vacation where we spent way more than we budgeted. We had to withdraw from our savings account to cover the difference. The following month when we used cash and debit cards, we were $250 under budget. It was eye opening how much we could save by including a little discipline in our spending plan.

After we learned to consistently live on our budget through our money date ritual, we eventually got back on the credit card train. Over the past decade, we've stayed true to our budget and earned cashback, points, and miles that we use to maximize our family experiences each year. Do we slip up here and there? Of course, we're not robots. We're human. Part of the budgeting process should include some grace in the form of a "Whoops!" category. This is a small amount of money budgeted each month that allows you to embrace the reality that you and your spouse are not perfect. Depending on your income, this "Whoops!" category could be set for $50, $250, or thousands of dollars.

Pick your ideal debt elimination method, increase your income, and methodically reduce your expenses, and you'll be well on your way to a debt-free future for your family.

CELEBRATE YOUR WINS TOGETHER

This debt-free path can feel long and tiring. There will be many days when you just want to give up. That's why it's important to consistently remind yourself why you are doing this and celebrate your wins along the way.

While extreme deprivation is never the goal, let's say you have decided to limit the amount of times you order takeout or visit a restaurant during your debt pay down journey. As you analyzed your budget, you found this was a trouble spot for overspending. You wouldn't be alone, as this is often a major area for overspending for many Americans.[18] Twenty-seven percent of those surveyed labeled food delivery as a recurring overindulgence of theirs. Since you personally don't enjoy cooking food, you decide that your delayed gratification reward for paying down your debt will be the following (let's assume you owe $45,000 of debt):

- $15,000 of debt paid off—Go in person and pick up food from your favorite takeout restaurant
- $30,000 of debt paid off—Get delivery of your favorite takeout restaurant from the comfort of your home
- $45,000 of debt paid off—Go to your favorite sit-down restaurant and enjoy a nice dinner served to you and your entire family

Of course, you'll need to budget out these celebrations along the way. You don't want to go back into debt just to celebrate.

Make this process fun. As humans, we need motivation to keep moving forward when times get tough. If we feel like life is all discipline and no fun, then we'll quit right away. But if we infuse some joy, celebration, and family experiences into the process, we're more likely to successfully complete our journey. Celebrating small victories and big victories reduces stress, creates happiness, and strengthens the bond in your family.[19]

A major bonus to this whole process is if your kids are along for the ride. They are watching you create a better life for yourself and for them. Your effort in creating debt freedom for your family today will mean your children will understand the importance of a debt-free future for themselves.

FROM THE PODCAST

Family: Leo and Faith, 27 years old from Georgia
Money Milestone: $224,000 of debt paid off in 36 months

Andy:	*How did you get into debt in the first place?*
Leo:	Back when we said, "I do," we got married with $211,000 worth of debt. That was a combination of student loans, credit cards, personal loans; you name it, we had it. While we carried that debt, we knew we didn't want to stay where we were. So, we got on the same page and decided to go after it.
Andy:	*What did you do to eliminate the debt?*
Leo:	We started budgeting. We needed a plan for our money. When we got married, Faith had just started working, and we started our debt-free journey as newlyweds. We still had to figure each other out and figure out those kinks as far as what was the grocery budget going to look like and all these other things.

Faith:	We cut our cable. We went to Walmart, and we bought an antenna. To this day, we still have that digital antenna. We worked on the same side of town, and so every single day we would carpool, and then Leo would come pick me up, and then we would head home. We packed our lunches every single day and still do. And we always ate at home.
Andy:	*Did you work to increase your income too?*
Leo:	Oh yeah absolutely. We had side hustles. Between Faith and I, we had five jobs during our debt-free journey. I worked extra shifts at the hospital on weekends and during the holidays and babysat and did overnight nursing in addition to her primary job, and we worked like crazy. I mean they were weeks when Faith was working 70–90 hours in a week.
Andy:	*That sounds rough. How did you guys sneak in some romance and fun?*
Leo:	During our first year [of] marriage, and I'll take blame for this, it was not the healthiest at all. We were so driven and determined. It did help us with our communication because we were forced to communicate to see how each other was doing. And see where we could pick up the slack for one another just so we can keep on going but that was not healthy and not something that I would recommend for anyone else … let alone newlyweds. Our second year we did much better by implementing small celebrations for our victories. We incorporated sinking funds for vacations and travel, date nights and all that stuff.
Andy:	*Now that you are debt free, what goals do you have for you and your family?*
Faith:	I love my job. I love what I do, but I really want to get back home with my babies. Cutting down like a couple

	days is my top priority, and that's what we're working towards. I think we're going to do it in phases.
Leo:	Being stuck at a job until 67 is not pleasing to my ears. To learn that there's a path that is contrary to what we've been told and taught and heard all of our lives is very reassuring. Our goal is to ultimately have the option not to work as much as we're working. But I have the time to do the things that we want. Time freedom.
Andy:	*What's one piece of advice you'd share with other families who want to become debt free like you have?*
Faith:	Sit down with yourself and come up with your "why" —why this is important to you. Don't even worry about the numbers. Don't even worry about how much debt you're in. There are so many bumps in the road. If you don't have a solid "why" that you can look back on, you're just not going to be successful.
Leo:	You are one decision away from a completely different life. When we look back on our journey, what we realize is that there were a series of choices that we made and with every "yes" that you say to something, you're saying "no" to a debt-free life. Examine the choices that you make because you're either choosing to become debt free and build wealth or you're choosing not to.

Carpe Diem Action Steps

- Review the benefits of a debt-free life that resonated with you in this chapter with your spouse. This is a good opportunity to dream of a better life together.
- Get an understanding of your current debt situation. Write down who you owe, how much you owe them, and your interest rates.

- Choose a debt destruction method and get to work.
- Explore some easy quick wins in reducing expenses without killing your joy. This will be motivation to keep moving forward.
- Sell 10 things around your house that have value that you don't use anymore. Use the proceeds to pay down your debt.
- Celebrate the small wins with your partner. Those celebrations will keep you moving forward.

NOTES

1. Peterson-Withorn, C. (2025). Forbes world's billionaire list 2025: The top 200. *Forbes.* Available at: https://www.forbes.com/sites/chasewithorn/2025/04/01/forbes-worlds-billionaires-list-2025-the-top-200/
2. Schulze, E. (2025, February 13). Americans' credit card debt reaches new record high: New York Federal Reserve. *ABC News.* Available at: https://abcnews.go.com/Business/americans-credit-card-debt-reaches-new-record-high/story?id=118788620
3. Martin, E. J. and Gage, S. (2023). *72% of higher earners are in credit card debt for at least a year: What is the best way to attack your credit card debt?* [Online]. Bankrate. Available at: https://www.bankrate.com/credit-cards/news/high-earners-in-debt/
4. Drentea, P. and Reynolds, J. R. (2014). Where does debt fit in the stress process model? *Sociology of Mental Health,* 28(5), pp. 16–32. Available at: https://pmc.ncbi.nlm.nih.gov/articles/PMC6521877/
5. England, M. J. and Sim, L. J. (Eds.). (2009). *Associations between depression in parents and parenting, child health, and child psychological functioning.* Washington, DC: National Library of Medicine. Available at: https://www.ncbi.nlm.nih.gov/books/NBK215128/
6. Collins, L. (2022). Job unhappiness is at a staggering all-time high, according to Gallup. *CNBC.* Available at: https://www.cnbc.com/2022/08/12/job-unhappiness-is-at-a-staggering-all-time-high-according-to-gallup.html
7. Davis, M. (2025). *It costs an additional $297,674 to raise a child over 18 years, up 25.3%* [Online]. LendingTree. Available at: https://www.lendingtree.com/debt-consolidation/raising-a-child-study/

8. Farrington, R. (2025). *Are MBAs worth it in 2025? How valuable is business school?* [Online]. The College Investor. Available at: https://thecollegeinvestor.com/1066/the-benefits-of-business-school/

9. Federal Reserve Bank of New York. (2025). *Household debt balances continue steady increase; delinquency transition rates remain elevated for auto and credit cards* [Online, Press Release]. Available at: https://www.newyorkfed.org/news events/news/research/2025/20250213

10. Federal Reserve Bank of St. Louis. (2025). *Average sales price of homes sold in the United States* [Online]. Available at: https://fred.stlouisfed.org/graph/?g= CpFW (accessed June 21, 2025).

11. Horymski, C. (2024). *HELOC balances surpass $45,000 in 2024* [Online]. Experian. Available at: https://www.experian.com/blogs/ask-experian/research/home-equity-line-of-credit-study/

12. Hanson, M. (2025). *Student loan debt statistics* [Online]. Education Data Initiative. Available at: https://educationdata.org/student-loan-debt-statistics

13. Davis, M. (2025). *Average car payment and auto loan statistics: 2025* [Online]. LendingTree. Available at: https://www.lendingtree.com/auto/debt-statistics/

14. Dickler, J. (2025). Americans' average credit card balance hits $6,580, but there are signs consumers are managing their debt relatively well. *CNBC*. Available at: https://www.cnbc.com/2025/02/20/transunion-americans-average-credit-card-balance-hits-6580.html

15. Freddie Mac. (2025). *Mortgage rates: Mortgage rates creep lower.* Available at: https://www.freddiemac.com/pmms (accessed June 21, 2025).

16. Schulz, M. (2025). *Average credit card interest rate in America today* [Online]. LendingTree. Available at: https://www.lendingtree.com/credit-cards/study/average-credit-card-interest-rate-in-america/

17. Zhang, C. (2024). *Credit card interest calculator* [Online]. LendingTree. Available at: https://www.lendingtree.com/credit-cards/articles/calculate-interest/

18. Empower. (2023). *Overindulge on everyday luxuries* [Online]. Available at: https://www.empower.com/the-currency/play/research-everyday-luxuries

19. Wildermuth, E. (n.d.). *The science of celebration: 5 reasons organizations should do it more* [Online]. Full Focus. Available at: https://fullfocus.co/science-of-celebration/

CHAPTER THREE

PROTECT YOUR FAMILY

"Love begins by taking care of the closest ones—the ones at home."
– Mother Teresa

I consider myself an optimist. Looking on the bright side of life just feels right. The reality is life can throw us curveballs when we least expect it.

We're living our lives, and things are going splendidly. Then all of sudden, disaster strikes. We're left thinking, "How could this happen to me?!"

It's fine to think life is good more often than not. But we can't ignore those times when things are bad or downright horrible.

We can wait for these terrible things to happen and have them shake us to our core. Or we can prepare for the worst and hope for the best.

After decades of adulting, I have learned that preparing for the worst is the best route to go. This is especially true when it comes to our family finances.

When there are more humans added into the mix, there is an increased chance of financial trouble. There's you. And you have a spouse. You've got kids. Maybe you're even caring for aging parents. All these people need to be protected. They are the rocks in your jar of life. We need to protect the people that matter to us most.

Lucky for us, we can take some simple steps to reduce the risks of financial ruin and even financial stress. When you know you've checked the box on these smart life choices, you will rest easier at night knowing you've protected your family the best you can.

BUILD A FAMILY EMERGENCY FUND

A smart place to start when it comes to financially protecting your family is with a family emergency fund. This is simply cash in the bank that you can easily access in case of emergency.

The word "emergency" can mean many different things to different people. This can be everything from a flat tire on the side of the road to your final burial expenses (and everything in between).

Smart reasons to have an emergency fund are as follows:

- **Job loss protection:** If you get laid off from your job and your family relies on your income to live, you need cash set aside. You can try your best to avoid being fired, but sometimes it has nothing to do with your performance. In 2025, there were mass layoffs in the federal government due to spending cuts (and had little to do with performance).[1] These once secure "dream jobs" suddenly became insecure. Tens of thousands of workers were suddenly out of work. For many of them, this was their first experience with unemployment. Having an emergency fund can set you up to weather the storm of job loss.

- **Keeps you from going back into debt:** When emergencies strike, many Americans rely on their credit card to help them get by. Unfortunately, credit card debt has reached an all-time high recently with many families paying more than 20% interest on their debt. This creates a debt cycle that is difficult to get out of. Having money in the bank for emergencies helps you use cash instead of credit. This is a life-long habit that will help you keep that coveted debt-free life we spoke about.

- **Protection from the unexpected:** This can come in the form of car accidents, medical emergencies, appliances breaking down, household repairs, and so much more. We can pretend these are unexpected, or we can embrace that these emergencies are actually things we should expect. As they say, stuff happens! (I think they use a different word, but this is a family book so …)

- **Higher deductible insurance plans:** If you have a higher deductible healthcare plan, you need to be able to cover the higher deductibles. Roof damage? You'll need to pay the deductible before your insurance kicks in. Someone crashed into the back of your car? Time to pay the deductible. This is another great reason to have an emergency fund.

- **Allows for more flexibility:** Let's say your great-grandfather who lives in another state just passed away. You love him, and you want to be there for his funeral. With an emergency fund, you have the cash to go. You don't even have to think about whether you can attend or not. This is one less issue you'll ever have to worry about.

- **Helps you become a calmer parent:** When my daughter was younger, she accidentally dropped a glass in our bathroom sink and cracked the porcelain. We needed to change out the whole sink, replace it with a new one, and it cost some money. As I'm writing this book, my son is in the other room playing with a friend. They just broke some dishes while throwing the football in the basement.

If I was stressed about money and feeling that every dollar was crucial to our survival, I may have lost my cool in these moments. Knowing we have money in the bank to take care of these things helps me approach the situation with a calm demeanor. After all, it's just stuff, and my kids are so much more important.

These reasons and so many more should get you motivated to build up your family emergency fund. As you start to pile in the funds, you'll feel the financial stress and anxiety begin to lift off your shoulders. This is because you know you're ready for whatever may come your family's way.

Emergency Fund Goals

Many financial experts recommend saving 3–6 months of expenses in an emergency fund. For those starting out on their family financial independence journey, a reasonable first goal is 1 month of expenses set aside.

Let's say after your first awesome money date, you find out your monthly expenses are around $10,000. With this newfound information, you can quickly do the math on your first emergency fund goal.

$10,000 of monthly expenses × 1 month = $10,000 emergency fund

This *beginner emergency fund* will help you with some of the smaller emergencies that may pop up. Also, it will more than likely keep you from going back into debt in the near term.

As you start to eliminate high-interest debt from your life (like credit cards), moving from a beginner emergency fund to a true emergency fund is important. This will protect you and your family from bigger emergencies like job loss, medical emergencies, and high-deductible payments.

If both you and your partner are working secure and full-time jobs, aim for 3 months of expenses saved. Using our example of a family who spends $10,000 per month, here's how the math shakes out.

$10,000 of monthly expenses × 3 months = $30,000 emergency fund

If you are a single income household with a family to take care of, aim for 6 months of expenses saved. This is because your family's household income is more vulnerable with only one income source.

$10,000 of monthly expenses × 6 months = $60,000 emergency fund

When you have no emergency fund, these dollar figures can feel insanely high. You wouldn't be alone either. According to a recent survey, 27% of Americans currently have no emergency savings at all.[2] This may feel like the norm, but it definitely keeps these families in a vulnerable position: vulnerable enough to stay working in a toxic environment and vulnerable enough to not feel confident during tough financial times.

When you have money in the bank, you move from a state of financial insecurity and anxiety to a state of security and confidence. That's what you want for yourself and your family.

So, if these large amounts of money feel intimidating, remember you don't need to hit these goals overnight. Just take it one step at a time.

Tips for Growing Your Emergency Fund

The first step is growing your confidence that you can actually do this. Start with action.

Just like we did with eliminating our debt, we need to increase our income and decrease our expenses. Once you see actual money making it into your account, you will start to believe that a 3- to 6-month emergency fund is possible for your family.

Remember the immediate money that can come into your life from selling stuff around your house that you don't use anymore. I believe you can easily make \$500–\$1,000 over the course of a weekend just selling your old stuff. This requires effort, but it will quite literally pay off. Once you earn that money, put it right in your bank account.

After earning a little bit of cash, it is time to examine your budget and see what expenses you have that you don't even use anymore. A recent survey of 1,100 Americans found that 85% of them have at least one monthly subscription they don't use anymore.[3] I'm willing to bet you might have some wasted money in your budget. Stop the drain on your account and put that savings into your emergency fund.

When money starts to roll into your life (both from earning income and reducing expenses), it is time to make a realistic goal for how long it will take you to achieve your starter emergency fund. Let's say you and your partner (who spend \$10k per month) have committed to finding \$1,000 of savings each month. Between earning more money and reducing unnecessary expenses, you think this amount is reasonable and realistic without burning out. With that commitment, you could have your starter emergency fund in just 10 months.

$$\$1,000 \text{ of savings} \times 10 \text{ months} = \$10,000 \text{ emergency fund}$$

Making the commitment as a couple to always keep an emergency fund is a big step on your family financial independence journey. Sometimes keeping our commitments is difficult. We are human after all, right?

That's why I like to take the "human" out of the process. Let's use automation and artificial intelligence to make our lives better. After making this commitment together as a couple and realizing that \$1,000 of savings is feasible for your budget, set up an automated monthly transfer from your checking to your emergency savings account. This way, you are specifically allocating money for emergencies only. Many banking partners allow you to do this easily. If your bank does not allow you to automatically add funds to your savings account, I would look for another banking partner.

Also, if your banking partner does not offer high-yield savings for your emergency fund, look for another place for your emergency savings. There has been a rise in customers abandoning their brick-and-mortar banks for high-yield savings account options online. One in four Americans do their banking entirely online.[4] Yes, you lose the convenience of being able to visit a bank in person, but you trade that for potentially thousands of dollars of interest (aka free money) each year.

For example, if you have your $50,000 emergency savings with a brick-and-mortar bank offering 0.01% APY on your savings, you will earn $5 per year in interest.

On the other hand, if you trade that situation for a relationship with an online banking partner offering 3% APY on your savings, you will earn $1,500 per year in interest.

When looking for a banking partner (brick-and-mortar or online), ensure your funds are protected through FDIC insurance. This will insure your funds up to $250,000, no matter what happens to this institution. If you have a joint bank account with two owners, you are protected up to $500,000. This will give you peace of mind knowing your funds are protected no matter what.

SECURE THE RIGHT INSURANCE COVERAGE

Having an emergency fund protects your family from the everyday small to medium-sized emergencies of life. But what about the really big emergencies?

That's where insurance comes in. Insurance definitely isn't the most exciting topic, but your family will be very happy that you have it when the big emergencies do happen.

These big emergencies can come in the form of car accidents, floods in your home, life changing personal injuries, people getting injured while on your property, and the untimely death of a spouse.

All of these incidents are horrible emotionally and financially. The sad reality is they do happen. We can work hard to avoid them, but many times things happen anyway. These devastating moments can make you feel broken inside. You don't also want to become financially broke as well. This is why we have insurance.

Let's review the types of insurance you should consider as a family.

Health Insurance

Protecting your health and the health of your family is crucial. Health insurance is meant to cover routine visits to the doctor all the way to cancer treatment.

Depending on your employment situation, or that of your spouse, health insurance is often provided as a workplace benefit. Employers can cover some or even all the premiums associated with being a part of the healthcare plan.

If you don't have a traditional employment situation where healthcare is offered, you can still sign up for health insurance. Small business owners or contractors can secure health insurance off the Health Insurance Marketplace (or healthcare.gov). Depending on your financial situation, you may be able to receive discounts making health insurance more affordable.

As you grow your emergency fund over time, you may want to consider going with a high-deductible insurance plan. With a high-deductible plan, your monthly premium payments are a lot lower than lower deductible plans. By paying a lower premium (monthly payment), your deductible (the amount you pay before insurance kicks in) becomes a lot higher. If you and your family are healthy, don't often visit the doctor, and have a sizable emergency fund, then a high-deductible plan could be right for you.

You can also get access to a Health Savings Account (HSA), which allows you to save on taxes when it comes to your healthcare expenses. In this tax advantaged account, you can save and even invest for your future healthcare costs.

If your family has frequent medical visits, your health is not the best, and your emergency fund is low or nonexistent, going with a lower deductible healthcare plan can make more sense. You may pay higher premiums each month, but your insurance can kick in quicker because your deductibles will be lower.

Homeowners/Renters Insurance

If you have a home, you need homeowners insurance. This covers your physical dwelling and your personal property inside your home and even provides liability coverage for you, your family, and your pets.

When seeking out a homeowner's insurance policy, find coverage that covers the entire cost to replace the home and the contents inside. This is important because tragic incidents like floods, wind damage, and fires can ruin your home and everything in it.

Having been a homeowner for more than 20 years now, homeowners insurance can feel like a waste of money when you're paying your bill month after month. Then on one random Michigan winter morning, you wake up to a flooded kitchen after your pipe bursts. Your floors, carpeting, furniture, and cupboards are ruined. All of sudden, homeowners insurance doesn't feel like such a waste of money anymore. It feels like you made a smart move.

If you are a renter and don't own a home, you still need insurance. While your landlord might have homeowners insurance, it doesn't cover the contents inside the home. As the renter, this is your responsibility to make sure your furniture, electronics, and belongings are insured.

Auto Insurance

Driving without insurance is illegal in most all states in the United States. Automobile insurance is a virtual necessity. If you live in a city that doesn't require a car, this is an excellent opportunity for savings. For a lot of us, this isn't an option.

Even if you have an older car and it doesn't have much value, it still makes sense to have auto insurance. It protects you from being sued if you're in a car accident and someone gets injured.

Long-term Disability Insurance

Often provided as a workplace benefit, long-term disability insurance covers you if you're unable to work because of injury or illness. Government benefits programs and workers' compensation can support you, but long-term disability can extend that financial support.

A lot of us won't think we'll need long-term disability support. Not surprisingly, we're more likely to have a disability during our working years than we are to die.[5] One in four workers will encounter a disability during their working years while only 13% will die during that same period. Unfortunately, more people have life insurance than long-term disability insurance.[6]

While an emergency fund can cover you and your family for a period, long-term disabilities can last anywhere from 2 to 10 years, or even longer.[7] That's not emergency fund territory.

Review your long-term disability coverage at work. You may want to consider purchasing additional coverage if your employer's coverage isn't sufficient for your needs.

Life Insurance

Remember memento mori?

The reality is that we're going to die someday. Personally, I hope it's later than sooner, but that may be out of my hands.

To support our families financially if we were to die unexpectedly, term life insurance can be a smart purchase. Term life insurance provides your family a financial payout in the event of your death for a term (or a period of time). For example, let's say you buy a 20-year term life insurance policy with a $1,000,000 payout. If you were to die during this 20-year period, your family would receive $1,000,000. To keep this policy active, you are required to make your annual premium payments.

You and your spouse should both consider term life insurance policies. This supports either one of you (and your children) with an income source if the other passes away.

Consider the impact of your spouse dying and how that would affect your family's finances. Having term life insurance removes the financial stress during an already emotionally stressful time.

Even if your partner is a stay-at-home parent and doesn't have an income, term life insurance is still an important purchase. Think of all the support they provide as a caretaker for the children and the dozens of roles at home. You will need financial support and the financial cushion to step away from work for a while if your stay-at-home partner dies.

In a podcast interview a few years ago, Juan from Michigan shared how term life insurance changed his life after his wife died in her thirties. No one was expecting it. Her death was untimely and emotionally devastating for Juan and his young daughter. Since his wife had a term life insurance policy, Juan was able to take time off work, eliminate all his family debt (including the mortgage), and eventually create a solopreneur business doing power washing. He was able to be there for his daughter when it mattered most. His solopreneur working hours are reasonable so he can be a present father as well. He's grateful for the time he had with his wife and that they both thought ahead to prepare for the worst.

For the majority of families, term life insurance is sufficient coverage in case of death. While whole life insurance is another option, it typically has more expensive premiums and provides a lower payout upon death. The positive side of whole life is that you get coverage for your entire life (whole) instead of just a portion of your life (term). Additionally, the policy grows a cash value over time.

Whole life can make sense as an investment for wealthier families after they have exhausted other better investment options like 401(k)s, IRAs, HSAs, and even taxable brokerage accounts. It's also worth exploring if you have children who require a lifetime of care (mental or physical disabilities) and would be financially disadvantaged when you pass away.

Again, for the majority of families, term life insurance is the better buy.

Umbrella Insurance

The last type of insurance you should consider as a family is umbrella insurance. This is essentially protection against getting sued.

Once you start to build up your assets and grow your net worth to around $500,000, it might make sense to get an umbrella policy.

Lawsuits are not fun. They are full of lawyers, money, arguments, more lawyers, and more money. Umbrella insurance helps protect you from the following:

- Slip and fall accidents at your house
- Major car accidents where your auto insurance does not cover all the damages
- Your dog attacking or biting someone else
- Ski, surf, or hunting accidents
- Parents who want to sue you while you serve as a youth sports coach

Some families have pools, trampolines, swing sets, and other outdoor adventure toys. If a child visiting the house gets injured and the parent decides to sue you, umbrella insurance is key.

Umbrella insurance is also relatively inexpensive. In most cases, you can get a lot of coverage for a small monthly fee. This makes sense because the insurance company is probably thinking anyone who buys this type of policy must already be very careful and smart people.

While hoping for the best is a plan, it may not be a financially savvy one. These big events may not happen often, but when they do, you're going to want to have the right insurance coverage to protect your family.

CRAFT A WILL AND TRUST

You know those movies where the older wealthy family member dies and their heirs wait patiently to see what they'll get when the executor reads the will? It's fun to see when you're watching a movie, but I think it's caused a lot of confusion for the majority of people.

When you watch a movie like that, you get the impression that wills and trusts are only for really rich people. That couldn't be farther from the truth.

If you're married, having a will is important because it ensures your spouse maintains possession of your assets and belongings after you die. With complex probate and estate planning laws, you're proactively helping reduce stress for your partner during a difficult time.

And if you're a parent, having a will specifies who should take care of your children in the event of your death. If this is left up to the courts, your children could be raised by someone both you and your kids don't agree with.

The sad truth is that just 22% of millennials have a will, with Gen X at 26% and the younger generation, Gen Z, at 15%.[8] The majority of parents are underprepared and are leaving their families vulnerable.

What Is a Will?

Before you go off and get a will, it's important to understand what it is first.

A will is a legal document that clarifies how you want your affairs to be handled after your death. Some of those affairs and important instructions include the following:

- **Assigning an executor:** This person will carry out the wishes of your will.
- **Appointing guardianship:** This clarifies who you desire to support and raise your children.
- **Laying out special arrangements:** This specifies things like if you'd rather be buried in a Superman suit or cremated or if you'd like a karaoke jam at your life celebration (my personal preference).
- **Determining who receives your property:** Depending on your state, law may require your spouse to receive everything upon your death, or it may not. It's important to outline who should receive your belongings, assets, and property in your will.

What Happens If I Don't Have a Will?

If you die without a will, you can create a lot of confusion and anger for your family. This is because when you die intestate (without a will), the court can get involved and decide how to proceed based on your state's laws.

A judge decides who the guardian of your children will be and who receives your property.

Probate court can be lengthy, confusing, and expensive. The entire process from petitioning for probate to final judgment typically takes several months or even up to a year.[9] Belinda, a commenter on my blog shared this story: "I've just been through almost 2 years of trying to resolve my

Dad's estate, where there wasn't a will. It has affected my health horribly. I had chronic physical health conditions prior to my lovely Dad's death, and the sheer labour, red tape and frustration of the last couple of years certainly contributed to worsening my health."

Where Do I Get a Will?

If you're ready to get a will but you're worried about how long the process will take, don't despair. Depending on the complexity of your family's finances, you can complete this process in under 30 minutes. I know this from experience. My wife and I cranked out our will during a relaxing weekend at home.

For straightforward financial situations, check out the online will makers that are available. My favorite is Trust & Will. You can complete your joint will all online from the comfort of your home.

For more complex financial situations including divorce, properties, or businesses in different states and children from previous marriages, consider meeting with a trusted estate planning lawyer.

The all-online solution will typically be less expensive than working with a lawyer. If your situation is more complex, it is worth the extra cost to have your estate plan set and your family protected.

When Do I Need a Trust?

Even with a will, your family still may end up in probate court. The process will be shorter than if you were to die without a will. With a will, the probate will review the document, assign an executor, and distribute the property accordingly.[10]

So how do you avoid probate court altogether? Consider a trust.

According to the head of legal at Trust & Will, Patrick Hicks, "The goal of a trust is to either eliminate probate entirely or to carve it down to such a small minor detail that you barely even know it happens."

A living revocable trust is one type of trust that families use. It is "living" because you create it during your lifetime, and it's "revocable" because you can cancel it at any time. This is a living document that allows you to modify it throughout your life as your life situation changes. It also supports the goal of keeping your family out of probate court.

Like umbrella insurance, seek out a trust as your assets start to grow. "If you get over $200,000, and that would include something like your house, that's the point where you should start at least considering a trust for the probate savings alone," suggests Hicks.

As parents, trusts are even more important. This legal document allows you to decide how and when your children will receive money and assets from your estate. Knowing that financial maturity can grow over time, you may decide to not burden your children with the heavy responsibility of an inheritance until they reach a certain age.

As parents, getting a will is a smart move you should make immediately. Protecting your children, honoring your final wishes, and distributing your assets is something you can do in a matter of minutes. The impact will last a lifetime.

When your assets grow (as they will over time), consider a trust to further protect your family's financial security and peace of mind.

FREEZE YOUR CREDIT

Building up a solid credit history can help us to get more competitive rates on loans. We discussed committing to a debt-free life in the previous chapter, but if we're pursuing homeownership and planning to secure a mortgage, having a good credit score is important.

If you're not actively applying for credit, I recommend freezing your credit. With more than one million cases of identity theft reported to the FTC annually, freezing your credit can prevent would-be thieves from using your stolen information to open up accounts in your name.[11]

While thieves can still use your stolen data to perform other acts of fraud, freezing your credit is one easy step you can take to protect your family.

How to Freeze Your Credit

Your credit profile is held by the three major credit bureaus. These are Equifax, Experian, and Transunion. When a credit profile is unfrozen at these three bureaus, you are able to apply for new lines of credit. This includes credit cards. If a cybercriminal has your data and applies online, they can get a credit card in your name and use it as they please. The problem is that you're on the hook for paying back the credit card debt, not them.

To freeze your credit, go the website of each of the three credit bureaus—Equifax (equifax.com), Experian (experian.com), and Transunion (transunion.com). There will be an option to freeze your credit. These credit bureaus don't make this process easy. They will try to sell you services you may not need. Freezing your credit is free. You should not have to pay for anything to do this. Complete the freeze at all three credit bureaus.

Once your credit is frozen, you can choose to unfreeze it at any time. It is also free to unfreeze your credit. You may want to do this if you are ready to apply for credit. I would recommend only unfreezing your credit for the period when you are considering applying for credit. After that time, freeze it up again.

Freezing and unfreezing your credit report does not affect your credit score.[12] You and your spouse should both freeze your credit.

Freezing Your Kids' Credit

Sad to say it, but major data breaches are becoming a common occurrence. Hospital systems, password protection sites, and even credit bureaus like Equifax have been hacked. Even more horrible, schools have been targets of data breaches as well.[13] This is usually due to poor cyber-security measures in the school system and lack of funding to support security enhancements.

Once your child's data are secured by cyber criminals, they can use it to open lines of credit in your child's name. According to Experian, 25% of children will become victims of identity theft before they reach the age of 18.[14]

While freezing your child's credit doesn't stop all the potential harms that could come their way through identity theft, it can help. Freezing your child's credit profile as early as possible ensures that thieves will not be able to open credit accounts in their name.

To freeze your children's credit, you would again work through each of the three credit bureaus previously mentioned. Unfortunately, they make this process even harder to complete. I did this for my children, and it took several hours. It is not an easy online process like freezing your own credit. You have to print out and physically mail in forms to each of the three bureaus.

Each bureau should freeze your child's credit after receiving the request in the mail within three business days.[15] Additionally, they will send a con-firmation of this freeze in the mail. Save this document in a secure loca-tion. When you or your child are ready to unfreeze their credit, this letter will come in handy as it provides instructions on how to do so.

Identity theft is often thought of as something that only happens to older people. This is far from the truth. The demographic that is the most impacted by identity theft is the age group of 30–39, with age groups 40–49 and 20–29 following right behind.[16] This age range is full of busy parents who spend a lot of time online.

While stopping wide-scale data breaches is not something in our con-trol, we can take some small steps, like freezing our credit, to ensure our family is at least a bit more protected.

HAVE THE MONEY TALK WITH YOUR AGING PARENTS

One of my more memorable podcast interviews was with Cameron Huddleston, the Author of *Mom and Dad We Need to Talk: How to Have Essential Conversations with Your Parents About Their Finances*. In our discussion, she shared how she learned the importance of knowing your parents' finances before it's too late.

Her mother was diagnosed with Alzheimer's at the age of 65. Cameron was only 35 years old at the time with three children at home. One of them was still in diapers.

Unfortunately, Cameron did not have a lot of conversations with her mother about her mother's finances before she was diagnosed. All of sudden, Cameron was thrust into managing her mother's financial situation and much more. She found herself trying to find accounts and passwords, all while taking care of her mother and her three children as well. This was the definition of the "sandwich generation."

Over time, she became more accustomed to managing her mother's financial situation. Having gone through the whole process, she shared with me that she wished she prepared better.

From her learnings, she shared this advice with me (which I ended up using for discussions with my parents).

- **Understand if they have a will and estate plan:** This conversation can be difficult for adult children to have with their parents. Try using yourself as an example. "Mom and Dad, we just read this book about getting a will and trust to protect our family. We're going to do it. By the way, do you have one?" This way, you're opening the door to a conversation where you can learn more about their estate plan. If they are willing to discuss it further and don't have anything set up, getting a will/trust and durable power of attorney are good starting points.

- **Determine if they have sufficient retirement planning:** Your father and mother may have a pension, Social Security, and investments to support them in retirement. Or they may only be relying on Social Security. This is good for you to know especially if your parents are not already financially secure. Use your situation again if it helps break the ice. "Mom and Dad, I'm investing for retirement and based on these online calculators I think we'll be in a good spot come retirement time. What income sources are you two using for retirement?" Whether they share the individual details of their retirement plans or not, your goal is to know if they are going to be financially stable in retirement.
- **Tread lightly and proceed with love:** Money can be a very sensitive topic for people. When you raised your children and all of sudden it feels like they are bossing you around with regard to your money, you might get defensive. Treat your parents with respect and kindness. Don't be condescending and don't issue an ultimatum about knowing their financial situation. You can support them in phases as they are ready. This is a conversation about you supporting them and helping them enjoy their golden years.

With Cameron's advice, I had "the talk" with my parents. I am glad I did. Today, I feel more confident knowing their financial situation and having the proper estate documents in place. I even helped them freeze their credit too. My parents and I can rest easier knowing this is one less thing we need to worry about.

FROM THE PODCAST

Family: Michael and Taylor, 34 years old from Texas
Money Milestone: 9-month emergency fund secured

Andy:	*When you guys got married, what was your financial situation?*
Michael:	When we got married, we both made a pretty decent income. I think combined we were about $120k or so, but we had no real structure of how we managed money. It was like, get it, spend it, and maybe save a little bit here and there. But for the most part, we were young, early twenties. We had started our careers, and we were just enjoying life, but no real vision for the future. And as a result, our finances took a hit for that.
Andy:	*What do mean they took a hit?*
Michael:	We racked up $61,000 worth of debt. It was silly stuff. My first encounter with debt actually came from a road trip. My car broke down. I was about 20 hours away from home with no savings. And all I had was just a credit card, you know, specifically set aside for emergencies.
	And so here I was in an emergency. The logical thing to do is just to swipe the credit card. So I did that. And it was like the flood gates just opened. From there, it was like emergencies just found me after that point. Everything that could go wrong for the next couple of years did go wrong. And then I got used to getting that statement in the mail. And so then after that, it wasn't just emergencies. It was TVs. It was new clothes for work. It was just all these other things that I was making a good enough income to buy.

Andy:	*After deciding you and Taylor wanted to pay off this debt, did you guys come across any roadblocks during your journey?*
Michael:	Yeah, a big one. I actually lost my job 8 months into the journey.

I'm in sales. I'm one of the top sales reps in the top market unit in this global company. And so I'm thinking I've got job security for life. And I take a few days off to just kind of breathe and relax. And while I'm on my vacation, I get a phone call and it's like, "Hey, we need you on a conference call at 8 a.m. tomorrow."

I get on the conference call, and they basically tell us, "We're restructuring, and some of you guys won't have jobs in six weeks." And I was one of the lucky ones that didn't have a job in six weeks.

And so another part of that was my wife actually has lupus, which is an autoimmune disease. And one of the triggers for that is stress. And so just dealing with my job loss and me feeling like, "Gosh, I'm not living up to everything that I'm supposed to be," she could feel that. And so she became stressed, and she got sick and missed about a month of work, which I think about two weeks or so of that was unpaid.

So I don't have a job, she's missing work, and it's just kind of this vicious cycle that we went through. And that was a really tough time for us.

Andy:	*What did you do to keep yourself motivated?*
Michael:	I really leaned into my wife. We really leaned into each other. I feel like that time period in our marriage was really pivotal for us because since then, going through that, nothing compares to that. We've not experienced

anything like that so anything that comes up now, it's like, okay, we can have a brief conversation. We can talk about anything. We can lay our feelings and emotions out there. And it's just unified us as a couple.

Andy: *Did you eventually pay off your debts? How long did it take?*

Michael: Sixteen months to the day after our wedding day. That was just an incredible moment for us. Hitting submit on the button, you kind of build it up in your mind. You're like, it's going to be this fantastic thing. And it, and it wasn't, it was kind of anticlimactic, but at the same time you have this realization that, okay, now from this point forward, everything that we earn is ours, and we get to direct it how we want to, and it's not obligated to pay for anything that we've done in the past.

We get to direct our money going forward and that was the big thing for us. Looking at our paychecks going, "Okay, what do we do now that we're not sending almost $4,000 a month towards credit cards and cars?"

Andy: *So you had all that extra money, what did you guys do with it?*

Michael: Having gone through the job loss and her illness and everything, it was just right for us to build our emergency fund. And I know a lot of people say 3 to 6 months, but for us, with my job volatility and everything, we felt comfortable with about nine months of our expenses saved up. And so that was our first priority.

And then once we took care of that, we just started sending all that money towards index funds. And it's been incredible just watching that grow over the last four years. It's just awesome.

Carpe Diem Action Steps

- Begin saving up your starter emergency fund. If you already have one, grow it to 3 to 6 months of expenses saved up. Find ways to make more money and reduce expenses without killing your happiness.
- Review your insurance coverage to make sure your family is protected.
- Secure a will or trust based on your family situation. Meet with a trusted lawyer if your finances are complex or use an online service like Trust & Will to complete it today.
- Freeze your credit. Do the same for your spouse and your kids. Identity theft is very real and damaging for over a million of Americans each year.
- Have the talk with your parents about their finances. Use a personal story or one from this book to open the door to this important conversation.

NOTES

1. Shao, E. and Wu, A. (2025, May 12). The federal work force cuts so far, agency by agency. *New York Times.* Available at: https://www.nytimes.com/interactive/2025/03/28/us/politics/trump-doge-federal-job-cuts.html
2. Gillespie, L. and Robloff, T. (2025). *Bankrate's 2025 annual emergency savings report* [Online]. Bankrate. Available at: https://www.bankrate.com/banking/savings/emergency-savings-report/
3. Self. (2024). *The cost of unused subscriptions 2024* [Online]. Available at: https://www.self.inc/info/cost-of-unused-paid-subscriptions/
4. Lisa, A. (2024). *Future of banking 2024: Will online banking eliminate brick & mortar branches?* [Online]. NASDAQ. Available at: https://www.nasdaq.com/articles/future-of-banking-2024:-will-online-banking-eliminate-brick-mortar-branches
5. Maleh, J. and Bosley, T. (2022). Disability and death probability tables for insured workers who attain age 20 in 2022. *Actuarial Note.* Available at: https://www.ssa.gov/oact/NOTES/ran6/an2022-6.pdf

6. Martin, A. (2024). *Life insurance statistics, facts, and industry trends for 2025* [Online]. Choice Mutual. Available at: https://choicemutual.com/blog/life-insurance-statistics/

7. Paychex. (2025). *Short-term disability insurance vs. long-term disability insurance* [Online]. Paychex. Available at: https://www.paychex.com/articles/employee-benefits/short-vs-long-term-disability-insurance

8. Trust & Will. (2025). *Redefining legacy* [Online]. Available at: https://trustandwill.com/learn/estate-planning-report-2025

9. Powers, M. (2025). *How long do you have to file for probate?* [Online]. Trust & Will. Available at: https://trustandwill.com/learn/how-long-do-you-have-to-file-probate-after-death

10. Bell, K., Tsosie, C., and Emmert, C. (2025). *What is probate? How it works with or without a will* [Online]. NerdWallet. Available at: https://www.nerdwallet.com/article/investing/estate-planning/what-is-how-avoid-probate

11. Caporal, J. (2025). *Identity theft and credit card fraud statistics for 2025* [Online]. Motley Fool. Available at: https://www.fool.com/money/research/identity-theft-credit-card-fraud-statistics/

12. Federal Trade Commission. (2025). *Credit freeze or fraud alert: what's right for your credit report?* [Online]. Available at: https://consumer.ftc.gov/articles/credit-freeze-or-fraud-alert-whats-right-your-credit-report

13. Greig, J. (2025). Thousands of Baltimore students, teachers affected by data breach following February ransomware attack [Online]. *The Record*. Available at: https://therecord.media/baltimore-public-schools-data-breach-ransomware

14. Weissman, S. (2024). *Child identity theft is a huge problem. The solutions are simple* [Online]. R Street. Available at: https://www.rstreet.org/commentary/child-identity-theft-is-a-huge-problem-the-solutions-are-simple/

15. Barroso, A. (2025). *Child identity theft: how to freeze and protect your child's credit* [Online]. NerdWallet. Available at: https://www.nerdwallet.com/article/finance/child-identity-theft

16. Roy, I. (2025, April 4). 11 ways to prevent identity theft. *US News & World Report*. Available at: https://www.usnews.com/360-reviews/privacy/identity-theft-protection/10-ways-to-prevent-identity-theft

PART 2

BUILD FAMILY WEALTH

CHAPTER FOUR

INVEST UNTIL COAST FIRE

"The stock market is designed to transfer money from the active to the patient."

– Warren Buffett

The problem with work is that it requires so much … work. You're at your job day in and day out for decades. Succeeding and thriving professionally requires consistent dedication to your employer's goals. Meeting those expectations and finding ways to innovate along the way can be downright exhausting. When you combine these expectations at work with your expectations at home, it's no wonder parental stress is out of control.

You can do this for a while, but eventually you ask the question, "When can I stop working so much and relax?" That's when conversations about retirement come into the picture. Traditionally, this is the time in our sixties or seventies when we stop working altogether and get started with living our lives. The only problem is there might not be a lot of life left to live at that point.

With the average lifespan in the United States at 78 years old, potentially less than a decade of defining how you want to live your life feels too short.[1] Also, these are typically not our peak years of health and vitality. So if you keep saying to yourself, "I'll go on that adventure when I'm retired," you may not feel up to it. If you've been investing for a while, you may have the funds to travel and try new experiences in traditional retirement, but you may not have the energy or the time. These are two very important resources we also have to consider.

While the traditional retirement model isn't all bad, I'd like to propose a different approach that can allow for more enjoyment while we're younger. It's something my wife and I have been experimenting with for the past 5 years.

Instead of working a corporate job for 40 years and relaxing for 15 years, let's work that corporate job for 15 years and relax for 40 years.

Who knows? If you have time to take better care of your health and not feel so stressed at work and home, you might extend that relaxation season a couple more decades.

How can we do this? Whether you retire from your corporate career in your sixties or in your forties, it starts by building your family wealth through the accumulation of assets. You then use those assets to make money for you. Instead of you making the money, your assets make the money. This is you transitioning from "active income" (making money through working at your corporate job) to "passive income" (your investments making money for you).

When you make enough passive income to cover your annual expenses, you are financially independent (FI). You don't need to work for money anymore (aka retirement).

CHOOSE YOUR OWN FINANCIAL INDEPENDENCE ADVENTURE

How quickly you get to financial independence is up to you. This all depends on your saving rate. If you earn $100,000 per year and save and invest $50,000 per year into the stock market, your saving rate is 50%. On the other hand, if you make $100,000 per year and save and invest $0 per year, your saving rate is 0%.

You can accelerate the time it takes for you to reach financial independence by increasing your saving rate. Let's review three different financial independence paths, and I'll share some pros and cons with all of them.

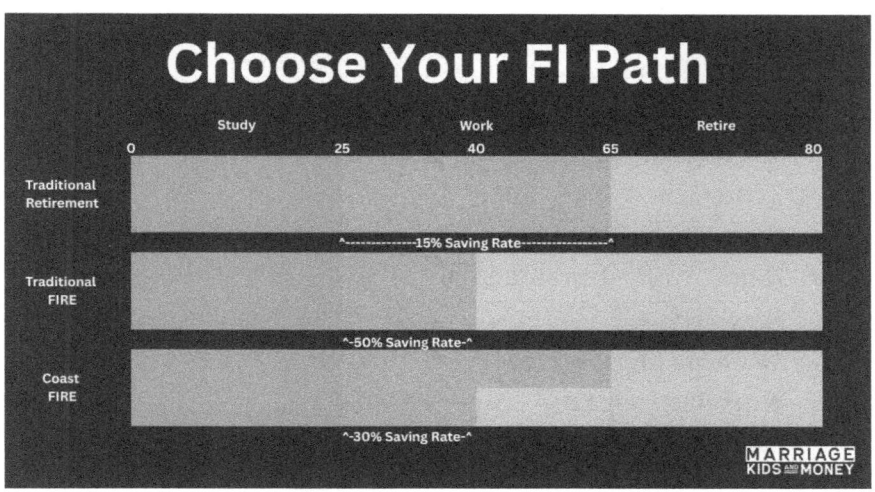

The Traditional Retirement Path

You are probably most familiar with this path. Your parents may have pursued this path or you might currently be on this path. Let's visualize this story with a fictional character named "Jacob."

Jacob is in twenties, and he's enjoying life. He spends all of his income each month because he's all about living for today. Sometimes he spends more than his income by taking on debt. He recently changed jobs for the third time in a few years after realizing he could make more money job hopping. This helps him to create a bigger gap between his income and expenses. Around this time, Jacob met the woman of his dreams, got married, and they are expecting their first child. With his job and family changes, he decides to finally live within his means, pay off his debt, and sign up for his workplace 401(k). He sets his saving rate at 15% of his household income and invests for the long haul. After 40 years of work in the corporate world, Jacob should have enough to retire comfortably at age 65.

- **Household Income (Annual)**: $100,000
- **Saving Amount/Rate (Annual)**: $15,000/15%
- **Retirement Investment Plan**: Workplace 401(k)
- **Starting Age**: 25
- **Retirement Age**: 65
- **Years Working Full-Time**: 40
- **Hours Worked in Total**: 80,000 (assumes 2,000 hours working per year)
- **Memento Mori Age**: 80
- **Years Relaxing After Corporate Life**: 15
- **Hours Relaxing Added After Corporate Life**: 30,000

If Jacob truly enjoys going to his job every day, this can be a desirable life path. He and his wife will be able to spend most of their money on things that make them happy. Putting away 15% each month takes some planning and intentionality on their part, but they are able to do this and still comfortably live their lives. They even have money to give generously to family, friends, and their favorite charities.

On the other hand, if Jacob doesn't like his job, this working situation could feel like a prison of his own making. He'll find himself getting more irritated with his job, bringing that stress home to his family, and overall feeling like he's missing out on life outside of the four walls of his office. At that point, Jacob may want to seek an alternative route. This becomes increasingly difficult if Jacob's wife, Emily, starts to lose her patience with her job too.

The FIRE (Financial Independence Retire Early) Path

When corporate careers start to lose their luster, employees begin to rebel against tradition. One movement that has gained a lot of interest over the past 15 years or so is the FIRE Movement. FIRE stands for "Financial Independence/Retire Early."

The FIRE Movement believes that humans are not meant to be working the majority of our lives doing jobs they don't enjoy. If we can harness the power of our saving rate, we can decrease our working years dramatically. This gives us more time to enjoy life and less time working. It's like the movie *Office Space* but with a much better financial exit strategy.

Over the years, this movement caught the attention of high-earning tech professionals. The grind of long days (and nights) working for startup companies and fast-growing corporations left them with an "all work and no play" life. Young parents in this working situation desperately started looking for a way out. The FIRE Movement became their saving grace.

Let's shift the story to Emily's perspective.

Emily has now been working for 5 years in the corporate world, and she's had it. Long days lead to even longer evenings of catching up on email at home. She's also pregnant and can't see how she's going to be able to keep up this pace with a newborn. As her career in the tech world has grown, she's received progressive levels of salary increases. Between her and her husband Jacob, they are now earning $150,000 as a household. They've been saving 15% for a few years now, but Emily is invigorated by the FIRE Movement and convinced this is her path out of the corporate world for good. Her plan is to save and invest 50% of her household income for 10–15 years and retire fully in her forties. This will leave her more time to breathe and enjoy special moments with her family. Maxing out her workplace 401(k) and having her husband do the same is a good starting point. They can also max out Roth IRAs and contribute to a taxable brokerage account to serve as a bridge account for their early retirement.

- **Household Income (Annual)**: $150,000
- **Saving Amount/Rate (Annual)**: $75,000/50%
- **Retirement Investment Plan**: Workplace 401(k), Roth IRAs, and Taxable Brokerage
- **Starting Age**: 25
- **Retirement Age**: 40
- **Years Working Full-Time**: 15
- **Hours Worked in Total**: 30,000
- **Memento Mori Age**: 80
- **Years Relaxing After Corporate Life**: 40
- **Hours Relaxing Added After Corporate Life**: 80,000

If Emily wants to retire at 40 years old and never work again, saving and investing upwards of 50% of her household income for 15 years can get her there. She'll have a wide open future in her forties with countless options on how she'll spend her time. The early portion of her daughter's life will require more daycare and support from her mother-in-law; the latter portion, Emily will be more available.

As Emily progresses down this path, she finds that her road to early retirement is a lot more difficult than she thought. With the arrival of her new child, new expenses have arrived as well. Daycare costs are astronomical, and her mother-in-law isn't as available as she hoped. In order to hit the aggressive saving rate of 50%, small pleasures start to get removed from their family budget. Date nights, vacation funds, hair coloring, nail appointments, evenings out with friends, and charitable giving all seem to take a backseat to their early retirement goal.

Increasing her income at work can support this early retirement goal, but she knows that means more hours working and proving herself to her supervisor. This is something she doesn't have the energy to do. She and Jacob want another child, but they both don't have the energy, time, and money to even fathom it.

If you feel overwhelmed reading about Emily's pursuit of FIRE based on your income, I can empathize with you. I tried this level of savings for nearly 10 years, and it caused some major issues in my marriage. I had a single focused goal of retiring early and a saving rate of 50% was the goal. Unfortunately, I took my eye off what mattered most: my relationship with my wife.

We had some heated arguments about me feeling trapped at my job. I felt like I was missing out on my children growing up. Instead of seeking out a new job or trying something new, I was convinced pushing toward Traditional FIRE was my only option.

This ultimately led to marriage counseling. At first, I felt like I was a failure. How could I let this happen? After 9 months of visits with our marriage counselor, I can honestly say it was the best thing for our marriage. We learned to communicate more effectively and really empathize with each other. What we were missing was time set aside to connect. With our busy schedule and two little kids at home, talking for an hour about our relationship was difficult. Marriage counseling was a blessing for us. It helped us realign our priorities and find ways to support each other.

The Coast FIRE Path

Some of us don't want to work for 40 years in the corporate world. But we also don't have enough income, energy, and patience to save 50% for 15 years. What then?

There is a middle way.

This way avoids the extremes of submitting to the corporate gods for 40 years (Traditional Retirement Path) and saving and investing until it hurts (the Traditional FIRE Path).

There is a growing community of people who appreciate the tenets and beliefs of FIRE but overall think they are a bit extreme and work better for people making multi-six-figure household incomes.

This community also believes life is for living. We should not be spending 80,000 hours of our lives working in offices typing on computers.

These folks are a part of the Coast FIRE Community. Since the word retirement can be a loaded word, I like to refer to Coast FIRE as "Coast to Financial Independence and Relax Early."

Coast FIRE is the point when you've saved and invested enough money in investment accounts that you can simply coast to retirement without any further contributions. After achieving this milestone (which is much easier than traditional FIRE to reach), many families move to part-time work. This middle way realizes that stopping work altogether may not be the most feasible solution and working until we're old and gray is not the most desirable solution.

This is the concept and plan our family adopted, and it's been the middle ground we never knew we needed. Coast FIRE, combined with a few other steps I'll share in the coming chapters, has allowed my wife and I to move away from full-time corporate jobs we dread and embrace part-time work we enjoy.

This concept combines the importance of a higher than average saving rate to create financial independence in your life with the reality that life is for living. Grinding away at work or grinding away investing is no way to live. Life should not feel like a grind.

Back to the story of Emily and Jacob.

Both 10 years into their careers, Emily and Jacob were now making a combined $180,000 household income. Their attempt at Traditional FIRE left them both feeling burned out. They liked the idea of FIRE because they wanted to work less and live more, but their income wasn't quite high enough to make it feasible based on their living expenses. The daycare costs were a major pain in their family budget. They were in desperate need of a solution. Sharing their experience with a friend, they learned about another FIRE path called Coast FIRE. This path would allow them to pull back on their aggressive investing goals and maybe even work fewer hours sooner than later. After all, Emily enjoyed the work she did, but she really didn't like the amount of work. If she could work half the time, she'd be happier at work and have more time with her kids. Jacob and Emily ran the numbers to see how much they were spending on daycare, commuting to work, and other work-related costs. They added that to the amount of money they could save by not maxing out all of their retirement accounts—going from a 50% saving rate to a 30% saving rate. Through this math exercise, the couple found out they could afford to go from two full-time jobs to two part-time jobs in the next couple of years. This was much better than continuing to grind it out for another decade or more on the FIRE path. Overall, this would cut down their household income, and it would require them to avoid lifestyle inflation in the future, but for the material possessions they might lack, it would allow both Jacob and Emily to own more of their time. This is the time when their growing family needs them most.

- **Household Income (Annual)**: $180,000
- **Saving Amount/Rate (Annual)**: $54,000/30%
- **Retirement Investment Plan**: Workplace 401(k), Roth IRAs, and Taxable Brokerage
- **Starting Age**: 25
- **"Relaxation" Age**: 40

- **Years Working Full-Time**: 15 (assumes 2,000 working hours per year)
- **Years Working Part-Time:** 25 (assumes 1,000 working hours per year)
- **Hours Worked in Total**: 55,000
- **Memento Mori Age**: 80
- **Years Relaxing After Corporate Life**: 27.5
- **Hours Relaxing Added After Corporate Life**: 55,000

Without a multi-six-figure household income, an inheritance from parents, or an extremely frugal lifestyle, Traditional FIRE can be very difficult for most people.

Coast FIRE is a more realistic path for parents. I've tried all three paths, and Coast FIRE is the best. It balances the importance of planning for tomorrow with the realization that living for today is also very important.

HOW TO ACHIEVE COAST FIRE

We've determined that reaching this happy-medium investing milestone of Coast FIRE requires a higher than average saving rate. Using Jacob and Emily's $180,000 household income as an example, a 30% saving rate would equal saving $54,000 per year.

So how do they use that $54,000 to achieve Coast FIRE?

After eliminating their high interest debt and allocating enough to eventually secure a family emergency fund, Jacob and Emily would invest this money to take advantage of the wealth-building power of the stock market.

Create Your Own Pension

Decades ago, there was a deal struck between corporations and their employees: "You work for us for 30 or 40 years of your life, and when you retire, we'll still pay your salary until you die." This was called a "Defined Benefit Plan" or "Pension."

While pensions still exist, they are quickly becoming a thing of the past. Only 15% of private sector employees have access to a pension today.[2] Compare this to 1990 when pension participation within corporations was at 43%, and you'll see how the trend is shifting away from this legacy benefit.[3] Evidently, the burden of paying someone's salary until they die got quite expensive and difficult for employers to handle.

To replace this benefit, corporations have adopted the retirement model of a "Defined Contribution Plan." Instead of the corporation being in charge of managing the pension and paying employees until they die, employees are now in charge of this process. Employees now need to invest in the stock market to create their own pension. The majority of private sector employees (67%) have access to these defined contribution plans, and around 49% participate in them.

In short, unless you're one of the lucky few who has a pension, you'll need to create your own.

Workplace 401(k)

The workplace retirement option that has become one of the most popular is the 401(k). This horribly boring sounding retirement plan comes from a section of IRS code that established the plan back in the 1970s.[4] Through some tax-wizardry, the 401(k) started to become the dominant way for employers to provide a tax-advantaged retirement benefit for their employees.[5] This saved companies money over time by decreasing the use of pensions and replacing them with 401(k)s instead.

My father worked for a company for 30 years, got his pension, and now gets to enjoy retirement as he pleases. For me and our generation, we're stuck with the 401(k).

Honestly, the 401(k) is not all that bad if you know how to take advantage of it.

For many employees, 401(k) plans are offered at the start of your employment or after a certain amount of time working at the company. These plans allow you to allocate a portion of your paycheck and invest it in the stock market. As years and decades pass, these contributions and the growth in your portfolio can turn into an impressive amount of money. If done properly, it can help you create your own pension.

As an employee perk, some companies offer a 401(k) match. For example, let's say Emily makes $90,000 and contributes $23,500 to her 401(k) each year. Her company matches dollar for dollar up to 3% of her salary. In this scenario, Emily would receive an additional $2,700 from her company as a 401(k) match. Between her contributions and her employer match, Emily's saving rate is close to 30%.

Another advantage to a 401(k) is regarding taxes. When you contribute to a traditional 401(k) plan, you can reduce your taxable income. In the eyes of the government, Emily's taxable income is reduced from $90,000 to $66,500 based on her contribution, thereby putting her in a lower tax bracket. Emily is investing for her future and paying fewer taxes today as well.

If you work at a nonprofit organization or for the government, you may be offered a 403(b) or 457 instead of a 401(k). They have different names but serve a similar purpose. All can reduce your taxable income and allow you to invest for your future retirement needs.

Roth IRA

Some employees don't have workplace retirement options available. There are also employees who don't receive an employer 401(k) match. Even those that do have 401(k) plans, some of the investment options offered within their plans are so laden with fees and subpar investment options that investing can feel counterproductive.

For those reasons and many others, it is important to invest for your retirement outside of your workplace as well. The Roth IRA (Individual Retirement Account) is an after-tax investment option that you can take advantage of outside of your employer. Within these accounts, you can invest for your future retirement needs.

When you work with a low-cost brokerage partner such as Vanguard, Fidelity, or Schwab for your Roth IRA, you may find the fees to be lower and the investment options broader when compared to your workplace 401(k) plan.

Roth IRAs allow your investments to grow tax-free, and since you already paid the tax when you contributed, you can withdraw your money tax-free in retirement too. Additionally, your contributions can be withdrawn anytime tax-free and penalty-free. If you take your investment earnings out before the age of 59.5, then you'll pay a 10% penalty. This encourages you to keep your money invested for retirement and not to use it for other things.

There are some restrictions with a Roth IRA, including income limitations and annual contribution limits. Be sure to examine those specific limits before contributing to your account as they change annually.

If you find your income is too high to participate in a Roth IRA, a traditional IRA may still be an option for you. Like a traditional 401(k), a traditional IRA invests your money pre-tax. The Roth IRA (and Roth 401(k)) invests your money after-tax.

Health Savings Account (HSA)

Another way to ensure your retirement is comfortable is to plan for health-care expenses. According to Fidelity, the average 65-year-old today should expect to pay $165,000 in healthcare expenses outside of their Medicare coverage in retirement.[6]

That's a lot of money to save up. Investing makes that healthcare savings goal a lot easier to attain.

With a Health Savings Account (HSA), you can save and invest for healthcare expenses now and in the future. HSAs can be available to folks who have a high-deductible healthcare plan. They take on more of the financial responsibility with higher deductibles in exchange for lower monthly premiums. These plans may not make sense for everyone, especially those with frequent medical needs.

Much like the 401(k) and IRA, the HSA provides you with tax benefits.

If you're signing up for an HSA through your employer, you can create pre-tax contributions that lower your taxable income. This is much like a traditional 401(k).

If your employer does not have an HSA, you can still sign up for one outside of your employer and make after-tax contributions. You will be able to take the tax deduction when you submit your tax return.

You can withdraw the money any time, tax-free and penalty-free, as long as you are using it for qualified medical purposes.

The money in an HSA grows tax-free as well. It can be saved in a savings account for short-term, easy access needs. The HSA contributions can also be invested for long-term growth and used in your golden years.

Keep Investing Simple

The world of investing can be very confusing. Watching the financial news can make you feel like you need a PhD to even think about jumping into the stock market.

I want to keep things incredibly simple. Because investing in the stock market really can be simple if we try.

Active vs. Passive Investing

When I started investing in my teens and twenties, I bought individual stocks on a platform called eTrade. I saw that rich people on TV owned stocks, so if I wanted to be rich, then I should buy stocks too.

The problem was I had no idea what I was doing. I would buy a stock of a company I liked. If I was lucky, it went up for a while. More often than not, the value of the stock would drop. This would cause me to freak out and sell the stock thereby ensuring my "on screen loss" was a true loss.

I did this for a while and eventually quit because I wasn't making money. It felt like gambling. I was spending a lot of time making bets, and I was losing.

This was active investing for me: spending a lot of time and money trading stocks in hopes of getting rich quickly.

I tried my best with the knowledge I had to make money trading stocks. There were three problems here:

- I didn't have the knowledge to trade stocks.
- I didn't have the time to dedicate to it.
- What I was doing wasn't actually investing; it was trading (also known as speculating or gambling).

If only there was a way where I could invest in the best stocks, dedicate minimal time and effort, and end up with the wealth I need to retire comfortably in the long run.

This exists, and it's actually less expensive and time consuming than active investing. It's called passive investing.

Active investing is buying and selling stocks so you can try to beat the overall return of the stock market. Passive investing is buying the entire stock market and mirroring its returns.

The overall stock market has returned around 10% during its entire history.[7] Instead of trying to actively beat out that 10% average return, passive investing suggests, "Hey, why don't you just take the 10% average and go back to living life?"

Not only does this prove to be a more relaxing strategy, it's also a more effective one too. According to Morningstar, only 14.2% of active managers have beat the overall market return over the last decade.[8] When you factor in the fees that these active managers charge their clients, it can make it hard to justify paying for their services.

These are professionals who do this every single day, and they have a difficult time beating the market. It's no wonder I had such a difficult time with my active investing plan!

The first step in simplifying investing is to go with a passive strategy. Ditch the active investing noise and enjoy the simplicity and benefits of passive investing.

Passive investing relies on investing for the long term through index funds.

An index fund is an investment option that allows you to buy into an entire market index like the S&P 500. Since the S&P 500 is a running list of the top 500 US companies, owning an S&P 500-based index fund allows you to own a piece of big companies like Apple, Nvidia, and Walmart. That means if you own one of these index funds, you have big money businesses working for you, the shareholder.

Although you'll hear the S&P 500 index referenced quite often, there are other market indices as well. There are indices for bonds, international stocks, and even stocks for small and growing companies.

Index funds typically have lower fees associated with them as well.

When you invest in mutual funds, there is a fee called an *Expense Ratio*. If you're not careful, these expense ratio fees can eat away at your earnings.

Some funds can have expense ratios as high as 1% or more. Index Funds on average have a much lower expense ratio. Vanguard's VFIAX[9] (their S&P 500 Index Fund) for example has a 0.04% expense ratio. This means for every $10,000 you invest, Vanguard gets $4 per year. Compare this to a mutual fund with a 1% expense ratio and you'll pay $100 per year.

"$100?! That doesn't sound like a lot." one might say. Let's demonstrate how the fees add up over time …

Annualized Rate of Return	Starting Balance at 22 yrs old	Annual Contribution for 40 yrs	Fund 1 Projected Ending Balance After 40 Years (Expense Ratio of 0.04%)	Fund 2 Projected Ending Balance After 40 Years (Expense Ratio of 1%)	Difference in Fees
7%	$1,000	$6,000	$1,282,796.63	$994,571.80	$288,224.83

Let's say you started investing with $1,000 at age 22 and contributed $6,000 annually until you were 62. If you chose the index fund with the lower expense ratio, you're looking at a savings of $288,224.83. That $100 adds up fast.

You'll also have $1,282,796 in your account at retirement.

Automate Your Investing

Outside of trying to beat the market and getting fleeced with fees, another problem investors come into is simply forgetting to invest consistently.

They know how important investing can be for their future, and they understand that's where family wealth is built, but they don't take time to allocate the money each month. I'm guilty of this too. Life gets busy. I have a lot of responsibilities. Sometimes the "to-do's" that are right in front of my face get handled before the other more important tasks.

Let's take the reality of our busy lives and our human tendencies to procrastinate on the important things and automate our investing.

During our money dates, we will allocate a certain amount of money to go toward investing. The goal percentage for the Coast FIRE life is 30%. You may not be able to invest that much straight away. Ten percent may be a more realistic starting point for you on your family financial independence journey. Over time though, this amount should be increased ever so slightly to achieve a higher saving rate. This higher saving rate will allow you to own your time faster.

Once you determine your desired investing amount, set an automated contribution to your investments. If this takes place in your workplace

401(k) for starters, ensure your contributions correspond to your investing goals. One bonus on this saving rate journey is your employer match counts toward your goal.

As an example, Emily decides to max out contributions to her 401(k) at work because she gets an employer match, her 401(k) plan has low fee options through Fidelity, and she can automate her contributions. She contributes $1,958.33 per month ($23,500 annually) to her 401(k) plan and gets a $2,700 annual employer match. With those decisions, she's already close to a 30% annual saving rate.

Unfortunately, her husband Jacob does not have the best 401(k) workplace options. There's no employer match and the funds available all have a 1% expense ratio or higher. Jacob decides to skip right over to investing in a Roth IRA and max that out. He sets up an automatic contribution of $583.33 per month ($7,000 annually). To increase his saving rate, he takes advantage of investing through an HSA and maxes out those contributions for the year as well. This is an additional $712.50 ($8,550 annually). To round out his portion of the 30% saving rate, he encourages Emily to also open a Roth IRA and max out her contributions too. This would be another $583.33 per month ($7,000 annually).

Between all of these automated investment decisions, Emily and Jacob are on track to invest close to 30% of their income each year. The best part of all, once they learn to live without this money, they won't notice they ever had access to it. They will adjust their lives and lifestyle accordingly.

Again, this may take some time to get used to. Going from a 0% saving rate to 30% would be a major shock to their financial life. What may be more realistic is starting off at 0% and shooting for a 5% saving rate in month 1. After month 1, you reassess things and find some additional areas for saving or increasing your income. Then you make the goal to increase to 10%. As the months or years roll on, you continue adjusting your life until 30% is feasible and realistic for your family situation. The entire time you use automated contributions to keep you committed to your investing goal of Coast FIRE.

By automating your investments, you're also taking advantage of dollar cost averaging (DCA). This concept ensures you buy a fixed amount of index funds on a regular basis no matter what. If the stock market is down, your human instinct might be to sell your stocks because you're afraid your portfolio will go down further. Dollar cost averaging helps you stay calm amid the chaos and continue buying index funds no matter if the market is up or down. In this case, buying index funds when they are priced lower is beneficial for you in the long run. Over time, this automated decision will help you to own more shares of the best companies in the United States (or the world for that matter). And those companies will continue to work hard for you, the shareholder, even when you're not working at all.

DETERMINE YOUR COAST FIRE NUMBER

We've reviewed how to create your own pension through Coast FIRE and how to keep the investing process simple.

Let's get focused on creating your own specific goal for Coast FIRE. That is determining your Coast FIRE number.

This is the amount of money you will need to have invested to drastically reduce or stop contributions going forward.

I remember investing for retirement for a while and asking myself that question, "When can I stop investing for retirement?" Searching for an answer to this question took a lot of wild turns.

There are a lot of voices laced in fear that will tell you that retirement will be out of reach for the majority and inflation will bury us all. So it's best to invest as much as you possibly can. While no one can predict the future, constantly living in a state of fear about our financial future is no way to live.

Then there are voices laced in optimism and YOLO that will tell you that living for today is the most important. They will lead you to believe that you can worry about retirement as you get closer to your fifties or sixties.

Through my research and interviews, I found Coast FIRE rides that middle way. It emphasizes the importance of saving and investing for tomorrow while realizing today should also be enjoyed. Coast FIRE also helps us find freedom from overworking and underliving sooner than most.

To help you achieve Coast FIRE faster, I believe it helps to have a goal number. When you know what you're aiming for, goals are a lot easier to achieve.

Let's jump back to our couple Jacob and Emily. Here are some of their financial details that you'll also need to know to determine your Coast FIRE number:

- Age(s): Emily (30) and Jacob (30)
- Target Retirement Age(s): 60
- Average Annual Spending: $100,000[10]
- Current Retirement Investments: $100,000

If this couple desires to spend $100,000 per year in retirement (adjusted for inflation of course), then they may need $2,000,000. This number is found through the 5% rule popularized by investment researcher Bill Bengen. His research found that in most cases retirees can comfortably withdraw 5% from their portfolio annually without fear of running out of money. Previously, 4% was a popular withdrawal rate, but it was found that many retirees not only did not run out of money, but they actually became wealthier in retirement after stopping work.

For Emily and Jacob, their $100,000 divided by 5% shows their FIRE number or retirement number should be $2,000,000. Another way to find out your FIRE number is taking your annual expenses and multiplying them by 20.

Hearing that a couple needs $2,000,000 to retire comfortably can make most people want to give up immediately. This is another reason Coast

FIRE is so powerful. By front loading your portfolio with contributions early, you can let time and compound interest do the heavy lifting for you.

If Emily and Jacob continue their near 30% saving rate for another 7 years, they can reach close to $560,000 in investments. This assumes a 6% real rate of return on their investments, which is fair given past stock market returns.

Once reaching this $560,000 point, Emily and Jacob can choose to stop or drastically slow down their retirement contributions and still get to around $2,000,000 by age 60.

At age 37, they can stop investing altogether and still reach their retirement goals. This is because compound interest helps their invested money continue to grow even without their contributions.

At this point in their life, this frees up more than $40,000 from their budget, and it helps them feel confident that their retirement years are covered.

To find your specific Coast FIRE number, we developed a free calculator on our website. You include information about your situation, hit the calculate button, and see how close you are to Coast FIRE. You can find that free calculator at MarriageKidsandMoney.com/Calculators/Coast-FIRE/. I'd include all the math in the book, but it might make your eyes glaze over. The important thing to know is that you don't need to invest for retirement forever. There will come a point in time when you've invested enough to coast to retirement. At that point, you have an important decision to make: Will you keep investing to build additional wealth for your retirement years? Or will you start to use your money to own your time today?

There's no wrong answer here.

If Emily and Jacob continue investing at the same rate, they could have around $4,500,000 in retirement. That could provide them with $225,000 per year in retirement. They would need to continue working full-time until age 60. If they like what they do for a living, then this should be no problem.

As we've determined though, they are not happy overall with their work situations, and they want more time back in their lives. Stopping or drastically slowing down their contributions after Coast FIRE will allow them to make future choices on how much time they are spending working. They can increase their hours living and decrease their hours working.

This could be Emily's ticket to part-time work in the short term and eventually Jacob as well.

If You're Not Coast FIRE Yet

Perhaps you've run the numbers with our calculator or you know you're not even close to these six-figure investment goals. No need to despair!

Continue to use your tax-advantaged retirement accounts to build up your investment portfolio. Slowly but surely increase your saving rate by investing in your workplace 401(k). Grab those employer matches if they offer them. That free money from your employer is an excellent boost to your saving rate.

Outside of your workplace retirement options, look into a Roth IRA, an HSA, and a taxable brokerage account. These investment opportunities are smart ways to get closer to your Coast FIRE goal.

If you're finding it difficult to increase your saving rate, it's time to take a deeper look at your budget.

Start by examining your income. What ways can you increase your income to make saving for Coast FIRE easier? The best place for corporate employees to increase their income is where they are already earning their money. Investigate ways of increasing your income with your employer through raises, bonuses, referrals, and commissions. When you help your employer win, they are usually more receptive to helping you win financially. Speak with your spouse about how they can increase their income at work as well. This can be a team effort.

Outside of your increasing your income, getting rid of waste in your budget is a smart move as well. Cancel those unused subscriptions, negotiate your bills, and increase deductibles to save more. Those moves can add thousands of dollars to your budget each year.

If you're finding your lifestyle is not conducive to a higher saving rate, but you desire to own your time, it may call for some more drastic changes. This is when you examine the "big three" expenses: housing, transportation, and food.

- **Food**: Can we re-examine our grocery store shopping habits? Are there ways we could save by eating more at home? Could we try meal prepping on Sunday nights so we're prepared for the week?
- **Transportation**: Are we spending too much money on our cars each month? What ways can we make this category less expensive without driving junky cars?
- **Housing**: Is our home and the bills that come with it making us "house poor"? Could we adjust or downsize our living situation and have a much more fulfilling life?

These discussions can be very difficult to have. I would recommend saving them for discussion after you exhaust all other options. The truth is that the "big three" can have the largest and quickest impact.

Better managing your food spending, going without luxury cars, or downsizing your home can be decisions that provide tens of thousands of dollars back in your life. While they are difficult decisions to make, they really move the needle quickly in owning more of your time. You just have to decide if the trade-off is worth it or not.

COAST FIRE PLUS PENSIONS AND SOCIAL SECURITY

While the pension is a relic of the past for the majority of us, others still have access to one. This retirement income source can massively change your future. If you have access to a pension or are eligible to receive one based on years of service, factor this into your Coast FIRE calculations.

Let's say Jacob is eligible for a pension at his place of employment if he stays for another 10 years at his job.[1] While not ideal because he wants to own more of his time, it may be a time sacrifice he's willing to make for long-term financial security. As he investigates things further, he realizes if he stays another 10 years, his pension will be $36,000 per year.

If he decides to stick around for those 10 years, this means Jacob and Emily won't need to cover $100,000 in annual living expenses in retirement anymore. They will only need to replace $64,000. This makes their Coast FIRE goal even easier to accomplish.

- Age(s): Emily (30) and Jacob (30)
- Target Retirement Age(s): 60
- Average Annual Spending: **$64,000** ($100,000 – $36,000)
- Current Retirement Investments: $100,000

Using the 5% rule, their new retirement number is only $1,280,000. Originally, their FIRE number was $2,000,000. By taking advantage of the pension option, Jacob and Emily have made their retirement goal $720,000 easier to reach.

With this decision, they can achieve Coast FIRE in just 4 years. They would need to continue to contribute as they have been until age 34 and reach around $340,000. That $340,000 could grow without any further contributions to well above $1,280,000 by age 60.

This is obviously more optimal financially, but only Jacob and Emily can decide if this is optimal emotionally and psychologically. Those difficult feelings of working in a job you don't enjoy day-in and day-out can weigh heavily on a person. And the "golden handcuffs" of the pension would force Jacob to stay with his employer instead of moving to a job that may be better for his overall well-being.

Jacob's scenario of receiving a pension is becoming rarer as time goes on. What about Social Security? How would receiving Social Security income in retirement impact Coast FIRE plans?

Similar to receiving a pension income, projected Social Security income could help make investing goals a lot easier to attain. Using SSA.gov, you can check to see your projected retirement income by age 62, 67, and 70. The current average monthly benefit from Social Security is around $1,900 per month.[12] If you are married, your spouse should check their projected retirement income as well. Depending on your spouse's lifetime earnings, this could substantially increase your household retirement income.

As an example, let's say both Jacob and Emily have earned enough credits to qualify for Social Security benefits. They check their statements on SSA.gov and discover that between the two of them, they will receive $3,000 per month ($1,500 each) if they decide to take their Social Security benefits at age 62.

Unfortunately, we all may not receive the "full" Social Security benefits we're seeing on our statements. According to the Social Security Board of Trustees, by the year 2033, the Trust Funds will be depleted based on current law.[13] This could change, but overall the math doesn't appear to be in the favor of workers receiving their full benefits. The ratio of workers to beneficiaries is decreasing fast as there are fewer babies being born and people living longer. The math for Social Security is not working out.

That being said, even if the funds are depleted and no laws are changed, the Social Security Administration feels confident they can still provide 77% of what is being shown in our statements. Keep in mind that this projection may change over time as laws and regulations adjust.

Similar to our previous example, here's how their new retirement investing scenario might play out:

- Age(s): Emily (30) and Jacob (30)
- Target Retirement Age(s): 60
- Average Annual Spending: **$72,280** ($100,000 − ($36,000 × 77%))
- Current Retirement Investments: $100,000

Factoring in potential Social Security income, Jacob and Emily's new retirement number is $1,445,600. Originally, their FIRE number was

$2,000,000. By factoring in their potential Social Security income, Jacob and Emily have made their retirement goal $554,400 easier to reach.

With this decision, they can achieve Coast FIRE in just 5 years. They would need to continue to contribute as they have been until age 35 and reach around $400,000. That $400,000 could grow without any further contributions to well over $1,445,600 by age 60.

While the Social Security system may be underfunded, it doesn't mean the entire benefit will be gone in the future. Ignoring the benefits, even if they are smaller than what is projected in your Social Security statement, may force you to work longer than you actually need to.

WORKING WITH A FINANCIAL ADVISOR— CONS AND PROS

If investing in the stock market feels intimidating and confusing, don't worry. You're not alone. Only 62% of US adults own stocks.[14] This leaves the other 38% out of one of the simplest ways to become wealthy and earn time freedom. When you invest consistently into the stock market, your investments will eventually pay you enough to comfortably live your life.

For many of us, working with a financial advisor can make the investing process easier. A financial advisor is a professional who supports your very personal investing journey. Instead of reading about the "Jacob and Emily's" of the world, your financial advisor tailors a specific plan that guides you on the path to family financial success.

Financial Advisor Cons

Unfortunately, not all financial advisors have your best interest in mind. A lot of money can be made in the world of investing, and sometimes financial advisors are more interested in that aspect than helping you win financially.

Recently, a Fishers Investments advisor in Indiana was sentenced to 4 years in federal prison for stealing more than $4 million of his clients' money.[15] Another financial advisor from Michigan lied to his clients, stole more than $3 million of their money, and did so for a period of 8 years. That "advisor" got 9 years in federal prison for his crimes.[16] (I use that word "advisor" loosely, of course.)

While these are some of the more egregious cases of financial fraud and embezzlement, around 10% of financial advisors have a bad record of serving their clients.[17] Even after committing illegal or immoral acts, many of these advisors find their way back into the investment world, often through insurance sales.

Fortunately, there are ways we can protect ourselves as consumers. Before working with a financial advisor, use the tool FINRA broker check. This website allows you to look up any registered financial advisor, find out their years of experience, the states where they are licensed, their credentials, and any disclosures they have on their record. If you do some poking around, you may find information about forging signatures, using client funds without permission, and other shady stuff.

Or you might find no disclosures at all. Either way, it's good to do your homework first. If they do have disclosures, ask them to explain what happened. Everyone makes mistakes. Perhaps it's something you can look past and create a relationship with the individual.

Financial Advisor Pros

For all the financial advisors out there that are doing wrong by their clients, there are tens of thousands of professionals who work in their client's best interest. They are tailoring financial plans to support their clients' overall financial well-being and giving them the wealthy future they deserve.

So how do you find a good financial advisor?

Look to see if they have signed a "fiduciary" oath to work in your best interest and not theirs. While this doesn't remove all questions regarding integrity, it definitely helps.

Also, find out how they are paid. This will help you understand more on motivation. If they are paid based on commissions from investments and products they sell to you, there may be a conflict of interest.

The "advice-only" financial advisor model has become more popular as of late. This ensures that that advisor is paid for their advice only (usually hourly) and does not receive commissions from products or investments they sell. Outside of hourly advice, they can develop a financial plan for you for a flat fee as well. For the DIY investor who needs assistance on their journey to family financial independence, this is my recommended model of financial advisor support. This way, you know what you're paying for.

Credentials are also a smart way to ensure your advisor has the knowledge to support you on your journey. Financial advisors who are certified financial planners (CFPs) have received one of the highest respected levels of financial advisor training. Out of all the degrees and certifications you might notice, CFP is an important one to look for.

Should I Use a Financial Advisor?

If not having the knowledge and expertise is holding you back from investing on your family financial independence journey, then yes, I would recommend you work with an advice-only financial advisor who has signed a fiduciary oath to work in your best interest.

If you've taken the time to read this entire chapter, I believe you have the interest and knowledge to start investing simply on your own. Start by using your workplace 401(k) or a Roth IRA and invest in low-cost index funds that track the US stock market. This simple plan can work for decades of your investing journey. Overanalyzing which funds to choose, the ideal asset allocation, and timing the market can lead to analysis paralysis. The best advice when it comes to investing? Just start.

FROM THE PODCAST

Family: Anders and Paige, 30 years old from Utah
Money Milestone: Coast FIRE achieved with $322,000 invested

Andy:	*What got you motivated to start investing?*
Anders:	What really got me motivated is frankly, I was working in a job that I just didn't love, and I really wanted to get away from it. The pay was great, but I just didn't love it. You know, there was no part of me that, that woke up and said, man, I'm so excited to get to work. It was more, you know, I'm going through the motions. I'm going to collect my paycheck at the end of the week and just come back next week and kind of rinse and repeat. So I was really motivated by this desire to just get out of the situation that I was in.

And then the other aspect that I think really motivated me to start investing at a young age was I watched my parents get hit pretty hard by the global financial crisis in 2008 and 2009. I was a senior in high school at the time.

I didn't fully understand what was happening, but I watched my dad lose his job. I watched my parents lose their house. They lost cars. Everything from a financial perspective in our lives changed. And that was a pretty formative experience for me where I took a step back and I said, I want to be financially bulletproof. And that carried through into my early 20s and really motivated me to start saving and investing at a fairly a young age.

And quick plug for my wife here, she actually started much, much younger. So she's the other half to this Coast FIRE equation in our family. And I really have to give her dad credit. He was the one that used to take her to the bank to help her get an investment account set up at like eight or nine years old. And her parents used to talk her through how to invest. Part of the birthday and Christmas money she would get and then spend part of it as well. But it wasn't just like they were talking about it. They were actually setting up a custodial account to start investing this money for my wife at a very young age. She talks about going to appointments as a young kid and how bored she would be sitting there at the bank. Looking back, how grateful she is to have parents that talked her through, "Hey, this is how you invest. And this is normal to invest and grow your wealth and save part of your income." So, you know she started much younger than I did and that put her in a very financially healthy position because she had so many years of contributions and growth and opportunity for that money to really compound.

Andy: *How do you guys get together to make sure you're on this journey together and then stay together?*

Anders: We've gotten to the point over the years where we don't have a standing meeting every week or anything like that. But there was a point in time where every Sunday we would sit down and even if it was just, you know, a 10- or 15-minute conversation, we would talk about our finances and what we're thinking about. We've gotten to a point now where we feel we've got the kinks really worked out and we know the plan that we have. We're on that trajectory now. In the beginning, it was once a week, and we were religious about it. So, I think that's very important.

If you're trying to figure out if you and your spouse aren't on the same page with money, or you just want to talk about it a little bit more, just go ahead and set up time. Like actually put it on the calendar, put it on each other's calendar. So you both know every week at this time, we'll be talking about money in some capacity. And it doesn't always have to be a huge conversation, but at least touching base and hearing what each other are thinking about or going through.

Andy: *How are things different now that you've achieved Coast FIRE?*

Anders: The way I like to think about it … I heard somebody describe coasting to financial independence, like you're driving down the freeway and you see this Coast FIRE exit as you're passing it. And you have the opportunity, if you want, you can downshift and just hop off the exit. So, we actually decided to do that two and a half years ago. When we reached Coast FIRE, we, took a look at our situation, and we said, okay, we don't have to take this exit, but we have the opportunity to, and what could this look like in our lives?

And ultimately we decided based on the things we want and the lifestyle we want to live right now, it would be smart to just go ahead and take this exit. And if it doesn't work out for any reason, who cares? We just loop back around and hop back on the freeway and that's okay. No harm, no foul. But at this time, I was working in a pretty stressful, high paying, but intense job, and I was earning a lot of money. It was the most money I'd ever made, and we were saving close to 50% of our income. So when we downshifted, I left that job and traded it in for a combination of freelance work and seasonal employment and took a pretty substantial pay cut in the process. But for us, that was fine. We have a pretty modest lifestyle. We don't have huge living expenses. So instead of continuing to save 50%, we just downshifted work and then covered our living expenses while coasting.

So for that first year, we really didn't save anything. We were truly coasting to financial independence. But over time, I've gotten better and better at my work, and I've earned more and more money. And we're getting back to that point where, we're still covering our living expenses, and I'm working the amount that fits our lifestyle, but we still have a little bit of excess. So we're starting to contribute that money into our Roth IRAs.

We really did lean in when we found out about Coast FIRE. We decided, "Hey, let's see what it would look like in our life. And let's lean into this fully."

Andy: *There's somebody listening right now and they want to hit Coast FIRE too. What is one step they could take to get themselves to Coast FIRE?*

Anders: The best place to start is just go ahead and calculate your Coast FIRE number. Get an idea of what it would actually take. So you can see where you are in relation to that goal.

And then you can start to draw a map to get you from point A to point B. And I think that's really the best place to start for anybody that's "coast curious" or interested in coasting to financial independence.

Carpe Diem Action Steps

- Review the different paths to financial independence with your spouse. Compare the pros and cons and start investing.
- Check in on your 401(k) plan at work. Ensure you're investing in low-cost index funds and taking advantage of any employer match available.

- As your financial situation allows, look into a Roth IRA for both you and your spouse. Even if your spouse is a "stay-at-home spouse" and not earning an income, they are still eligible to open a Roth IRA for retirement investing purposes.

- Calculate your FIRE number and your Coast FIRE number using our calculator: MarriageKidsandMoney.com/Calculators/Coast-FIRE/. This will give you an investing goal to pursue. Factor in any pensions or Social Security you may receive as well.

- Meet with an advice-only financial advisor if you need assistance on your investing journey. Sometimes paying for 1 hour of support could be all you need to launch you in the right direction.

NOTES

1. CDC. (2025). *Life expectancy* [Online]. Available at: https://www.cdc.gov/nchs/fastats/life-expectancy.htm

2. BLS. (2024). *15 percent of private industry workers had access to a defined benefit retirement plan* [Online]. Available at: https://www.bls.gov/opub/ted/2024/15-percent-of-private-industry-workers-had-access-to-a-defined-benefit-retirement-plan.htm

3. Davidson, L. (2016). *The history of retirement benefits* [Online]. Workforce. Available at: https://workforce.com/news/the-history-of-retirement-benefits

4. Conde, A. (2025). *Why is it called a 401(k)?* [Online]. Smart Asset. Available at: https://smartasset.com/retirement/why-is-it-called-a-401k

5. Elkins, K. (2017). A brief history of the 401(k), which changed how Americans retire [Online]. *CNBC*. Available at: https://www.cnbc.com/2017/01/04/a-brief-history-of-the-401k-which-changed-how-americans-retire.html

6. Fidelity. (2025). *How to plan for rising health care costs* [Online]. Available at: https://www.fidelity.com/viewpoints/personal-finance/plan-for-rising-health-care-costs

7. NerdWallet. (2025). *What is the average stock market return?* [Online]. Available at: https://www.nerdwallet.com/article/investing/average-stock-market-return

8. Morningstar. (2024). *US active/passive barometer report: Year-end 2024* [Online]. Available at: https://www.morningstar.com/lp/active-passive-barometer

9. Vanguard. (n.d.). *Vanguard 500 Index Fund Admiral Shares* [Online]. Available at: https://investor.vanguard.com/investment-products/mutual-funds/profile/vfiax (accessed 7/3/2025).

10. Smart Asset. (2025). *Federal income tax calculator—estimator for 2024–2025 taxes* [Online]. Available at: https://smartasset.com/taxes/income-taxes

11. Equable. (2019). *Pension basics: How pension benefits are calculated* [Online]. Available at: https://equable.org/pension-basics-how-pension-benefits-are-calculated/

12. Moorhead, C. (2025). *Here's the average Social Security benefit at every age.* Yahoo Finance. Available at: https://finance.yahoo.com/news/average-social-security-benefit-every-120016509.html

13. SSA.gov. (2025). *Social Security Board of Trustees: Projection for Combined Trust Funds One Year Sooner than Last Year* [Online]. Available at: https://blog.ssa.gov/social-security-board-of-trustees-projection-for-combined-trust-funds-one-year-sooner-than-last-year/

14. Brumley, J. (2025). *Roughly 62% of U.S. adults hold stocks. Those who don't could be missing out on millions.* Motley Fool. Available at: https://www.nasdaq.com/articles/roughly-62-us-adults-hold-stocks-those-who-dont-could-be-missing-out-millions

15. United States Attorneys Office. (2024). *Fishers investment advisor sentenced to four years in federal prison for embezzling $4.6 million* [Online]. Available at: https://www.justice.gov/usao-sdin/pr/fishers-investment-advisor-sentenced-four-years-federal-prison-embezzling-46-million

16. United States Attorneys Office. (2019). *Financial advisor who pled guilty to embezzling more than 3.7 million dollars from his clients sentenced to 9 years in prison* [Online]. Available at: https://www.justice.gov/usao-edmi/pr/financial-advisor-who-pled-guilty-embezzling-more-37-million-dollars-his-clients

17. Crawford, K. (2022). *Investors beware: Crooked financial advisors can slip through regulatory cracks* [Online]. Stanford. Available at: https://siepr.stanford.edu/news/investors-beware-crooked-financial-advisors-can-slip-through-regulatory-cracks

CHAPTER FIVE

LIVE MORTGAGE FREE

"Home is the nicest word there is."

– Laura Ingalls Wilder

Homeownership can be a beautiful thing. You find a house that works well for you and your family. After buying it, you can modify and design your humble abode to your specific preferences. Over time, you provide it tender love and care until your house starts to feel like a home.

You make family memories in your home over the years and decades. This is where family dinners, movie nights, and birthday parties take place. First steps, first words, and first attempts on the bike all start at home.

When you're having a rough day out in the busy world we live in, you know that you can always go home and things will be better.

This is the type of homeownership experience that many families desire. Unfortunately, without the proper financial preparation and planning, homeownership can go from a dream to a nightmare.

I remember this well with my first-time homeowner experience.

"Buy a house as soon as you can! It's the best investment ever!" This was the refrain I heard throughout our society when I was in my early twenties. While this may be true for some, it was not the experience I had.

With a full-time job and an interest in "doing the smart financial thing," I decided it was time to buy my first home. Having saved up years of cash in savings, I had enough money to put a 10% down payment on the house. The mortgage lender seemed to think it was enough for me, so I secured a 30-year loan and went for it.

Little did I know that my mortgage payment wasn't the only expense I'd be dealing with as a homeowner. There were utility bills, home updates, appliances that were broken, a roof that needed to be replaced, furniture purchases, outdoor maintenance to do, and dozens of other things.

Underestimating the true cost of homeownership was a huge mistake. Quickly, I started to learn what I had gotten myself into. Most of my budget and time were taken over by the responsibilities of homeownership. I started to take on additional debt outside of my mortgage just to pay my bills and enjoy life.

My home owned me instead of the other way around.

When I got my second opportunity with homeownership with my wife, I vowed to do it differently. I promised myself that I wouldn't buy a house we couldn't afford. This required a much higher down payment and some patience in the home purchasing process.

When we found the house we wanted, we agreed that we would buy it as long as we could pay off the mortgage in 5 years, not 30 years. Having a home mortgage for 30 years when I already didn't like my job was not something I was willing to do. I wanted freedom and independence not loan commitments that lasted multiple decades. This would make me feel bound to my corporate job even longer.

Remember our fun mortgage fact: The literal translation of "mortgage" in French is "death pledge." You are signing a pledge to pay this debt until you die.

Not us. We wanted financial independence for our family much sooner than that. Without a mortgage (aka, the largest debt we'll ever have in our lives), we could make some decisions that were in the best interest of our family.

HOW WE PAID OFF OUR MORTGAGE IN 5 YEARS

To tackle the largest debt we'd ever have in our lives, we needed to start off by lowering it as much as possible. This started with our home down payment.

Larger Home Down Payment

Instead of a 10% down payment like I did with my first go around with homeownership, we went with a 45% down payment. This cut our mortgage nearly in half. Our monthly payments were lower, and homeownership felt easier straight away.

Putting this much down on a home is not required, but if you desire to live mortgage free in the near future, it definitely helps. Twenty percent down should be the minimum starting point.

Our larger down payment took us years of saving more than 50% of our income on average. It was difficult to deny ourselves the "lifestyle inflation" we desired as DINKs (Double Income No Kids), but we knew we wanted our home to be a blessing and not a curse.

15-year Mortgage

Instead of going with a 30-year mortgage, we decided to take out a 15-year instead. This significantly lowered the amount of years in our "death pledge." It also forced us into higher monthly payments. Those higher monthly payments ensured we paid more money toward the principal of our loan each month and less toward interest.

As an example, using a $500,000 home, a 15-year mortgage might have a 6% interest rate (with a $400,000 original principal).[1] If you let the loan play out for the entire 15 years, you will pay $207,576.92 in interest.

Another option is a 30-year mortgage. This may come in slightly higher at around a 7% interest rate. This is because it is a slightly riskier loan for the lender. If you let that loan play out for the entire 30 years, you will pay $558,035.59 in interest.

This is almost three times as much interest: more than a half million dollars going to the bank over your lifetime instead of that half million working toward you owning your time.

While the 15-year mortgage sounds better than the 30-year for interest savings over time, it's important to ensure you can actually make the larger monthly payments without feeling too strapped.

Using our previous example, the 15-year mortgage monthly payment (including principal, interest, taxes, and insurance) could be closer to $3,800 while the 30-year payment would be closer to $3,100.

If you can financially afford the larger payments of the 15-year mortgage and time freedom is your goal, they are well worth it in the long run.

Make Additional Principal Payments

Although our mortgage-free life was set up 15 years in the future, I wanted to accelerate that timeline to reach financial freedom faster. To do this, we set up an automated payment of $500 each month in additional principal payments. This way, we wouldn't forget.

It was important for us to designate that this extra money was to go to the principal of the mortgage and not the interest. You might be surprised that the bank needs this specificity, but they do. Yolanda, a listener of my podcast, made repeated extra payments on her mortgage for a series of months. Her mortgage provider decided to not apply these payments to her principal only and instead applied them as future mortgage payments. This unfortunately set Yolanda back on her path toward mortgage freedom. It is best to clearly specify that the extra payments be made to the principal and not the interest. You can do this in writing, through online payments, over the phone, or in person if your mortgage is with your brick-and-mortar bank.

Outside of the regular principal payments, we also took advantage of newfound money during this period. Money from tax refunds, bonuses, referral payments, and selling stuff around the house we didn't use anymore all went to pay down the mortgage early.

We also did a little psychological paycheck trick as well. Some employees get paid twice per month (or 24 paychecks per year). And some employees (like me) get paid every other week (or 26 paychecks per year). During our mortgage payoff journey, we just pretended that we only got paid 24 times per year. We crafted our budget as if we only had the income from those 24 paychecks. When those two extra paychecks came in, we would throw them both at the mortgage principal. These were impactful moments where the overall mortgage principal went down significantly.

Keep the Money Date Alive

In order to pay off this mortgage in 5 years, my wife and I had to work together. With two small kids at home, time for conversation was limited.

Setting up a twice monthly "budget party" was my idea for keeping the communication going and trying make the process more fun. My wife saw through my marketing tricks and did not buy that this money date was a "party," but she showed up anyway, and I love her for that. I tried to make it fun in the beginning by ordering pizza, opening a bottle of wine, and ensuring we didn't just talk about money. I definitely wasn't perfect or consistent with the "party" part, but I gave it my best effort!

As for the budget part, we would review how we did from the previous month, create a plan for the next month, and discuss family plans. Outside of the "money" portion of the budget party, we could discuss weekend plans, upcoming family events, date nights, and future goals.

By setting up this time together, it helped us stay synced up with our mortgage payoff plans and our relationship overall.

Celebrate with the Family

If we kept consistent with our goal, made sure to still have fun, and kept dreaming of a brighter future for our family, we knew we'd pay off our 15-year mortgage early.

And we did. Just shy of 4 years actually.

We had an epic mortgage payoff celebration together as a family to commemorate this big moment in our lives. My wife created a piñata out of the mortgage papers so our kids could "crush the mortgage" too. When they did, candy, toys, and money came crashing down to the floor. It was symbolic. When you destroy the mortgage, you get rewarded.

After becoming mortgage free, we decided to travel more, give more, and live more. We went to Cabo San Lucas with the family for an all-inclusive getaway. We increased our giving from 1% to our own form of 10% giving. And we both moved toward a life of part-time working and full-time living.

Between achieving Coast FIRE and becoming mortgage free, we just didn't need full-time jobs anymore. When you save half of your income and then you achieve your goals, you now only need to earn half the income. It's a beautiful math problem.

THE BENEFITS OF A PAID-OFF HOME

There are so many opinions on whether you should pay off your mortgage early. Some say that paying off your mortgage is a bad idea because you could make a lot more money in the stock market. With the incredible stock market returns over the past decade, there's a lot of truth to that. And others appreciate the peace that comes with not owing anything to the bank each month. The benefits of a paid-off house are hard to deny as well.

I believe this conversation of "right and wrong" can be squashed after families achieve Coast FIRE. Unless your goal is to leave your children with a large inheritance as opposed to owning more of your time, there's little point in investing for retirement after Coast FIRE. You've secured your retirement future. Now it's time to focus on enjoying more of today.

That's why I'm such a big advocate for paying off your mortgage early, but only after you hit Coast FIRE.

If you're on the fence with this decision, here are the benefits of a paid-off home. These aren't just my opinions either. They are the opinions of more than 50 mortgage-free families that I've interviewed across the world as well.

Decreased Annual Living Expenses

According to the US Department of Labor, the largest expense in the typical American family's household budget is their mortgage or rent.[2] When that is completely wiped from your annual expenses, it is such weight off your shoulders.

That leaves you more money for fun, vacations, investing for the future, contributing to your kids' college funds, and, of course, working less and owning your time.

Since our mortgage and extra principal payments were around 35% of our living expenses (outside of our investments), we are breathing much easier with our mortgage gone.

Makes Saving for Retirement Easier

Let's say before paying off your mortgage, your annual expenses were around $100,000 per year. With that type of lifestyle, we would need to save around $2,000,000 to retire comfortably using the 5% rule.

By removing your mortgage from the equation, your annual expenses could get to around $70,000 per year if you had a $2,500 mortgage payment (principal and interest only). In theory, this means we would only need to save up to $1,400,000 for retirement to live a comfortable lifestyle.

There are a lot of factors that can throw that convenient math problem off (inflation, lifestyle change, etc.), but when all is said and done, it's going to be easier for you to retire, $600,000 easier.

Increased Net Worth

February 2018								
Assets			**Liabilities**			**Net Worth**		
Home	$396,000		Mortgage	$0		Assets	$679,000	
Andy's Roth IRA	$75,000					Liabilities	$0	
Andy's 401k	$105,000							
Nicole's Roth IRA	$52,000							
HSA	$2,000							
Cash	$30,000							
Nicole's Car	$8,000							
Andy's Car	$11,000							
Total Assets	$679,000		**Total Liabilities**	$0		**Total Net Worth**	$679,000	

When you don't have debt, you avoid the negative drain on your net worth. And without a mortgage, this is doubly true.

When we started our journey of financial betterment, we had a −$50,000 net worth. After eliminating our debt, saving cash for emergencies, investing for Coast FIRE, and then paying off our mortgage, our net worth skyrocketed.

Have More Fun

My wife loves to do design projects in our home. I love vacations. With more available cash flow, we were able to enjoy life and reward ourselves more.

My wife was able to update our laundry room, update our kitchen, buy new furniture guilt-free, and we even got the hot tub we always wanted. Our paid off home now feels like a palace, and it's ours.

We've traveled a lot more as well. Disney World, Cabo San Lucas, Los Angeles, Ft. Lauderdale, Cancun, and many trips to Northern Michigan have been some of our favorite destinations since paying off our mortgage.

Having the extra cash available has helped us travel without restriction. Getting out of town during our Michigan winters is now a must for our family.

Reduced Stress

I got really stressed out about the size of my mortgage. Having such a large payment each month made me feel worried.

- *"What if I lose my job and we're not able to make the payments?!"*
- *"Or what if I get a new boss and he's a complete jerk, but I can't leave because of the mortgage?!"*
- *"What if a recession rolls in and severely impacts our income?"*

These were real recurring thoughts I had. And I couldn't just tell myself to calm down or not think about it.

When our mortgage payment was gone, my stress level decreased dramatically. There are still other bills we have to pay for the rest of our lives, but none will ever be as big as our mortgage.

Never Worry About Refinancing Your Mortgage

You know when the interest rates drop and all you hear is chatter about refinancing your mortgage? Well, when you don't have a mortgage, you don't even have to wrestle with the decision of whether you should refinance your mortgage or not.

That is one less decision you have to make for the rest of your life.

There are major benefits to reducing the number of decisions you need to make in your day.[3] You'll be more productive, your mind will feel clearer, and life will feel easier.

Ownership Pride

The fact that we own our home outright fills me with so much pride. The peace of mind that comes with true homeownership is incredible.

I've even found myself standing on my front lawn staring at my house and saying, "That's our house. We own all of it. My kids will always have a place to call home."

Those declarations are fun to say.

Design a New Lifestyle

One of the most impressive things I've learned about how mortgage freedom has changed things for the families I've interviewed is their overall lifestyle design.

Many have gone from working full-time jobs to just part-time jobs. Now that they don't need as much money to live, they don't want to work as much.

Others completely changed career paths altogether. It's as if they now had the confidence and financial cushion to make bolder lifestyle decisions. That's what mortgage freedom did for them.

Not having a mortgage gives you the confidence to take major lifestyle leaps.

Easier Path to Family Financial Independence

With a paid-off mortgage, you don't have to save as much money to reach financial independence. Your expenses are now significantly lower.

Using our previous example, if your family spends $100,000 to live each year and then pays off your mortgage with a $2,500 payment per month (principal and interest only), your new annual living expenses are only $70,000.

That means you only need to create $5,833 of monthly income to become financially independent.

How can you get there?

Two spouses working part-time at home. Split this number in two, and you both only need to earn slightly less than $3,000.

This is around $40 per hour for only 80 hours per month: a 20-hour workweek.

That's 80 hours of less working and 80 hours of more living.

ALTERNATIVES TO PAYING OFF YOUR MORTGAGE EARLY

Perhaps the idea of paying off your mortgage early sounds unappealing to you. Maybe you have a super-low interest rate loan or you despise the idea of not growing your next dollar in the stock market despite hitting Coast FIRE. Maybe a 15-year loan is just not in the cards and 30 years feels more feasible for your life.

Never fear. There are alternatives to paying off your mortgage early that support the goal of owning more of your time.

Recasting Your Mortgage

You've heard of paying off your mortgage early. Also, you're probably aware of refinancing your mortgage. But you might not be aware of recasting your mortgage.

A mortgage recast can reduce what you pay in interest and, overall, decrease your monthly payment amounts. This lowers your overall annual expenses giving you the option to redefine your work life.

To recast your mortgage, you will make a large payment on the principal of the loan. After that, your mortgage lender reruns your mortgage numbers in what is called a reamortization. The reamortization (or new repayment schedule) should lower your monthly payments.

To illustrate how this works, let's use some simple math. You originally have a $500,000 mortgage that charges 3% interest for 30 years. That means you pay $2,108 (principal and interest only) each month.

Now, you recast by putting a lump sum of $50,000 toward the principal. That drops your payments to $1,897 per month, which means you're paying more than $200 less per month for the entire life of the loan.

This could take place if you move into a new home before your original house sells, land a very generous bonus at work, or perhaps an inheritance comes your way.

Recasting is not nearly as involved as refinancing or getting a new mortgage. Usually, it only involves requesting a recast and being able to make a lump-sum payment.

There is typically a small cost. Depending on your lender, you can expect to pay anywhere from $100 to $500 for a recast. I've heard from some viewers on my YouTube channel that they have gotten this done for free with their lender.

Overall, recasting can be an excellent option for families who have the ability to put a lump sum down on their mortgage principal, want to save on their monthly payments, but don't want to go all the way to complete debt freedom.

Downsizing Your Home

Another way to reduce your overall cost of homeownership is to downsize. You may feel excited to own more of your time because between work, kids, and taking care of your house, you have very little time left. You may want to consider the advantages that come with downsizing or put another way, rightsizing.

As our incomes grow over time, our lifestyles tend to inflate as well. What used to be "enough house" is not enough anymore. So, we upgrade, update, and up level our domiciles until we panic and say, "Homeownership is expensive!" By rightsizing our living situations, we can accomplish the following:

- Reduce our annual expenses
- Save more time cleaning, maintaining, and updating our properties
- Eliminate clutter and waste that is taking our time and money

Some families started off with a bigger home and realized they just didn't need all the space they had. After rightsizing her home in Texas, Sandra shared with me that a large lot size used to be appealing to her in the beginning, but that changed over time. "I used to always want the biggest lot. Besides sitting out on my patio and looking at my backyard, I didn't really make a whole lot of use of that square footage. And there's landscaping cost, fertilizer, and you have to get it mowed. And I hate gardening. I pay people to do that anyway. So, when I moved, the square footage of the home didn't necessarily change but the lot size did."

Other families may have planned for three or four children, but after one or two kids, they realized they were content. If the home purchase happened as family planning was still happening, their homes might be bigger than they need.

According to Rocket, the appropriate square footage per person ranges from 500 to 700 square feet per person.[4] Of course, "appropriate" is in the eye of the beholder so adjust as you'd like.

A family of three may want to find a house in the 1,500–2,100 square foot range.

If another child is in your future and you become a family of four, consider something in the 2,000–2,800 range.

We have a family of four, and our house is around 2,700 square feet. It feels like the right size for us right now.

Here's a quick recap of the home square footage suggested per person:

- Family of 2: 1,000–1,400 sq. ft.
- Family of 3: 1,500–2,100 sq. ft.
- Family of 4: 2,000–2,800 sq. ft.
- Family of 5: 2,500–3,500 sq. ft.
- Family of 6: 3,000–4,200 sq. ft.

When you own a smaller home, you'll potentially have fewer things to fix, fewer upgrades to make, and fewer costs to incur. This all depends on the home you would downsize to, but the goal is with a smaller home you'll get smaller problems.

To put some math around this idea, a general rule of thumb is to save up 1–4% of the value of your home each year for home maintenance.[5] Let's say you have a bigger, more expensive $700,000 home and you're considering downsizing.

For a $700,000 home, that's $7,000–$28,000 per year. A few years of not updating your home will make that number creep up fast.

Let's say you found a $300,000–$400,000 home that you were able to buy outright with no mortgage because of all the equity you built up over time. Then you'd be looking at $3,000–$16,000 per year instead.

That sounds a lot more comfortable and much more in line with owning your time.

Renting Instead of Buying

Homeownership can be great, but renting gives you flexibility. You have the ability to change where you live after your lease is up. The changes can be big or small. You can change what type of housing you have or even change the city, state, or country you live in.

You can't say the same for homeownership.

It's not just a mortgage, though that's certainly a big part of it. When you buy a home, you're stuck with a mortgage, homeowners insurance, property taxes, and maybe even PMI.

Plus, let's not forget about all those closing costs and fees. If you buy a home and want to sell a year or two later when you get bored of where you live, that's not only cumbersome, but it's cost prohibitive as well. Those fees that you paid to buy a home are waiting for you when you sell too.

Depending on where you live, renting may be less expensive than owning your home when you factor in all the true costs of homeownership.

Outside of cost, time is an important consideration.

I've been a homeowner for 21 years now, and I'll tell you the truth: I wish I was a renter sometimes. The amount of home maintenance and repairs I've had to do over that time frame has been insane.

I'm already longing for the day where I can become a renter again so I don't have to:

- Cut my lawn
- Edge my lawn
- Weed my lawn
- Treat my lawn (See how annoying lawns are?)
- Trim my trees
- Repair or replace broken appliances
- Replace my cracking driveway
- Save up thousands of dollars to replace my roof
- Paint my house

The list feels never-ending … probably because it is. My point is that all that home equity and net worth growth comes with work as well as costs.

With renting, when something breaks, your landlord *should* take care of it. There's either no lawn to cut or it's taken care of by the landlord too.

When you consider the time and cost of home maintenance and repairs, renting feels more relaxing to me.

That said, I know that renting can come with rent hikes, design rules, and the feeling that don't really own your home. It's less work because it's not truly yours. You're not building equity, and you don't have a home as an asset on your net worth statement.

That may be a freeing feeling for you or an upsetting one.

Choosing whether to rent or buy is a very personal decision.

In my single time in my twenties, all I wanted was freedom. As I learned, homeownership was the exact opposite of that. Fast forward to when I got married, and we started our family. All of a sudden, I really cared about school systems, communities, and laying down roots. I wanted to have a place for my kids to call home for good.

And maybe when the kids are grown and gone, maybe I'll want to be a renter again.

It all depends on your season in life.

Either way, running the math on renting versus buying could be a smart move as you look to own more of your time.

FROM THE PODCAST

Family: Amber and TJ, 43 years old from North Carolina
Money Milestone: Mortgage free on their $600k home in 7 years

Andy:	*Why did you want to become mortgage free?*
Amber:	Well, for us, it was very much an insurance policy. That's how we're thinking about being mortgage free. We had done a lot of work to get out of debt and the mortgage free part, it was something that was really important to us because both sides of our family, we've had several family members who have experienced homelessness.
	And you know, I think a lot of people think its drugs, it's alcohol, it's all these vices that cause that. In our case, our family members had medical emergencies.

It was cancer. It was a debilitating car accident. It was a number of things. They were working. They were doing all the things you're supposed to do in life. But then they got hit with this thing and eventually lost their homes. And so we just wanted an insurance policy against that. If something like that were to happen, you know, of course we're saving, we're doing all the things, but as long as I can pay my taxes and my HOA and my insurance, nobody can take a house from me at this point. So, it was very psychological.

Andy: *What did you do to pay this off in 7 years?*

Amber: We used the same techniques that we used as we were paying off debt. We certainly did try to increase our income. We both moved jobs and moved into higher paying industries, and both of us increased our income by about 30% by doing that. I did side hustles.

My husband did not. Instead, his side hustle was taking on the bulk of the childcare tasks. Because his career is very flexible. He gets to work when he wants; he gets to work as much as he wants, as long as his goals are met. I'm in HR, so mine is much more, "You need to be in a certain place at a certain time."

And of course, we reduced our expenses, and for me personally, part of that, was I needed to go through therapy. I went through a year and a half of therapy because we are an adoptive family. When we adopted our children, we went from zero children to two one-year-olds. Very, very big change. I had also just started a new job and was not eligible for FMLA and so I didn't get that leave.

They were like, "I mean, we'll give you 4 weeks of unpaid leave." So here I was with two new babies that were one years old, special needs because of their foster situation. And so I wasn't sleeping. I didn't have any time to myself. It was work, it was doctors, it was all the things. And I developed a very detrimental shopping habit as a way to cope.

A very bad coping mechanism. And that was obviously really not helping. And so, I went to therapy to figure out what that was about. And really what it was is when I was going to the store or out shopping, that was the only time that nobody needed something from me. My husband wasn't there, kids weren't there, and work wasn't there. It was the only time that I could just be alone by myself with nobody touching me or asking me for something.

And so, through therapy, I was really able to get a lot of techniques and work through a lot of that and develop better coping habits. And that decreased our expenses as well. Of course, we looked at the more traditional expenses that people look at and how can we lower those and what we can cut back on. But that therapy piece was extremely important for me personally.

Andy: *How is life different after becoming mortgage free? Did you guys celebrate?*

Amber: Well, we celebrated by opening a Vanguard brokerage account. And we paid the mortgage off during our anniversary month. And for our anniversary, my husband got me index fund shares. So, we're boring, but that's fine.

That's my kind of romance. I like it.

When he got me the shares, he calculated it out to 20 years, and he was like, this is how much I'm giving you. It was fabulous. And so, it is such a pressure off now that we have the mortgage paid off. And what we're doing with the money is a couple of different things. One is we completed saving for our kids' college.

We are doing a brokerage account and because FIRE is our goal.

And then actually we funded a 6-month sabbatical for me, which I am currently on coming up on that 6-month mark for me where I will be re-entering the workforce. But it was just an opportunity to have that career break, and it has been such a gift. It was completely worth everything we needed to do to pay off debt and go mortgage free for me to be able to do this.

Andy: *There's somebody listening right now, and they want to become mortgage free too. What is one step they could take?*

Amber: As a family, decide, "What are the things that matter to us? And are there ways to do those things that don't involve money?" We changed so many things about our lives that cost money. We eliminated those, but we still kept those core things that were so, so important and just found ways to do those low cost, and no cost.

And that way we did not feel denied or deprived in any way when we were on that journey, because 7 years is a long time. And you can't feel denied for that whole time. And so really making those decisions upfront, I would recommend a family do that for themselves.

Carpe Diem Action Steps

- Calculate your annual mortgage principal and interest payments and dream with your spouse about what you would do with extra money back in your lives.
- Review the benefits of a paid-off mortgage with your spouse and see which ones resonate most with them.

- Calculate how extra principal payments could cut down the duration of your mortgage. Use our free mortgage payoff calculator at MarriageKidsandMoney.com/Calculators/Mortgage-Payoff/.
- Make a plan with your spouse regarding newfound money in your relationship (tax refunds, bonuses, commissions, inheritances, etc.) and see how you can use this to become mortgage free faster.
- Explore recasting, downsizing, or renting as annual expense reduction alternatives thereby allowing you to own more of your time.

NOTES

1. Majaksi, C. (2025). *15-year vs. 30-year mortgage: What's the difference?* Investopedia. Available at: https://www.investopedia.com/articles/personal-finance/042015/comparison-30year-vs-15year-mortgage.asp
2. BLS. (2023). *Consumer expenditures* [Online]. Available at: https://www.bls.gov/news.release/cesan.nr0.htm
3. Clear, J. (n.d.). *How willpower works: how to avoid bad decisions* [Online]. Available at: https://jamesclear.com/willpower-decision-fatigue
4. Johnson, J. (2023). *How big of a house do I need?* Rocket. Available at: https://www.rockethomes.com/blog/home-buying/key-factors-to-find-right-size-home
5. Wentland, M. (2023). *Solved! Here's how much to budget for a home maintenance fund.* Bob Vila. Available at: https://www.bobvila.com/articles/how-much-to-budget-for-home-maintenance/

CHAPTER SIX

STOCKPILE FU MONEY

"I got gas in the tank. I got money in the bank. I got news for you baby.
You're looking at the man."
— Brandon Flowers (The Killers, Lyrics from "The Man")

As corporate employees, we make a life-changing arrangement with our employers when we start our careers. We exchange our time, energy, and autonomy for money. That deal can work for a while and provide us with many benefits we wouldn't have had otherwise.

But there may come a day when that deal feels out of balance. This is when you start to feel that your employer is getting much more out of the deal than you are. You're working longer hours than you used to, and you're not getting paid for it. The amount of work you're asked to do has increased, but your pay has not kept pace. You've addressed these issues with your supervisor, but no real change is happening. And now, the amount of money you're receiving for the time, energy, and loss of freedom you're providing is simply not worth it anymore.

This is about the time you start thinking, "This isn't working for me. How do I get out of this arrangement?" Quitting doesn't work because you need money. You have a family that relies on your income. Getting another job could work, but what if the same situation repeats itself somewhere else?

Since those questions were so complicated and felt impossible, you lean back into work and resign that this work imbalance is just the way it is. And this is something that you just need to get used to. The negativity and low-grade depression takes over.

Phrases like "Life is tough" and "Everyone works jobs they hate" start to become part of your everyday vernacular. You find yourself repeating these phrases to your children, or they simply observe that your pride and confidence in yourself starts to fade.

If this sounds familiar, you're not alone.

Toxic workplaces can drain our souls. The light, joy, and hopefulness we once had can be replaced with darkness, anxiety, and fear. In a recent survey from the American Psychological Association, 15% of workers labeled their workplaces as "somewhat or very toxic."[1] The same survey found that nearly 60% of employers thought their workplace was mentally healthier than it actually was. Evidently, there's an imbalance in communication between workers and their employees as well.

Prolonged stressful situations like these can have so many negative effects. Stress can be brought home and affect relationships with your spouse and children. Mental health issues can also lead to physical health issues, including cardiovascular disease and even cancer.[2]

That is until we decide enough is enough. Everyone has their breaking point. For many of the families I've spoken to over the past decade, it's usually a moment when they are feeling low and their supervisors just take it too far.

That's when quitting feels like the only option.

Unfortunately, without the right financial safety net in place, this can lead to further stress, anxiety, and depression. We may own our time quickly by quitting our jobs, but we immediately become financially vulnerable.

So how do we solve this? We stockpile FU Money.

WHAT IS FU MONEY?

FU Money is money stashed away in a savings account that allows you to say goodbye to a job that isn't serving you anymore. By saving enough money, you can cover your expenses for a while.

It is essentially a bridge that helps you transition from a place of hardship and stress to a place of peace and prosperity. When you have enough money set aside, for a time of your choosing, you can say "FU."

FU, of course stands for "Forget U" job. This is a family book after all.

Leaving Corporate for a Solopreneur Life

I was rescued by FU Money.

A decade or so ago, I felt trapped working in an industry that I didn't enjoy. I needed the six-figure income I was making in order to sustain my family's six-figure lifestyle.

Through some experimentation outside of work, I found a new passion that I was interested in. Podcasting was a hobby of mine, but I was finding small ways to make money with it. I was optimistic about a future where I worked for myself as a podcaster, but I was also realistic. This was not a lucrative venture. Making the money I was bringing in as a senior corporate marketer was going to be very difficult. I needed time and space to figure out how to grow my solopreneur business.

That's what FU Money afforded me. By saving up more than 12 months of expenses in a separate savings account, I was able to buy myself time to figure it all out.

It also bought me more confidence. With money in the bank, I knew that I wasn't beholden to my employer like I used to be. I knew that I wouldn't have to lower my head after getting scolded for failing to "read my boss's mind" yet again.

Then the day came when I had enough. It was my breaking point.

After years of feeling unmotivated and drained at work, I was asked by my supervisor to take on an additional task where I had no prior experience. This was outside of my typical responsibilities, but he told me to just do my best. I did just that, and unfortunately for both of us, he hated the way I executed the project. He called me into his office after work hours and scolded me for my performance. As I tried to explain my reasoning and actions, it only made the situation worse.

Already, I didn't like my job. The benefits and pay were excellent, but the work was unfulfilling, the hours were long, and my time away from family on weekends was just too much as a young father. Now add in getting yelled at for a project I took on outside of my area of expertise, I was done.

I didn't quit that day, but I did mentally check out. My focus shifted away from being the best employee I could be and over to getting out of this situation as quickly (and safely) as possible. I was able to hold my head up high after being berated by my boss because I knew I had done my best with the information I had and I knew that my FU Money was going to come in handy soon.

Over the years that followed, my wife and I saved the equivalent of a year's worth of expenses. This money became my bridge to leave my place of hardship (the corporate life) and walk slowly to a place of peace and time freedom (my solopreneur life).

When I told my boss I was leaving, he was surprisingly very supportive. In my cortisol spiked mind, I made him out to be a villain, but he was anything but that. He wished me the best and even gave me my work laptop as a thank you gift as I started my new business. Perhaps he was just as stressed out and strapped for time as I was in the corporate world. Maybe he felt trapped like I did.

After my 2 weeks were up, I took some time to breathe. Owning my time outside of work was a true blessing, and I didn't want to mess it up. I focused on becoming a better husband, a more present father, exercising more and reuniting with friends I had lost touch with.

Unfortunately, my breath was cut short.

Two months after I let my employer know I was leaving my secure job, the global pandemic came in, and the whole world went sideways. My small business income plummeted. I lost solid client contracts, my advertising dollars decreased, and my hopes for a prosperous first full year as a business owner were crushed.

I was so glad I had my FU Money to help us during this crazy time. Not only did it help us take care of our family's expenses for a few months while my business was right-sized, but it allowed me not to panic and jump back into my old corporate life.

Fast forward to today, I'm a solopreneur working 20–25 hours per week, and I enjoy what I do for a living. More importantly, I enjoy having more hours back in my week to live my life. This would not have been possible without my FU Money.

Transition from Double-income to Single-income Household

Starting your own solopreneur business is not the only use for FU Money. Many couples I've interviewed over the years have used FU Money to transition from a two-income household to a one-income household. They just needed the financial cushion to allow that big transition to happen.

Let's jump back to our couple, Jacob and Emily. After they achieved Coast FIRE and paid off their mortgage early, they were feeling a lot more confident with their financial situation. Their expenses were lower, and they were ready for a life change.

Emily wanted to become a stay-at-home mom and raise her two small kids before they went off to elementary school. They decided that using FU Money would allow them to have a bridge out of Emily's corporate job.

The couple was used to spending $10,000 per month to live their comfortable lives. Without Emily's income, they would only have $6,000 per month.

Jumping directly from a monthly budget of $10,000 per month to $6,000 per month would have been quite difficult for them. So instead, they decided together to use an FU Money bridge that would allow them to slowly but surely get used to living on less.

By saving up $18,000 in an FU Money fund, they were able to utilize the funds as a bridge to become a single-income family.

FU Money Bridge

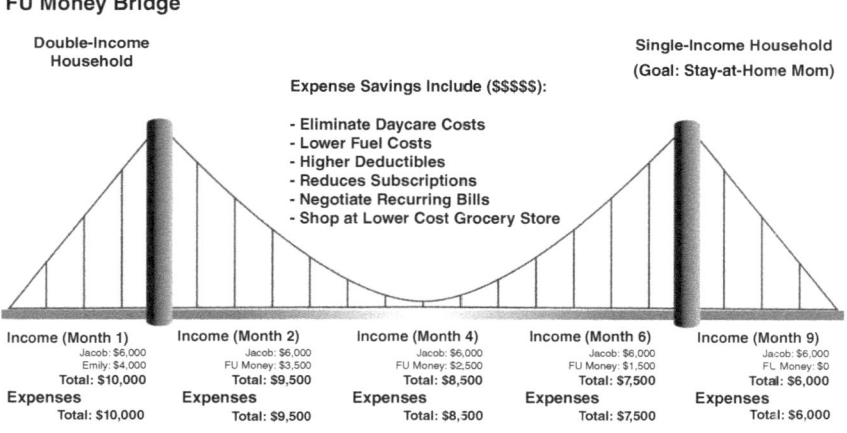

Each month, they would find ways to decrease their spending by $500.

In the beginning, it would be easier because they found immediate savings by eliminating daycare costs. With less commuting to work, there were savings on gas. They found ways to save on their insurance by going with higher deductibles.

And as the months rolled on, they got thriftier with grocery shopping and, overall, just paid more attention to where their money was going.

Over 9 months, they would be ready to live on $6,000 per month. But during their time of transition, that FU Money helped ease them into their new lives. And Jacob was able to increase his income over time as well.

In the end, Jacob and Emily were able to transition to a single income successfully. It was a difficult road and required some partnership, but the plan worked.

Pursue a New Career Path

After years of doing the stay-at-home mom thing, my wife was ready to go back to work. Checking emails at a desk and drinking coffee sounded like heaven compared to having no time to yourself at home with toddlers.

She started working in the advertising industry as an office manager and found the work to be enjoyable and not too overwhelming.

When the pandemic hit, everything seemed to change quickly. Her relaxing and manageable job became stressful and demanding.

She transitioned to another company in hopes it would be better, but it was more of the same. She knew that this industry was not for her anymore, and she wanted to change career paths altogether.

For a long time, she wanted to transition into a job where she could use her hands, get out of the email grind, and truly help people. She had her heart set on becoming an aesthetician.

That's when our FU Money came in handy once again. Since we still had more than $30,000 of FU Money left after my solopreneur leap, we decided that we could use this money to help cover our expenses while my wife went back to school for 6 months to pursue her new trade.

She is now a licensed aesthetician working 20–25 hours per week. We're grateful for the time and space we had with this big life change, and it wouldn't have been possible without our FU Money.

HOW MUCH FU MONEY DO I NEED?

The amount of FU Money you need depends on your goal. For example, let's say you're hoping to become a stay-at-home parent for a period. You're bringing home $3,000 per month in income, and you're paying $3,000 per month in daycare costs. This becomes an easy math problem as you may not need any FU Money to make this transition. Cancel daycare and leave the job.

Unfortunately, not all situations fit that conveniently. Here are a few scenarios and a range of FU Money that may support your transition.

Family Transition (3–6 Months of Your Income)

There may come a time when you need to take a break from work for an extended period. This may be to take care of an aging parent or raise your children at home. While this period could last anywhere from 1 year to 10 years, it's not necessary to save up your annual income for that entire period. While that would be ideal, it's not necessary if you have a spouse that is supporting you. Without a spouse supporting you during this transition, saving up the entire amount would be necessary.

If you do have an income-generating partner willing to support this family time, try to think of your FU Money as "transition money." You are transitioning into a new way of life and your expenses will need to adjust to that new life over time.

Saving up 3–6 months of your income can help with this change. This money should be outside of your emergency fund. Your FU Money should be in a separate account.

Over time, you'll find that you are able to reduce expenses to better align with your new way of living.

Sabbatical (3–12 Months of Your Income)

Outside of family transition times, you may just need a break from work that's longer than your allotted paid time off. Perhaps your corporate burnout has reached a peak and you're ready for a break. Or you have other life adventures you want to take advantage of before you're in your traditional retirement years. When you have a pile of FU Money, this is a lot easier.

While some companies have paid sabbaticals, many do not. According to the Society for Human Resource Management, only 7% of companies offer paid sabbatical leave.[3] You could go unpaid and still have your job waiting for you, but that is only offered by 8% of companies. The majority of the time, you will need to foot the bill for your sabbatical.

Depending on how long you want your break to be, that's how much you'll need to save up. If you want a year off, then save up 1 year of your income. If you take home $90,000 per year after taxes, you'll want to put away $90,000 to get that year off.

You could save less, but your supportive spouse may also want to take some time off as well. So be sure to thoroughly discuss the idea of a sabbatical during your next money date.

Career Transition (9 Months–2 Years of Your Income Plus Cost of School)

Let's say you've had it with your career and you're ready to try something completely new. This new career path may take some further education and career training. Depending on how long this education process takes, you'll need to cover your income during that time.

If school lasts 6 months, build your FU Money pot up to 6 months of income plus another 3 months of income to allow for the new job search. You'll also want to factor in the training costs or university fees.

Perhaps school takes much longer to complete. Your FU Money savings needs to pair up with the costs of transitioning. This will reduce stress in your marriage and allow you to focus on your studies and launching successfully into your new career.

Launch a Small Business (6–12 Months of Your Income Plus Startup Costs)

Uncertainty abounds when it comes to launching your own business. Close to one quarter of businesses fail within the first year.[4] The number climbs to nearly 50% by year 5.

While there are many factors that lead to small business failure, they all come back to money. Small business owners may not have enough money to keep the business running, or they simply aren't proficient in handling the money well.

Having 6–12 months of FU Money set aside will allow for you to transition into your new business. It won't make your business successful, but it will make it easier for you to become successful. Also, include appropriate startup costs based on your business type. I'm a fan of businesses that have low startup costs and businesses that get their first sale before spending money.

The old saying, "You have to spend money to make money," can be true, but it can also be abused by new business owners. They will spend so much time and money creating the perfect website, storefront, business card, and logo (aka "playing business") that they forget getting someone to actually buy something is the true definition of a business. Make more than you spend and always pay yourself first.

HOW TO CREATE YOUR FU MONEY STOCKPILE

In most cases, the FU Money we're discussing is easily tens of thousands and in some cases hundreds of thousands of dollars. This is not a small amount of money.

After achieving Coast FIRE and becoming mortgage free, most corporate employees should be able to save up a large amount of money each month. Thousands of dollars saved each month can easily turn into tens of thousands in a year and hundreds of thousands in 5 years.

For example, after achieving Coast FIRE, our fictional friends Jacob and Emily now have more than $40,000 available each year.

They also paid off their mortgage early. Their monthly payment of $2,500 (principal and interest only) is now gone. This mortgage-free situation allows them to save $30,000 per year.

You can see how much easier it is to save tens of thousands per year after achieving these family financial independence milestones.

Automate Your FU Savings

Now that you've created such a large gap between your income and your expenses by achieving Coast FIRE and mortgage freedom, it's time to save. You don't want lifestyle inflation to take over and move you away from your goal of owning your time.

Take this decision out of your hands and create some automated savings. Just as we've done with our emergency savings, our investing, and our mortgage payoff process, use automation to help you build up your FU Money.

If you have a gap of $4,000 between your income and your expenses, send that $4,000 directly to savings automatically at the beginning of the month. This way, you're not tempted to spend it or use it for something else.

Continue Your Money Dates

As you're banking money each month, the dreams start to feel more real. Early on in the process, it might have felt like a fantasy to think you'd be able to own your time and escape the corporate world. The reality now is you are a matter of months away from a better life.

Celebrate these moments with your spouse during your money dates. These bi-monthly meetings can be a time for marital check-ins, financial progress updates, and dreaming sessions.

Use a High-yield Savings Account

When you're saving for any big near-term goal like a home down payment, a new-to-you car, or emergency fund, using a high-yield savings account is a smart move. That's because you get a lot more interest for your savings than a typical brick-and-mortar bank.

As of the time of this writing, many high-yield savings accounts are offering 3% APY or more on your savings, while big banks like Chase and Bank of America are offering 0.01% APY on your savings.[5] Saving $50,000 in a high-yield savings account earning 3% APY can net you $1,500 in interest annually. For the big banks with 0.01%, that will net you $5.

Saving up your FU Money stockpile becomes a lot easier when you have a higher interest rate. Whichever bank you choose, make sure your money is FDIC-insured. This protects your savings up $250,000 and up to $500,000 for a joint account with two spouses.[6] So if you and your spouse pooled up $500,000 and your bank fails, your money is insured by the federal government, and it's protected.

You Gotta Keep It Separated

Comingling your FU Money with your checking account or emergency savings is not recommended. Without ironclad discipline, you may fall victim to using your FU Money for other purposes.

Ideally, this money would be saved in a separate high-yield savings account and labeled as "FU Money." Many accounts allow you to put an actual name or purpose to your savings account. So instead of "savings account," it's called "FU Money." That way, you're reminded what it's for, especially when temptation comes knocking at your door.

One week, you may have had a slower time at the office, and you start to think, "Eh, work isn't so bad. Maybe I'll use these tens of thousands or hundreds of thousands to upgrade my home instead!" Or you're in mid-life crisis mode and you decide that a brand-new car will make you feel better about your job you hate. Spoiler alert: it won't!

Materialism and consumer culture can convince us that more stuff or upgraded stuff will make us happier. The opposite is actually true. When we let go of material things and instead allocate time, space, and money toward the things that really matter, we will become happier in the long run.

Leave the Money Liquid

While you may be tempted to invest this FU Money to get a higher return, I wouldn't recommend it. This is money you want to easily access in the event of your departure from the corporate world.

You don't want to worry about selling shares of stock in order to pay for life's expenses in your transition time. Also, you'd hate to be in the middle of a bear market, which is an extended period of price declines that severely affect investor portfolios. These on average last up to 289 days.

Your $50,000 invested in a bear market could drop to $40,000 just when you're ready to say goodbye to your 9-to-5.

Keep this FU Money liquid in cash and in a savings account.

Celebrate Your Milestones

As you get closer to your FU Money goal, be sure to make mini moments for celebration with the ones you love. If your goal is $50,000 of FU Money, be sure to celebrate three to five times along the way.

These don't have to be wild blowout parties, but they should be moments of recognition and happiness. You're doing something you never thought was possible. Recognize that with your spouse, smile, dance, eat, drink, and be merry! You are strengthening your family tree and about to become financially free.

FROM THE PODCAST

Family: Jamila and Woody Souffrant, 40 years old from New York
Money Milestone: Saved $160k of FU Money to start a solopreneur business (*Journey to Launch*)

> **Andy:** *You and your husband saved $85,000 per year consistently for a period of time. What was your motivation?*

Jamila:	I wanted to quit my job. I had a long commute from Brooklyn to New Jersey, a very demanding career. And then I had three kids at this point. And so, the plan was already set in motion before I had my third child. But I like to say each child when I got pregnant with them prompted me further into my journey. And so really my pursuit of financial independence was to attain the freedom that I essentially have now, which is more time and energy autonomy where I can decide what I do instead of being in a car, on a commute and answering to a boss. Now I just answer to myself, which is still not fun because I still don't want to work.
	But at least it's on my own terms.
Andy:	*Was that difficult for you and your husband to do? Did it feel like a stretch?*
Jamila:	I had a six-figure job with bonuses working in corporate America. And my husband actually is a teacher in New York City and also earned six figures. So, we had a healthy income as a two-parent household. So, I always like to bring that up. In order for us to save $169,000 in 2 years, that was a function of our income and our discipline in hitting those goals that we set for ourselves.
	It was a change from what we were doing before. We definitely reeled in our expenses. At the time, we both had more expensive cars. He had a very expensive lease. I owned my car, but the maintenance on it was very expensive, especially at the time driving from Brooklyn to New Jersey. And so, we cut all that out and got a budget together. And the pain and discomfort of having the commute, which was an hour and a half one way and working at this job I just didn't love was more uncomfortable than saving and investing the money we needed to get out of the situation I was in. And so, it was worth it. It was uncomfortable,

but it was worth it. But also, we did have the income to help support that. We did have to make some small term changes.

Andy: *This practice of saving and investing a large percentage of your income, what did that allow you to do eventually?*

Jamila: I first started *Journey to Launch* to document what I was doing because I wanted to reach financial independence and quit my job by 40 years old. And so, I officially started the blog in 2016 and the podcast in 2017. And that's when I aggressively started to save with my husband. And so, over the course of the 2 years, that's where we saved $169,000. But when we realized we were pregnant with my third, we readjusted to say, "Well, what if we could achieve more freedom earlier, have an income cut if I'm able to quit my job, but achieve freedom quicker by switching our investing strategy?"

So instead of putting all our money into investment accounts, what if we save up this FU Fund in a high yield savings account to help cover what I knew I would be doing, which was quitting my job. And for me to leave my job, that's cutting off more than half our income.

And so, what do we need to be secure over the next year or two while I figure out this business, but still now have three kids at this point to raise and what that looks like. So, starting the journey, even though I didn't reach financial independence when I quit my job, it allowed me to take the risk of leaving my job because I knew I had the safety net of money to help support us and the family as I made this transition.

But also, what we did was we reached Coast FIRE.

Coast FIRE is the ability to not have to invest ever again because on autopilot our investments accumulate over time. And so, all that made us feel comfortable that I would walk away and try entrepreneurship, which I'm still trying out.

Andy: *When did you realize the extra money you had was better served as liquid cash than invested in the market?*

Jamila: When I realized that quitting my job was possible. Because we have responsibilities, we own our home, and we have three kids, we had to make sure we had to at least be able to pay for our expenses. And so, I thought, what does a more balanced approach to financial independence look like? Whereas beginning of the journey, it was really all about saving and investing and optimizing for numbers and just bearing through it, you know.

I had the mindset of "if I just stay here for 7 years and focus on the income, we could reach a really great spot into financial independence." But then I realized it wasn't sustainable. The lifestyle we want to live in New York, also realizing it's not just my life. I have a partner who wants to do different things where we don't want to feel as constricted. And so, we thought about what that life could look like. If it takes us longer to reach it, but we can enjoy it and I have more freedom, then isn't that the same benefit?

Carpe Diem Action Steps
- Calculate how much FU Money you need to achieve your "own your time" goal.
- Set up an automated deposit each month into a high-yield savings account.

- Continue to meet with your spouse for your money dates to gauge your progress.
- Celebrate your money milestones along the way and be sure to celebrate with your kids too so they are watching you win.
- During your money dates, take time to recognize your progress, and continue dreaming about your future life with your corporate career behind you.

NOTES

1. Sleek, S. (2024). *Toxic workplaces leave employees sick, scared, and looking for an exit. Here's how to combat unhealthy conditions* [Online]. APA. Available at: https://www.apa.org/topics/healthy-workplaces/toxic-workplace
2. Solan, M. (2023). *Prolonged stress may increase the risk of death from cancer* [Online]. Harvard Health Publishing, Harvard Medical School. Available at: https://www.health.harvard.edu/cancer/prolonged-stress-may-increase-the-risk-of-death-from-cancer
3. SHRM. (2023). *State of work/life balance benefits* [Online]. Available at: https://www.shrm.org/content/dam/en/shrm/executive-network/en-insights-forums/June%202023%20Insights%20Forum.pdf
4. Davis, M. (2025). *Percentage of businesses that fail—and how to boost chances of success* [Online]. LendingTree. Available at: https://www.lendingtree.com/business/small/failure-rate/
5. Mitchner, R. (2025). *What is the average savings account interest rate?* [Online]. MarketWatch. Available at: https://www.marketwatch.com/financial-guides/banking/average-savings-account-interest-rate/
6. FDIC. (2025). *Joint accounts* [Online]. Available at: https://www.fdic.gov/financial-institution-employees-guide-deposit-insurance/joint-accounts

PART 3

ENJOY TIME FREEDOM

CHAPTER SEVEN

CREATE YOUR 3-DAY WORKWEEK

"Lead a life of your own design, on your own terms.
Not one that others or the environment have scripted for you."
– Tony Robbins

E ach week, we get 7 days to live our lives. A lot of us work 5 days and take 2 days to relax, enjoy our hobbies, and spend time with the ones we love.

This begs the question, "Why don't we have more days for relaxation and fewer days for work?" It feels lopsided. Why not something like 4 days for relaxation, socializing and fun, and 3 days for work? A permanent 4-day weekend does have a nice ring to it.

The reason most people don't do this usually comes back to their lifestyle and money. Most people can't afford to work fewer days each week based on the lifestyle they choose to live.

It is possible though. Our ancestors definitely worked less than we do. I'm not talking about our grandparents or even great-grandparents. Prior to the Industrial Revolution and capitalistic societies that dominate our way of life now, a 1,400-hour work-year was typical.[1] Holiday time in medieval England spanned one-third of a typical year. France and Spain had an even more generous holiday schedule. And the workday almost always included a mid-day nap.

Our ancestors may have not had all the material goods and technological advances that we enjoy today, but they definitely had more leisure time.

As you come to this financial crossroads in your family financial independence journey, you have a choice to make. Do you double down on building your wealth, continue working at your current pace, and inflate your lifestyle further? Or do you choose to slow down, own more of your time, and embrace the comforts of a simpler life now?

There are plenty of books that will show you how to maximize your wealth; this one is focused on using your money to maximize your time.

At this point in your journey, you're debt free, you have an emergency fund of 3–6 months, you're Coast FIRE, you're mortgage free, and you even have FU Money to launch into a new work life you enjoy. You have financial strength, and you have financial options.

Let's explore them.

FAMILY BUDGET—BEFORE AND AFTER THIS JOURNEY

With no debt and no near-term need to save or invest, your budget opens up. The possibilities abound. Your family is protected now and in the future.

The only things left to pay for are your daily expenses.

To highlight this point further, let's take a look at a typical American budget from a household earning $10,000 per month and compare it to what the budget might look like after going through our previous steps.

If we use our friends Jacob and Emily as an example, their budget might look something like this prior to their work on improving their family financial lives.

Budget—Before Family FI Journey				
	Monthly	Annually	Percentage	Notes
Income				
Emily	$ 5,000	$ 60,000	50%	
Jacob	$ 5,000	$ 60,000	50%	
TOTAL INCOME	$ 10,000	$ 120,000		
Expenses				
	Monthly	Annually	Percentage	Notes
Housing	$ 3,500	$ 42,000	35%	Mortgage, bills, etc.
Transportation	$ 1,500	$ 18,000	15%	Two cars with payments or leases
Food	$ 1,200	$ 14,400	12%	Groceries for family of 3, food out of the house
Daycare	$ 1,150	$ 13,800	12%	One child in daycare
Savings, investments + Insurance	$ 1,100	$ 13,200	11%	Investing 10% and paying for personal insurance
Entertainment	$ 800	$ 9,600	8%	
Giving (family, friends, charities)	$ 300	$ 3,600	3%	
Clothing + services	$ 200	$ 2,400	2%	
Personal care	$ 150	$ 1,800	2%	

(*Continued*)

(Continued)

Budget—Before Family FI Journey			
Miscellaneous	$ 100	$ 1,200	1%
Left Over	$ 0	$ 0	0%
TOTAL EXPENSES	**$10,000**	**$120,000**	

They are earning $10,000 per month and allocating it toward most everything they want in life. The only issue is that they both desire more time freedom now and in the future.

Their housing costs total up to $3,500 per month or 35% of their budget. While this is higher than average compared to data from the Bureau of Labor Statistics,[2] Jacob and Emily have inflated their lifestyles over the years. They got a mortgage on a house they want to grow into with a slightly higher interest rate than their peers, and they underestimated the costs of home maintenance and utility bills.

Transportation costs for this couple come in around 15% or $1,500 of their monthly expenses. They went with slightly nicer cars than they needed, and Emily's commute to and from work eats up more gas than they had planned originally. Auto insurance rates have recently increased as well, making it harder to grow the gap between their income and expenses.

Between grocery prices, eating out at restaurants, and food delivery, Jacob and Emily spend around 12% of their budget on food. Spending $1,200 per month feels like a lot when they look at their budget, but it all adds up.

Daycare for their child also comes in around 12% of their monthly budget as well. They've tried to work out an arrangement with Grandma to watch a couple of days per week, but the driving distance back and forth has made planning difficult. This $1,150 per month daycare bill is here to stay for the moment.

Jacob and Emily have been stocking away investments and paying for personal insurance to the tune of $1,100 per month or 11% of their budget. This has gotten their investment journey started off on the right foot.

Entertainment, vacations, and relaxation get 8% of their budget or $800 per month. After long days at work, they both wish they had a bigger allocation here.

The remaining $800 or 8% goes toward giving, clothing, personal care, and the general miscellaneous costs of life.

When all is said and done, they are spending $10,000 per month or $120,000 per year.

Now let's compare this to their budget after completing the previous steps.

Budget—After Family FI Journey				
	Monthly	Annually	Percentage	Notes
Income				
Emily	$ 5,000	$ 60,000	50%	
Jacob	$ 5,000	$ 60,000	50%	
TOTAL INCOME	$ 10,000	$ 120,000		
Expenses				
	Monthly	Annually	Percentage	Notes
Housing	$ 1,400	$ 16,800	14%	No mortgage
Transportation	$ 500	$ 6,000	5%	No car payments
Food	$ 1,200	$ 14,400	12%	
Daycare	$ 1,150	$ 13,800	12%	
Savings, investments + Insurance	$ 350	$ 4,200	4%	No need to invest for retirement anymore after achieving Coast FIRE

(Continued)

(Continued)

Budget—After Family FI Journey			
Entertainment	$ 800	$ 9,600	8%
Giving (family, friends, charities)	$ 300	$ 3,600	3%
Clothing + services	$ 200	$ 2,400	2%
Personal care	$ 150	$ 1,800	2%
Miscellaneous	$ 100	$ 1,200	1%
Left over	$ 3,850	$ 46,200	39%
TOTAL EXPENSES	**$10,000**	**$120,000**	

Housing expenses have gone down significantly after paying off their mortgage early. Conservatively, Jacob and Emily might spend $1,400 on home maintenance, bills, property taxes, insurance, and other home costs on their paid-off home. Going from 35% of the budget to 14% is a nice change.

Assuming the couple decided to buy reasonably priced new-to-them cars, the transportation budget would decrease as well. This category could easily go to 5% instead of 15%, knowing that the couple will still need to save up for their next car and pay for fuel, maintenance, and insurance needs. So this category is $500 instead of $1,500.

For the purposes of this exercise, let's assume food costs remain the same. This category could easily go down through shopping at lower cost grocery stores, reducing or eliminating food delivery services and trips to restaurants. It could very well go up as well. More children might mean more mouths to feed over the years that their family grows. Let's go with 12% or $1,200 then and now.

Daycare is still a large chunk of the budget for Jacob and Emily. Let's assume part of owning more time at this stage in their lives means Emily taking on the role of stay-at-home mom for a time. The trend of stay-at-home fathers has been steadily increasing over the past few decades, rising to 20% of stay-at-home parents. The role of full-time caretaker at home is still dominated by women.[3] With the savings available plus the cost of day-care, Emily stepping away from work completely is a choice they can make safely. The couple is still thinking about the right decision and might start with a 3-day workweek for starters.

With no need to save for near-term emergencies or invest for long-term retirement goals, this line item can decrease to 4% of the overall budget. There will be some insurance payments and small savings goals to consider.

All other categories remain the same with Entertainment at 8%, Giving at 3%, Clothing and services at 2%, Personal care at 2%, and Miscellaneous at 1%.

This leaves our couple with 39% or $3,850 per month left over in their budget. This totals up to $46,200 per year of free available cash.

They are debt free, mortgage free, and have no need to continue investing for retirement. They have three paths they can take at this point:

1. Double down, keep working, and growing their family wealth even more
2. Increase their lifestyle with more entertainment, more generosity, and maximize family experiences
3. Work less so they have more time to enjoy those family memories

I'm going to leave behind option 1 because our focus is owning more of your time sooner than later. Let's pursue a combination of 2 and 3 so we can work less and enjoy more life now.

To do this, we need to shift from a full-time work schedule to a part-time work schedule.

CHOOSE YOUR 3-DAY WORKWEEK ADVENTURE

If you are in a position to financially afford it, consider the benefits of a 3-day workweek instead of a 5-day workweek. As our previous guest, Author Simone Stolzoff stated so well: "You exist on this planet to do more than just create economic value."

I love that statement. You're not just a worker. You also may be a …

- Father
- Mother
- Brother
- Sister
- Son
- Daughter
- Community leader
- Volunteer
- Teacher
- Friend
- Athlete
- Musician
- Writer
- Singer
- And so much more

When we work the majority of our days and do these other roles just two of the days, we're limiting our life potential.

I've heard too many stories of people at the end of their lives talking about working too much being their biggest regret.

Once you reach this financially privileged stage in your family financial independence journey, consider these four ideas to help you create your own 3-day workweek. While everyone's situation is different, these ideas may trigger some thoughts that could make "future you" quite happy.

Ask for a Part-time Schedule Where You Currently Work

If you've been determined, focused, and successful enough to achieve complete debt freedom and Coast FIRE, there's a good chance you're a great employee.

Before you up and quit your job in a financial independence blaze of glory, use the rapport you've built up with your supervisor to have a candid chat about going part-time instead.

Of course, this assumes you enjoy what you do but you'd prefer to (and can afford to) do less of it. Be prepared to discuss a decrease in your salary as that may be a requirement as a fair exchange for fewer hours worked each week.

When I interviewed Angela Rozmyn from Tread Lightly Retire Early, she shared that her employer was surprisingly open to the idea of her working fewer hours. "As long as I could keep my core stuff, then we found ways to shift (my work schedule) around," recalled Rozmyn. "And as I've worked less for 3.5 years, now I'm finding more and more people that have different schedules and hours than you would think."

Seek Part-time Work at Another Company (with Your Skill Set)

Perhaps you're burnt out at your current company, but you don't want to waste the skills and network you've built. Well, it might be time to look for a new job in your industry or at least with your skill set.

Use your current network and start having conversations with people about opportunities for part-time work. Although there may not be job listings officially set for part-time work, conversations and negotiations are always possible.

While this is probably an easier sell at your current employer because they know your work ethic, you may find employers looking to hire part-time to save on costs.

My wife was hired as a part-time employee at a dermatologist's office. She was seeking part-time work, and they were hiring for it. The arrangement required conversation and negotiation, but these opportunities are out there. She's now enjoying a 3-day workweek.

In an interview together, she shared the part-time work benefits she's found. "I went for a run this morning and did some yard work," she shared. "It's a nice break in the middle of the week. I'm not sure I'd be able to do all of this on a Saturday when we're running to kid's soccer games or birthday parties."

Become a Part-time Contract Worker or Freelancer (with Your Skill Set)

This idea steps you away from the employee side of things and more toward self-employment. While leaving an employment situation and moving toward an entrepreneurial life is quite challenging, the rewards of lifestyle design can be worth it.

Essentially, you would be in charge of finding clients, making sure those clients paid you, and managing your own work schedule. This autonomy can be freeing and liberating for some and terrifying and scary for others.

Since going down this path personally, I've realized the disadvantages of solopreneurship. It requires a lot of discipline and systems that

I wasn't used to as an employee. Over time, I've found a good path, and I'm very happy with my decision to leave full-time employment for part-time solopreneurship.

While I'm yet to earn a salary comparable to what I used to earn at my previous corporate job, I'm still very happy because I've gained a lot more of my time back.

Eric Rosenberg, a freelance writer who earns well over $10k per month, shared how his time flexibility as a freelancer helps him to be a more present dad. Rosenberg shared this awesome freelancer dad milestone with us in our interview: "Now if I finish a big project and I feel like I've earned taking my daughter for ice cream at 3 p.m., I can do that!"

Start a Solopreneur Business Based on Your "Ikigai"

If your 3-day workweek is going to come from starting a small business, know that it requires a bit more patience since around half of US businesses fail within the first 5 years.[4]

Let's say you've had enough of working as an employee and you've had enough working in your industry. You could start your own business based on a passion or interest you have.

You'll want to ensure your passion or interest can actually make money though.

I like looking at it through the lens of the Japanese term "Ikigai" or your purpose for being.[5] This is where the following four ideas intersect:

- You love it.
- The world needs it.
- You are paid for it.
- You are great at it.

If I had to think of someone I've spoken to over the past 7 years who exemplifies this Ikigai well, it would be Chad Carson. He built a real estate business and the systems to go with it that allowed him to drastically increase his time freedom.

"It's a combination of good people on the ground and technology," shared Carson. "I typically spend an hour or two a week. On Thursdays, I usually do my bill paying and bookkeeping. The rest of the week I might get a text here and there asking a question."

Ultimately, I see this 3-day workweek discussion as a pathway to a more intentional life. Not a life where you only feel accomplished when you've piled millions upon millions of dollars. Because honestly, that type of life doesn't really ever have a destination. You can always make more money, save more, or invest more. That path is truly never-ending.

The Own Your Time framework allows you to find a saving and investing goal that fits your family's needs and a lot of your wants too. And then, it encourages you to go back to enjoying life. Because life is for living.

THREE-DAY WORKWEEK SOLOPRENEUR OR JOB IDEAS

The easiest choice is to ask for part-time work at your current employer. They know you, they trust you, and you are already being paid by them. The most difficult of all the options is to go out on your own and start a business. But if you are completely sick of the industry that you're working in and you can't see yourself doing it any longer, it may be the best for your family and your mental health.

Here are seven solopreneur type businesses you could start where you could make a decent living depending on your skills, experience, and willingness to stick with it over time.

Bookkeeper

Bookkeeping is an incredible job that has a lot of flexibility to work from home and the income growth potential is huge. Tiffany Higgins earned well over $5,000 per month as a bookkeeper before she decided to go full-on with her small business. She shared with me, "I was making about $5,000 per month. And then things kept growing and growing. After about 3 years, we were making $20,000 per month with our bookkeeping business." Tiffany was previously a bookkeeper, so her skill set was a good fit for her new business.

If you'd prefer to avoid the whole "business ownership" side of bookkeeping, you can take your current bookkeeping skills to the marketplace and work for a company. Owning your bookkeeping practice will be more difficult but could be more lucrative in the long run.

Freelance Writer

I've had the opportunity to interview many freelance writers on my podcast who make a very good living. The majority of them work from home. For example, a recent interview we did on the podcast with Miranda Marquit showed her making more than $10,000 per month on a part-time schedule. This came with over a decade of experience, but freelance writing over the long term can produce quality rates. Writing gigs can be paid "by word" or "per hour."

Financial Coach

I can share this solopreneur business idea from experience. I've been a financial coach for the past 7 years and make more than enough to cover our family expenses after achieving our family financial independence goals.

Helping people win with money brings me a lot of joy. You can receive an accreditation from the AFCPE like I did; however, many financial coaches I know do not have a specific accreditation.[6] Guest of the podcast, Whitney Hansen, earns well over $100,000 per year as a financial coach.

Financial Advisor

As a financial advisor, you would support people with their investments and retirement plans. The most well-respected designation for a financial advisor is a Certified Financial Planner (CFP).[7] This can take up to 3 years to complete, so do your homework and research before going down this path.

Real Estate Agent

Real estate agents often manage their schedules and can significantly increase their income over time. This does require you to have more of an entrepreneurial spirit due to the commission-only nature of the job. You'll need a good network and the willingness to grow your network further. Depending on how much money you want to earn, this business could fit into a part-time work lifestyle.

Graphic Designer

With graphic design skills and experience, you can command a higher hourly rate. Look for industries like advertising, film, and engineering where higher rates are more often provided.

Programmer

Supporting small business owners with their programming needs can be a great part-time job from home. I've paid well over $40 per hour for programming on my website. Follow the money and offer services in specialized high-paying industries like healthcare, IT, banking, and cybersecurity.

Will these 3-day workweek jobs guarantee you a high hourly rate right away? No.

Are these specific ideas immune to the increased adoption of artificial intelligence in the marketplace? No.

And will they all guarantee you a part-time schedule right away? No.

But over time, through small 1% improvements, you'll increase your hourly rate and decrease your hours worked. That way, you can spend more time living life and less time working.

The best option is to talk with your supervisor about a future where you're working fewer hours each week. That is the easiest and quickest way to secure a higher-paying part-time job.

SOLOPRENEURSHIP PROS AND CONS

I've had the pleasure of owning my own one-person business for the past decade. It's grown over the years, and my pride in what I've built has grown as well. The reality is it's not all roses and sunshine as a solopreneur. There are good days and bad days. Depending on how you run your business, the good days can definitely outweigh the bad.

Let's go over some pros and cons of solopreneurship that I've experienced. I'll go back and forth between pros and cons so you can experience the reality of the ups and downs of solopreneurship. If your stomach gets queasy on this "pros/cons rollercoaster," then a part-time job may be a better option for you.

Con 1: Making Less Money (a Lot Less)

During my corporate career, I was able to grow my salary immensely. My last role had my salary around $180,000.

All I had to do was sell stuff and make clients happy. Was it hard? At times, it was difficult, but mostly, it was something I was skilled at and therefore, I should have been happy. But I wasn't.

I really didn't enjoy what I did.

Today, I pay myself a salary of around $90,000 to run my business as its sole employee. If I perform well, sell stuff, and make my clients happy, I'll consider giving myself a raise.

But for now, I'm in growth mode, and therefore, I need to keep investing time, money, and resources into the business.

I hope to make more in the future, but I don't want to compromise my shorter workweek. With my wife working part-time as well, we have enough for us to live comfortably right now.

Pro 1: Time Freedom

While you might trade fewer dollars in your life as a solopreneur in the beginning, you can earn much more time back in my life.

I typically work 20–25 hours per week and do the bulk of my work Tuesday through Thursday during the day. After my kids are off to school, I typically exercise every day. I've never felt so healthy in my entire life.

When I want to take a vacation, there's only one person I have to ask ... Me.

I still have to get my work done, but I'm in control of that work. I'm in control of what I want to do with my time. And I love that.

When I was side hustling this solopreneur business of mine, working in the evenings and weekends was a must. Now that's a rarity.

I've prioritized more of my time toward my family, health, and social life.

Con 2: Complacency Isn't an Option

There were times in my career when I was working hard, driving sales, leading teams, and making my employer proud. And there were other times when I wasn't as much of a go-getter, and I wasn't exceeding my goals.

The awesome thing about being an employee is that I still got paid the same amount of money either way.

That is definitely not the case with solopreneurship. If I'm not hustling during my 20- to 25-hour workweek, then I'm not making money.

And even though my wife and I prepared well for this career leap, we still need to make money to live. So, if Daddy isn't earning, we're hurting.

I'm so thankful that my wife works part-time as well. That has taken a lot of the pressure off. We're a good team together.

Without her and my drive to see this business grow, we wouldn't be doing so hot. Complacency is not an option.

Pro 2: You Are in Charge

For the longest time, I did not like my job. It was a fine industry with fine people, but I was so done with it.

I fell into corporate event marketing out of college based on an internship opportunity I got from my dad (thanks, Dad!). It was fun because I traveled a lot, and I met a lot of younger people like me to hang out with.

Once I had a family, I realized it wasn't the best career for me. At that point though, I really needed the money. I was a dad. I was a husband, and I needed to provide.

For the next 10 years, I grew my career, my position, and my salary the best I could. And it worked.

We became millionaires in our thirties, we paid off our mortgage early, and we're now in a position to coast into retirement based on our investments thus far.

I'm thankful for all that. Truly. But I was done with my job, my industry, and the emotional grind.

Today, I absolutely love what I do. I get to help families win with money. That's fun to me.

Every other week, I interview really interesting and intelligent people who help me grow.

I can't tell you how much I've learned from doing my podcast. It's definitely more than I learned in my 6-year MBA program.

So, I may make half the money I used to make, but I wouldn't trade it for the world. I love my new job.

Con 3: Solopreneurship Can Be Volatile

When I decided to leap from my 9-to-5 job, I did it with a few parachutes packed away (outside of the financial and emotional support from my wife):

- $100,000 in savings (aka, our FU Money)
- No debt
- Enough investments to Coast FIRE
- A paid-off house
- And a sizable contract from a client

The savings made me feel comfortable knowing that we could always dip into it if needed.

Paying off our mortgage early gave me confidence in knowing that we'll never lose our house.

The client contract helped my wife and I know that my income would be solid. Even though it was a lot less than I was making in my full-time job, it was an excellent starting contract.

Unfortunately, that little global pandemic came rolling through in my first year of solopreneurship. That contract was canceled due to loss of revenue after about a half year of working together.

This was a huge blow to our family's income, my company's overall revenue, and my mental health. It was a tough one to come back from. There were sleepless nights and even some tears. I was feeling low.

But after some time, some advice from friends and family, I realized that this experience was a blessing.

I'm no scientist, but I believe global pandemics are pretty rare. So, if I can make it through that in my first full year as a solopreneur, then I've got a good chance of succeeding.

Since then, I've diversified my clients, opened up several new income streams, and my business future is looking bright.

Pro 3: The Sky Is the Limit

From time to time, I do think about the tremendous salary and benefits I used to have and I get a little jealous of "Employee Andy."

After my jealousy subsides, I get motivated, and I think: "Can't I eventually make more than 'Employee Andy'?"

Learning from and seeing many of my solopreneur superheroes, I not only think it's possible, I think it's an inevitability.

I have the drive. I have the will. My heart is in this.

Here are some of the heroes who've inspired me along the way:

- Denis Trufin makes more than $10,000 per month through affiliate marketing on YouTube.
- Kristen Sweeting makes more than $300,000 per year as a photographer working only 20 hours per week.
- Tiffany Aliche started off unemployed and broke and grew a $10,000,000 digital business.

I've had the chance to interview these folks and many more who've inspired me to grow and win for my family.

And they really enjoy what they do. They are helping people and getting paid well doing it.

Growth, work-life integration, and happiness. That's what I'm striving for.

But even if I don't make another dime, I'm happy. I love what I do, and I'm making enough money for our family to enjoy our lives to the fullest.

Without a mortgage or a need to invest for our retirement, our comfortable expenses sit at around $84,000 per year. So, anything on top of this is just gravy. Gravy does taste really good though, so I'm going for it.

SOLOPRENEUR BEST FINANCIAL PRACTICES

Through a decade of solopreneurship, I've made a lot of mistakes. Those mistakes helped me learn not to do certain things again. It's like touching a hot stove. Solopreneur mistakes hurt, so you don't want to repeat them.

Since many businesses fail due to financial reasons, let's review my 10 best financial practices for solopreneurs.[8] This way, you can avoid my mistakes and become more profitable earlier than I did.

Get Someone to Pay You for Something First

Before creating a fancy website, logo, or designing your ideal workspace, get someone to actually pay you for something. A person or business needs to give you money for your product or service for you to actually have a business. Many of us like to "play business" before actually "doing business." What I mean by that is we enjoy spending time and money on business-like activities without actually focusing on the purpose of the business. And that purpose is for you to earn a decent income and go back to enjoying your life outside of work.

Oftentimes, we can earn money faster than we think. For example, let's say you're considering a video editing business. Instead of spending time and money on building a website, logo, social media presence, and buying the latest video editing software and equipment, try emailing 10 prospective clients about your editing services instead. Get someone to take a chance on you (of course at a much lower rate than your competitors) and get paid sooner than later.

Business ownership is a lot easier when you have more income coming in than expenses. Lead with income and support with expenses as you grow.

Separate Your Accounts

Once that money starts to come in, it's time to create a separate bank account for your business. Mixing your business income and expenses with your personal bank account is a really bad idea long term. This makes things more difficult when it comes to taxes and overall business management.

Get a business checking account for the everyday income and expenses of your business. With this account, you'll be given a business debit card that you can use for expenses. Don't get a business credit card until you've proven you can pay yourself first and stay on budget. Those steps are coming up.

Also, snag a business savings account as well. This is where you can create a business emergency fund as well as a place for long-term savings. Just like other savings accounts, there are the brick-and-mortar business savings accounts, and there are the high-yield business savings accounts. When possible, consider a high-yield business savings account that is FDIC-insured to grow your business savings faster.

Build a Business Budget

Your business can be similar to your personal finances. The concept is simple. Grow the gap between your income and your expenses so you can profit.

When you have more income coming in than you have expenses, you win the business game. The difficult part is understanding your true expenses and diligently tracking them. Utilizing an automated budgeting tool can make this a lot easier. QuickBooks, Freshbooks, Monarch, and YNAB are some of the more popular options available.

If you don't want to pay for an automated budget tool, create your own business budget in a spreadsheet. You'll need to manually track your income and expenses, but that more laborious process will help you identify areas for improvement along your solopreneur journey.

Pay Yourself First

As you are budgeting for your business, the most important line item needs to be your salary. Many business owners build a thriving enterprise with dozens of employees but fail to pay themselves first. According to CNBC, 26% of small business owners don't pay themselves a salary.[9] This leads to financial stress and ultimately, small business burnout.

In order to make your solopreneur business worth it, start by allocating an appropriate percentage toward your employees. Luckily in your business, you're the only employee. Personally, I allocate 50–60% of my business budget toward my salary and benefits. No matter what happens, I'm ensuring this whole business idea is worth it.

Keep Expenses Low

Over time you may be tempted to add recurring expenses to your business budget. These come in the form of subscription services, equipment, and marketing expenses.

Do your best to stay lean with these expenses. Ask yourself if these add-ons are "nice to haves" or "must haves" for your one-person business. Consider used equipment instead of brand new. Barter for services if you can. If you're a financial advisor and need a website, see if you can exchange a financial plan for website design.

Again, business ownership is a lot easier when your income is high and your expenses are low.

Build a Business Emergency Fund

Remember those rocky times I talked about? Well, it's time to prepare for them. Just like our personal emergency fund, we need a business emergency fund.

You may have a solid client that pays you well month-after-month and then, suddenly, that relationship is gone. Your business emergency fund will help you as you ramp up your sales efforts to find your next client.

There may be a complete industry shift in how your business makes money. And now you need to pivot your entire business strategy. This may sound unrealistic, but think about the small businesses that required in-person interactions during the pandemic. These folks were forced to pivot. I know a small business owner (Ralph) who owns a gym for little kids to get exercise and play. During the pandemic, Ralph was forced to take his business out of the gym due to the restrictions in place and get outside. He started planning outdoor birthday parties with the same equipment and ended up thriving because of it. Having a business emergency fund surely supported his business pivot. With the indoor restrictions lifted, he now has two business income streams instead of one. If we can survive the tough times, we can thrive on the other end.

Because business ownership can be more volatile than being an employee, I recommend saving up 6–12 months of business expenses (your salary should be included in those expenses). This can take some time to build up. Set incremental goals for your business to build up from 1 month of expenses all the way to 12 months of expenses. Easily accessible money in the bank will give you confidence to succeed as a solopreneur.

Diversify Your Income Streams

Relying on one income source can be easy when you're an employee. When you're a solopreneur, losing one client can spell disaster for your business.

Bake time into your solopreneur schedule for sales growth and networking. Having multiple clients can diversify your revenue and leave you feeling more secure as a business owner.

Even if your client roster is full, it can't hurt to continue networking and seeking out new future clients. If you are unable to service the new client opportunities due to your limited work schedule, it may be time for strategic outsourcing.

Use a CRM (customer relationship management) tool to track your sales progress over time. A system like this will hold you accountable for following up on new leads and ensuring your sales go from initial talks to clients.

Outsource to Grow and Own More Time

When you feel like you can't take on any more clients, but you're interested in increasing your revenue and ultimately your profits, outsourcing is the way. As I've grown my business over the years, I've seen areas where I am weaker and areas where I'm stronger. For the areas where I lack expertise and speed like accounting, editing, and social media support, I outsource.

This doesn't mean you're going from a one-person business to business with many employees. I would recommend hiring contractors for the services you need only when you need them.

An example of this would be website design. I'm not a graphic designer. I don't know how to code. But I do have a vision for how my website should look and operate. By working with a professional website designer, I can strategically outsource my website design and go back to doing what I do best.

Of course, you want to make sure you actually have enough money for outsourcing. This comes with advanced planning and smart business budgeting.

Utilize Project Management Software

As your business and team grows, consider project management software to track the dozens of tasks you may need to do in order to have a functioning business. When you automate the tasks you and your team need to complete, it decreases the amount of overwhelm happening in your solopreneur brain.

Remembering to check in on your budget, paying vendors, reaching out to clients, creating marketing campaigns, and much more are all tasks you can set up in a project management system. These recurring tasks automatically show up so that you know exactly what you need to do each workday.

I even have tasks set up to remind myself to shut down and go back to living life. After all, that's the whole point of working really. Work to live. Don't live to work.

Be the Boss You've Always Wanted

Picture this. You've been working on your business for a while, keeping true to that 3-day workweek, and you're starting to make some excellent progress. To really grow your income faster, you begin adding a fourth workday. This increases your revenue, profit, and your overall salary, but you also have to scale back your health routine. You say to yourself, "I already workout more than most people. I'm fine." Then you add a fifth day to your workweek. This increases your salary even further because you're able to take on an additional client. The walks you used to take with your spouse get kicked to the curb and your progress on your health wanes.

You see where this is going.

We've been trained for so long that "hard work" is an incredible virtue we should all strive for. While that can be true, I don't believe we should sacrifice the important values we hold as a family because of this "hard work" virtue.

Once you're earning enough money to live happily, more money at the expense of time with family, friends, and taking care of your health is not worth it.

Be the boss you've always wanted to have. When your workday is done, stop checking email. If you've decided your workday is 3 days after becoming debt free, mortgage free, and hit Coast FIRE, then stick to your 3-day workweek.

If you've always wanted to slow down your work in the summer, but you've never been able to, this is your opportunity. Design your work life the way you want. You are in charge now. You are the architect of your best life. It's time to act like it.

ONE SPOUSE FIRST, THEN THE OTHER

I wish I could tell you that you and your spouse could both jump to a 3-day workweek at the same time. While that might work, I'm more cautious than that.

Whether your 3-day workweek is at your current job, a new job, or a solopreneur venture you're creating, it's important to adhere to a step-by-step process to ensure financial stability and success for your family. Depending on your income and your ability to save and invest, this entire timeline could take anywhere from 10 to 20 years to complete.

Two and a Half Income Household

Jacob: 1.5 full-time jobs (corporate full-time job, and a part-time side hustle)
Emily: 1 full-time job (corporate full-time job)

Before one spouse drops down to part-time, it may be necessary at first for one spouse to have a full-time job plus a side gig. This way, you're increasing income and using that additional income to pay down debt, invest for the future, and build emergency savings. In a sense, you might start off your family financial independence journey by going from two full-time incomes to two and a half full-time incomes.

It may feel like a step backward at first, but over time the additional income will propel you forward down a path of more time ownership.

Two Income Household

Jacob: 1 full-time job (corporate full-time job)
Emily: 1 full-time job (corporate full-time job)

Once you've made significant financial progress on your goals, you can eliminate that extra side hustle or that side hustle can become your new full-time job. This all depends on how well you've done in building your solopreneur business.

Alternatively, one spouse keeps their full-time job and side hustle while the other goes down to part-time work. This may be the case when a couple has children. Two full-time working parents may just be too many hours dedicated to working and not enough to taking care of your child.

However you slice the two-income household, this decrease in income will have an impact on the family budget so plan accordingly. Of course, this becomes so much easier without debt and with emergency funds in place.

One and a Half Income Household

Jacob: 1 full-time job (corporate full-time job)
Emily: 0.5 full-time job (corporate part-time job)

Congratulations! You were able to successfully negotiate a transition from full-time corporate worker to part-time worker. This comes with a decrease in income, but you were fully prepared for it by investing for Coast FIRE at an early age. You have no need to continue investing for retirement since your projections show you may have enough to fund your comfortable retirement decades in the future.

By reducing your investment contributions and finding other ways to save on life's expenses, you have bought yourself a part-time work life. More time for yourself, your family and friends, and less time working.

One Income Household

Jacob: 0.5 full-time job (solopreneur part-time business)
Emily: 0.5 full-time job (corporate part-time job)

After years of plugging away at the mortgage, you've earned a paid off home. That money you were paying in principal, interest, as well as the extra mortgage principal payments starts to get stocked away as FU Money.

You're feeling financially confident, protected, and ready for another financial leap forward in owning your time. With one part-time solopreneur and one part-time corporate employee, your household can now be funded by one full-time income.

Full disclosure: This is where my wife and I are in the timeline.

Half Income Household

Jacob: 0.25 full-time job (solopreneur part-time business)
Emily: 0.25 full-time job (solopreneur part-time business)

Your solopreneur business is doing so well that you invite your spouse to join you in working. Your combined efforts increase your overall household income and drop the need for both of you to work in any corporate capacity. The business emergency fund you've been building now exceeds 12 months of expenses, so you're ready for any business uncertainties that may come your way.

To buy back more time, you strategically outsource the more time-consuming or complicated tasks involved in your business. This reduces your household workweek from 40 hours combined to 20 hours combined.

With your newfound time freedom, you invest more time in your health, marriage, kids, aging parents, social circle, and you start learning how to solve the Rubik's cube in under 5 minutes. After all, you've always wanted new skills.

FROM THE PODCAST

Family: Sarah and Laird, 35 years old from Florida
Money Milestone: Making $100,000 per year working 25 hours per week

Andy:	*How did you and your husband get together originally?*
Sarah:	So, we actually met in China. Funny story, I had just moved to China a week before he did. And when I met him, he was severely jet-lagged. He arrived about 10 p.m. that night and then had to go to school the next day at about 7 a.m. So, he barely had any sleep. And I don't think he remembers meeting me, but his version of the story was I fell in love. It was love at first sight.
Andy:	*What were you guys doing for work at the time?*
Sarah:	So, I was teaching grade two, and he was teaching middle school English.
Andy:	*So, when did you guys decide to become parents?*
Sarah:	So, I was actually very anti-children for a long time after we got married. My husband knew that, and he was okay with that for quite a while. And I think it was until, I would like to say 5 years ago that I was like, "Oh, I've started changing my mind." And then I got into a fight with him. I was picking a fight with him for no reason. So of course we're just bickering. All of a sudden, I was like, "I want children." And he said, "I want children too." And then that was kind of the end. That was our decision right there.

Andy: *There's lots of conversations that happen with spouses as they're deciding to become parents. "What are we gonna do for work?" What type of conversations were you guys having right around this time when your son came into the world?*

Sarah: I was still doing freelancing as a side hustle. This was for fun at the time. And then we decided, OK, let's go to the US. Let's try it for a few years, see how we like it. And so, because my teaching license was from Canada, I just assumed it was really difficult to get my degree equivalent. And so, I thought, "Okay, well, maybe I can do this freelance writing thing until that happens." And so, the more freelance writing I did, the more clients I got, the more I thought, "You know what, I really actually want to stay home with my son. Maybe I can make a go of this."

I wasn't that motivated until after he was born. I remember going back to work, and I would just start missing him. And I know it's natural to do that, but it was really like, "No, I just want to walk home. It's only a 10-minute walk. And so, I would do that during my prep periods." And I was like, "Okay, if I can replace my salary, we have 2 years' worth of expenses in an emergency fund. I can make a go of this."

And so, my husband and I had a very long chat. We ended up in North Carolina for the first year that we were here. So, I said, "Okay, you get your teaching job, I'm gonna do freelance writing. We set a deadline for me. We decided that if in 6 to 8 months, I wasn't making a dime, I would go back to a full-time job."

Andy: *Got it. Then after that 6 to 8 months, you made a good go at it?*

Sarah: Yeah, and I essentially replaced my teaching salary and then this year I doubled it so that was really exciting. As of September, I invoiced six figures worth of work.

Andy:	*How many hours a week are you working then?*
Sarah:	It took quite a few years to get to the point where I've got some pretty decent systems going. I think it's hard to say definitively how much I work sometimes because I do get distracted when my son's home. I try to cap it like 25 hours a week.
Andy:	*So, you're working 25 hours a week, and you're making six figures?*
Sarah:	Yeah, yeah, that's a dream, right?

Carpe Diem Action Steps

- Review your current budget and see what life options you would have if you did not have a mortgage, didn't need to pay off debt, or save or invest for anything. Dream about what type of lifestyle you would want with your spouse.
- Examine the different 3-day workweek options and see which appeals to you the most.
- If starting a solopreneur business sounds appealing, review the pros, cons, and financial best practices shared so you are prepared.
- Discuss with your spouse about eventually moving from full-time work to part-time work. Have fun conversations about what that extra time would mean for your lives together.

NOTES

1. Schor, J. B. (2003). Pre-industrial workers had a shorter workweek than today's, from *The Overworked American: The Unexpected Decline of Leisure.* MIT. Available at: https://groups.csail.mit.edu/mac/users/rauch/worktime/hours_workweek.html
2. BLS. (2023). *Consumer expenditures* [Online]. Available at: https://www.bls.gov/news.release/cesan.nr0.htm

3. Pew Research. (2023). *Almost 1 in 5 stay-at-home parents in the U.S. are dads* [Online]. Available at: https://www.pewresearch.org/short-reads/2023/08/03/almost-1-in-5-stay-at-home-parents-in-the-us-are-dads/

4. BLS. (2024). *Survival of private sector establishments by opening year* [Online]. Available at: https://www.bls.gov/bdm/us_age_naics_00_table7.txt

5. Gaines, M. (2020). *The philosophy of Ikigai: 3 examples about finding purpose.* Positive Psychology. Available at: https://positivepsychology.com/ikigai/

6. AFCPE. (2025). *Become an AFC* [Online]. Available at: https://www.afcpe.org/

7. CFP. (2025). *CFP Board* [Online]. Available at: https://www.cfp.net/

8. Heaslip, E. (2025). *Reasons why small businesses fail and how to avoid them* [Online]. US Chamber of Commerce. Available at: https://www.uschamber.com/co/start/strategy/why-small-businesses-fail

9. Munk, C. W. (2022). The small business employee who often gets paid last and the least. *CNBC.* Available at: https://www.cnbc.com/2022/10/20/how-much-small-business-owners-should-pay-themselves.html

CHAPTER EIGHT

EMBRACE THE SIMPLE LIFE

"It is not daily increase but daily decrease. Hack away the unessential."

– Bruce Lee

We have a cat named Pishi. Her day mostly consists of the following activities: eating, sleeping, spending time outside, and, when she feels like it, cuddling with her family. She leads a simple life and doesn't require much.

As odd as it may sound, I admire Pishi's life. She has a few daily activities that make her feel content, and she doesn't fret about the purpose and meaning of life. She's also not worried about what people think about her plump body size or if her collar is fashionable or not.

While she is a bit of a freeloader with her food and healthcare expenses, overall she doesn't require much to live a happy life.

It's not possible for me to live Pishi's life of course. My human brain and needs are much different than hers. But that doesn't mean I can't think of her as an excellent teacher.

When she rubs on my leg asking me to pick her up and scratch her belly, she's teaching me to slow down and enjoy the small pleasures in life.

When I see her spending time outside chasing animals and rolling in the grass, she reminds me that you don't need any money to enjoy time in nature.

And when I see her napping in the middle of the day without a care in the world, she's showing me that rest is important and always free.

As we start to move away from the idea that work is meant to consume the majority of our days, our income will likely decline in the beginning as our working hours decrease. Psychologically, this would be a smart time for us to start embracing the simple life (like Pishi).

If we only equate the purchase of material things with happiness, then this path to family financial independence will be a rough one. If we learn to spend time aligning our core values with happiness, the journey will be easier.

RECOGNIZE THE PRESSURE TO CONSUME EXISTS

One of the most iconic visuals in the United States is Times Square in New York City. At any time of day or night, countless people are in and around the streets surrounded by gigantic physical or digital billboards. While standing in the heart of one of America's greatest cities can feel exciting, this many advertisements piercing into our brains can be a lot to handle.

Let's leave the chaos of Times Square for a moment, take a seat on a park bench, and look at your phone. Instinctively, you check your email. While there are some messages from family, friends, and work colleagues, you notice the majority of your email is filled with ads: emails about new clothes to buy, courses to sign up for, and the latest innovations in mattress technology.

Your email box starts to feel overwhelming, so you try zoning out with your favorite social media app. As you flip through some funny videos, one video catches your attention and suggests buying their product will solve the problems you have. And if you act now and use coupon code "BUYNOW," you'll get an additional 20% off.

Even though that thing sounds really great, you've been trying to reduce frivolous purchases lately to pile up FU Money to leave your corporate job you don't like. You decide to close out that social media app, throw on a podcast, and go for a walk in Central Park. A bit of nature and fresh air is always good for you. Fifteen minutes in your walk, you arrive at the park and enjoy the sunny day. The podcast conversation you're enjoying starts to take a turn as they thank their sponsors. Now suddenly, you're thinking about buying new bed sheets and a mattress because the host is raving all about how excellent their sleep has gotten since purchasing these items totaling more than one thousand dollars.

Exhausted, you decide it's time to head back home. You get in a cab and try to relax with no digital distractions. With your renewed focus on family financial independence, these ads really aren't helping you. Unfortunately, staring right in front of you in the cab is a small screen with advertising disguised as a news story. The audio is so loud. You try to turn it off or mute it, but the touchscreen buttons are confusing or simply don't work.

You finally arrive at home feeling run down and tired. After grabbing the mail, you find that 100% of today's letters are advertisements. There are credit card offers, home decor discounts, and a letter from your alma mater asking for donations to the university. You rip that one up really fast because you just recently paid off your last student loan.

After pushing a few brown Amazon boxes you've yet to open off the couch, you sit down and turn on the TV to watch your favorite sports team. After the day you've just had, your brain starts to recognize something. The stadium is sponsored. The player's jerseys have ads on them. Billboards surround the stadium with messages of things you should buy. Each segment between the plays with player stats has a sponsor. And of course, as the team takes a time out, they jump to another 3 minutes of commercials.

It becomes nighttime, and you're done with this day. You lay down and scroll through your phone one last time before trying to fall asleep. You close your eyes but can't seem to actually sleep. Your mind is racing. Thinking about the events and visuals of the day and the fact that you can't sleep seems to make it worse.

You decide to pick up your phone again after you see a notification come through. In what feels like no time at all, you drop $1,000 on that new mattress you learned about earlier today.

After all, what else could be the reason you are not sleeping?

I share this hyperbolic story to demonstrate that advertising is a very powerful tool. With consumer spending making up the majority of US Gross Domestic Product (GDP), advertising is a tool that keeps our country alive.[1] Our consumption is at the core of our country's stability.

But there does come a point where we need to decide, "While my consumption supports my country, are my consumption habits at odds with my family goals? Am I buying things because I want or need to buy them? Or am I buying them because I'm being convinced to buy them?"

GET CLEAR ON YOUR FAMILY VALUES

Recently, I had a discussion with my wife on our podcast about the "pillars of our family." She mentioned that she believes family dinners are one of the most important rituals in her eyes. This is a focused time where we can all sit down, eat some delicious and nutritious food, and catch up about our day. No distractions. No phones. Just time for family, conversation, and a nice meal.

Since this is important to her and the rest of our family, this is an area where we feel happy to spend money. Consumption isn't inherently bad. We all consume on a daily basis. If family dinner is important, then our family should feel content spending freely here.

Think About Your Family Rituals and Values

The idea of family dinner as a strong family ritual is one that has been around for millennia.[2] In fact, scientific benefits prove that family dinner is worth the work behind it.[3] At a young age, family dinners help with language and social skills. As kids get older, they are more likely to get good grades if family dinners are a cornerstone of their home life. For parents, there is lower risk of depression, less need for dieting, improved communication in marriage, and higher self-esteem overall.

Outside of this excellent family ritual promoted by my lovely wife (spouse-brag), think about the other important rituals and values you want in your family life. When you think of the "good life," what comes to mind?

Take some time to write down your ideas. This can be a cathartic process as it will help you gain more clarity on what you feel is missing from your life.

To walk the talk, here are a few of my core family values and rituals outside of family dinner:

Time Together as a Family

Family Movie Night: Every Friday, we take turns picking out a movie to watch together as a family. When it's your turn to the pick the movie, you are the king or queen of the night. You also get to choose where we watch the movie, what our dinner will be (no cooking on movie night—takeout only), and what the dessert will be.

Family Vacations: In the summer, we like to visit family and friends around the Midwest. The weather is beautiful so taking advantage of nature and spending time outside together as a family is important. In the winter, we enjoy flying south to Florida or Mexico to spend time on a beach and by the pool.

Birthday Celebrations: During birthdays, we carve out time in our schedule to celebrate the birthday boy or girl and make them feel special. Since these days are so important, we do our very best to not book anything else. When our kids were younger, we'd even pull them out of school early and go do something fun.

Time Together as a Couple

Date Night/Days: Getting a babysitter for the night or a few hours during the day has helped my wife and I get away for a bit and have fun. In the beginning of our relationship, we spent so much time together focusing on us. With kids in the mix, that important time dedication to our marriage can get lost at times. When things feel out of balance, we know it's time for our date night.

Coffee Talk: The mornings can feel rushed. Carving out moments throughout the week where we can sit down, have a cup of coffee, and talk about life has become a must-have in our relationship. Without it, our marriage feels drained—both caffeine-wise and marriage-wise.

Morning Runs: My wife and I are runners. It helps us stay in shape, enjoy the fresh air and make memories together. For the past 10 years, we've done a series of races together as well. Half marathons are our jam typically. We did one marathon. That was enough.

These are just a small amount of the rituals we have as a family. With these starter ideas in mind, see which ones resonate with you. Consider how they align with your current family values and rituals. If there are ones that you feel are missing, write them down and have a conversation with your spouse about them.

For example, I would like to be spending more time together as a family volunteering in our community. We don't do this very often currently, and I believe it is an excellent way to help our kids learn empathy for our neighbors and also a sense of gratitude for the life they have.

Share Your Ideal Family Values with Your Spouse

After getting clear on your family values and the rituals that come along with them, share with your spouse. This conversation will undoubtedly spark new ideas, enhance your existing ones, and help you gain insight into your spouse's family values.

Much like the money date we've spoken about, this conversation shouldn't happen in passing. Dedicate time for it during uninterrupted moments together. Chatting during our coffee time, date night, or morning runs works for us. That may be different for your relationship. Either way, make time for it.

Outside of time together as a family and as a couple, it's important for you to have solo time too. This helps you maintain a sense of identity and autonomy. Your "me-time" can be literal time alone, time with friends, or time with extended family. It's important for your spouse and your kids not to think you'd fall apart without being with them every waking moment. That's a lot of pressure to bear. If you find yourself feeling lopsided in this department, exploring hobbies and reaching out to new or old friends can be a smart idea.

This idea of "me-time" as a family value can feel contradictory, but I believe it's crucial for a good relationship with both your spouse and your kids. This also demonstrates to your children that they are not always the center of your world. You have multiple identities outside of

Mom or Dad. It's good for them to see this because you also want this for their lives. Parenting is more about modeling than preaching. This would be an opportunity for us to show our kids what a well-rounded life looks like.

SPEND FREELY IN ACCORDANCE WITH THOSE VALUES

Once you've determined your core family values and the rituals that you'd like to tie to those values, it's time to plan for them. Block off time in your calendar. Also, plan for them financially.

If you say date night with your spouse is an important marital ritual of yours, it needs to be in your budget. Without scheduling the time and allocating the money, it won't happen.

The same goes with family vacations. If you want to make memories in a sunny location with your loved ones, start saving up money each month to make this a reality.

You are what you do. Not what you say you will do. The same goes for your family.

Once you've financially planned for these family rituals ahead of time, you can spend freely. There's no feeling bad about spending money anymore because you are spending according to your family values.

The other day, my family went to Top Golf to celebrate my son's birthday. We took him out of school early, picked up my daughter after her school ended, and headed out to hit some balls. We got our own golf bay, breathed in the fresh spring air, and enjoyed some food and drinks. When the bill came, it was around $100 for our time together. Since we talk about money openly in our family, my son wondered, "Hey Dad, is that a lot for my birthday?" It was a good question. Was it a lot? Or was it a little? Since we had saved up for my son's birthday in our budget, as it's a family ritual of ours, $100 was just fine. We put money away monthly for the past year to prepare for this moment so that we didn't have to penny-pinch and worry about spending money.

This is the beauty of planning your finances according to our values. Ahead of time, we said, "Celebrating our son's birthday is important to us. Let's save up!" By doing this, we're defining the life we want to live and then we're using our money to financially support that life. There's no better use of money.

And this goes for your "me-time" as well. If you want to spend quality time with friends, plan for that financially. My wife and I give each other "Fun Money" buckets in our budget that allow us to do whatever we want without checking in with each other. This is individual money to use how we please. I'm a Detroit Lions fan, so I'm often spending money on tickets, food, and parking. Also, I like to host get-togethers with my friends where we play cards and board games and watch sports. My wife likes getting together for lunches with her girlfriends and treating herself with nice self-care indulgences. With money set aside for these important rituals of ours, we avoid money fights and ensure we're both getting the joy we want out of life.

WHAT TO DO WHEN LIFE GETS TOO EXPENSIVE

You might be thinking, "Okay Andy, you are making sense, but I've lined up all the things I want for my family life and it's not adding up. My income is not enough to pay for all the things I want."

You are not alone my friend. I'd venture to say that this is most of us out there. Those advertisements, as annoying as they may be, are very enticing. More often than not, they are talking about products and services that would make our lives better.

It's true. We're a consumer-driven culture for a reason. Consuming can be fun, addicting, and overall, enjoyable. I like that saying, "They say money can't buy happiness … but have you ever seen a sad person on a jet ski?"

We do need to balance things out though. If we want more than we can afford, then we need to figure a way we can still get what we need and most of what we want.

Let's explore some smart ways to do this.

Embrace Free

Because advertising and marketing is so incredibly powerful, we can forget that many of life's greatest pleasures are absolutely free. The reason that there are no commercials or ads about the free things in life is because there's no money to be made in advertising free stuff. That is unless the product or service is free but then they use your data to sell to advertisers who will eventually sell you "not free stuff." There's a whole doom-loop there we won't go down.

My point is we often forget free is all around us. To inspire you to think outside the spending box, here are 10 things I do for free that truly make me happy:

- Taking a nap on the hammock on a sunny day
- Visiting my local library to check out a new book (a good thing to do after the nap is over)
- Going for a walk with my dad
- Throwing the ball with my son in the yard
- Meditating in the morning to start my day
- Exercising at home with my favorite fitness YouTuber
- Going for a run in my favorite park

- Listening to an audiobook (on our library app) while cutting my lawn
- Gathering wood in the forest and making a fire in our backyard
- Volunteering my time at my kid's school or with their sports teams

It is true that some of these things I mention above do have some upfront costs. I need shoes to go running or walking. Napping on a hammock without an actual hammock would be tough. But you get the idea.

Think Inexpensive Alternatives Before Expensive Conveniences

Eating out at restaurants is a lot of fun. Someone cooks for you, and there are no dishes to clean. But eating out for every meal of the day might be difficult for people looking to prioritize their family values and rituals. Instead, ask yourself, "What is a more realistic and inexpensive way for me to eat today?" While it might take more of your time, preparing meals to eat throughout the week on Sunday could help you meet more of your other financial goals. Also, it'll more than likely encourage you to eat healthier. You don't need to give up eating at restaurants completely, but it should be something to consider as a periodic expense, not a daily one.

This doesn't have to be limited to food either. Our daily coffee habit, where we shop for our clothes, and even reducing shipping costs if we're willing to wait a bit longer for packages can all be simple ways to save daily.

Consider Used Before New

Brand-new stuff can be very enticing. It's shiny, clean, and many new items even have a "new smell." Cars, for example, have a first impression smell that is an off-gassing of plastics and adhesives.[4] Weird, yes, but who doesn't love that "new car smell"?

The problem is new cars and used cars are wildly different in pricing. An average new car costs close to $50,000,[5] while an average used car costs comes in at around $25,000.[6] That's half the price. If all things were equal, everyone would take the new car. It has fewer miles, less wear and tear, and has the new car smell.

But used cars coming at 50% off the cost of new cars and typically having lower insurance payments than new cars are a smart alternative for someone interested in owning more of their time.

Cars are just one example. Pre-owned phones, furniture, clothes, baby gear, bikes, and more can be purchased at a steep discount. This type of lifestyle is also excellent for the environment. When we give something a new life instead of throwing it in a landfill, we're taking care of ourselves, our planet, and our children's future.

Downsize, Rightsize, and Declutter

Homeownership and the costs that comes with it can be the most expensive budget line item for American families. We may come to a crossroads where we find that our house is the reason we're not able to afford our family goals. While it might not be fun and could hurt our egos, rightsizing our homes could mean a world of a difference in our financial lives. If shifting your housing situation could mean you don't have to work at your toxic job anymore that might be a path worth pursuing.

If the idea of moving from your home becomes more harm than good to your family unit, consider the life-changing benefits of decluttering.

When I interviewed decluttering expert Tracy McCubbin, she said something that was really profound: "We expand to meet the space we have."

This statement blew me away when I heard it. When we buy our houses, we find a way to fill it with all sorts of stuff. The more stuff we have in our lives, the more time it takes to manage it, store it, update it, maintain it, and so much more.

As an example, I upgraded my iPhone recently. While it didn't take up a lot of extra space, it took up a lot of extra time.

- Time to move all my photos over to the cloud
- Time to move the apps and contacts over to the new phone
- And time to transfer my old phone into a usable phone for someone else

And honestly, that messed up my whole week. I was looking for this new phone to be a time saver over the long term, but in the short term, it was a time suck.

Think about that with the potentially dozens of things we buy every month, time draining from your life to take care of, update, and maintain stuff.

Before decluttering all the things we've gathered in our homes, we need to pause before buying more things. We need to ask ourselves:

- Do I need this?
- Is there something else around my house right now that can solve the problem this item is supposed to solve?
- How much maintenance and extra work is involved with this purchase?
- Do I have unopened boxes or packages from things I've bought recently that I haven't even attended to?

Simple questions like these can save us a lot of time and money in the long run. They can take our minds out of the mindless consumption loop and transition to a conscious consumer life.

As for the stuff we already have in our homes that we don't use, it's time to sell, donate, or throw them away. Clutter in your home drains your energy and your space. Take time each month to reduce the clutter in your home. This can put money in your pocket, add space in your home, and free up time on your calendar.

Do Less

Busyness is engrained in our culture. The "work hard" mantra is strong. I'm all about living life to the fullest, but I believe that includes time for relaxation, time with family, and time margin between activities.

When our schedules are not packed, we have more time to breathe and end up spending less money as well. If you're feeling overwhelmed lately and you're looking to save more to pay for those important family rituals, I encourage you to ask yourself and your family the following questions:

- Do we need to do all the things on our schedule?
- Can we say "No, thank you" more than we do right now?
- What are ways we can slowly but surely get more of our time back?

This is your life. This is your time.

Also, if you feel overwhelmed in life more than you'd like, it's possible your kids might be feeling that way too.

Are you running from swim practice to school, to soccer, to band practice, to volunteer time, to who knows what else, and not allowing for more time to just relax?

More days with no plans may be just what your family needs to get re-centered and have more time for unstructured fun.

Say "No, Thank You, but How About This …"

This new simple life might start to feel like a warm blanket for you. It feels just right. But your extended family or friends might lead different lives than you. Their idea of a good time might not fit in your new life plan.

Saying "no" can be really hard. During our family financial independence path, we had to say no to family and friends more than I liked. It impacted how much time we spent together and ultimately created more distance between us.

There were many times I said "yes" to the expensive dinner, concert, or vacation when it didn't fit in our family budget. And that hurt even worse than saying "no" to those invitations.

What I wish I would have done more often is say, "No, thank you, but how about this instead?"

- Dinner at that restaurant doesn't work for me, but how about a coffee tomorrow morning instead?
- That concert sounds like a blast. We're unable to make it, but we'd love to have you and your family over for a barbeque next Saturday. Would that work for you?
- That 7-day vacation won't work for us right now, but we could do 3 days. What do you think?

This isn't saying "no" and missing out completely. And this isn't saying "yes" and breaking promises you've made to yourself and your family. It's a middle ground that hopefully gives you the social life you need and most of what you want while honoring your ideal family life.

Cancel the Obvious Nonessentials

We've defined our priorities and lined up our budgets to support them. Our lives are starting to come more into balance. As this happens, we'll start to see some obvious outliers that just don't fit anymore:

- Subscriptions we don't use anymore
- Memberships you once used but haven't gotten value from in some time
- Commitments on your calendar that you and your family don't enjoy

- Relationships that pull you away from your family-first mission
- Obligations that no longer serve you

It's time to cancel, unsubscribe, and say goodbye. You are in a season of life simplification, and there will be some casualties. As long as we remember our main priorities (remember those big rocks), these things you're saying "no" to won't feel so bad. That's because you're saying "yes" to what matters most.

EXPERIENCES OVER THINGS

In our quest to advance the essential and hack away at the unessential, I recommend selecting experiences over things. Choose the family weekend getaway over the latest phone. Commit to the lunch with a friend over a new outfit. Go to that concert with your spouse instead of upgrading your headphones.

There is scientific research that backs up this thinking. A 5,000-person study by the University of Texas at Austin concluded that "people are happier with experiential purchases over material ones irrespective of when you measure happiness: before, during or after consumption."[7]

The happy feeling was due in part to the fact that experiential purchases lasted longer in our memories compared to material ones. Also, purchasing experiences brings us closer to friends and family. When you make those lasting memories with your favorite people in life, the happiness becomes amplified.

When we're making this happiness comparison, be sure to line up financial decisions that are comparable. A brand-new $100,000 car might beat out $5 trip to the candy store with your kid. The same goes for the $10,000 vacation beating out $100 pair of pants. They just aren't in the same league.

If you do decide to purchase a material good over an experience, see if you can make that purchase an experience that aligns with your family values. A few years ago, we bought our first hot tub. We saved up for years to make this purchase a reality. Living in Michigan, our hot tub gets us outside during the cold winters and creates moments of connection when we would otherwise be huddled inside staring at phones. While a hot tub is a material purchase, it has become an experiential one because it sparks family bonding moments. We play cards in the hot tub with our water-proof deck, we relax and talk after going for runs, and our kids invite their friends over to enjoy it as well. It was worth every penny.

I'm not saying don't spend money on material things. Material things are important, but they shouldn't be the most important. If you're presented with the choice and all things are equal, vote for experiences. There's better bang for your buck.

FROM THE PODCAST

Family: Angela and Greg, 30 years old from Washington
Money Milestone: Working part-time on the path to family financial independence

Andy: *How did your life change financially when you became a mother?*

Angela: So financially, not so much. I had a list of like 30 things I needed to get done before I got pregnant. Part of it was to have separate funds specifically to pay hospital bills and make sure that I could stay home for some amount of maternity leave.

I actually ramped up very early and then was full-time when he was 5 months old, and at that point, I was working about half-time in the office and then half-time trying to work during nap time and after bedtime.

I was so exhausted dealing with the baby all day, and then he'd finally go to sleep and then I'd have to open my laptop and do a bunch of work. And so Monday through Friday I was either working or taking care of the kid or attempting to do a few house chores and errand stuff. But it meant that it bled into the weekends and life was a blur and it wasn't very fun. It was really overwhelming.

Andy: *What changes did you make that helped with your schedule as a working mother?*

Angela: I had the opportunity to put him into preschool a couple of days a week when he turned a year old. And we're really lucky to have family support for the other days.

And so, we started paying for preschool at the same time that I then cut my hours but still went into the office. So, I am there Monday through Friday, but I'm there shorter days.

We have our mornings together, we can have breakfast together, and then I pick him up in the early afternoon and we have the rest of the day. Or occasionally I will sneak into work early and do a podcast interview, or after work, I'll go for a run before I grab him. Life has a lot more balance these days.

Andy: *How did you develop a flexible working arrangement with your employer?*

Angela: I think it was more just talking about what I wanted and what I was hoping. There are more employers that might be open to that sort of thing if you can talk them through it like, "Well, I can do all of these things at this amount of time. I just would have to give up X, Y, and Z, but I'm also willing to give up this significant chunk of my income to do it."

But as long as I could keep my core stuff, then we found ways to shift it around. And as I've worked less for 3.5 years, now I'm finding more and more people that have different schedules and hours than you would think. A lot of people don't realize that I don't work full time because I'm in the office 5 days a week and I'm there when they see me, so they don't really notice, especially people that don't work in my office.

They can't tell I'm not working full time. But then as you get into conversations with people, even with city staff, like government employees, private employees, across the board, if you start paying attention and talking to people more and more, there are more flexible working agreements, and I think it's just not talked about and the expectation is that everybody works full time, but a lot of people don't.

Andy: *How much of your income was decreased?*

Angela: I went to 80% time, so I cut my hours by 20% and my pay by 20%. Though, it's probably more than 20% because there is some additional value to being full time.

So, it's probably more like a 25, 30% pay cut.

Andy: *Where do you spend your money that makes you super happy?*

Angela: I don't know about super happy, but I'm super happy that my dog is still alive. She's been very expensive for the last couple of years. She had some heart problems a couple of years ago and that cost a lot of money, and then she, most recently, had to have a couple of toes amputated because she's got this autoimmune thing going on.

I realized that we've spent a lot of money on her already this year. So, our savings rate is a little bit lower, but I'm glad to do it. I enjoy having dogs in my life, and I think it's part of being a responsible pet owner is taking care of them.

Andy: *Where do you not spend money that maybe the typical person does?*

Angela: As of last week, I'm at two-and-a-half years of a clothes-buying ban. So, I've not spent a dollar on clothing for myself in two and a half years. I do have a few new things from hand-me-downs from friends and whatnot but that budget for me has been zero.

And then my husband works in construction, so when he wears out a pair of Carhartt's he buys new ones. But other than that, he doesn't really spend money on clothes.

And then my son's clothes come from either hand-me-downs or other stores. So that's oftentimes a zero on our budget monthly. I think we're under a couple of hundred dollars for the year so far.

Andy: *If you had $1,000,000 more today, would you buy more clothes?*

Angela: No. I've had people offer me like "I will buy you something so you have something new." And I'm like, "I don't need anything new."

I get new things from people that are getting rid of their old stuff. It's new to me and the clothing ban started out as trying to get to a more minimalist wardrobe initially but wanting to do it in the most sustainable way possible. That means wearing out the clothes I already have.

And by the time I'd hit that year-mark, I decided that I was going to go past a year and just kind of see where it took me, and it has kind of morphed into not just a money savings thing and not just a shrinking closet thing, but really the sustainable bit.

The most sustainable thing is to not have new stuff to begin with. It doesn't matter how sustainable it is. The best is just to not have a new thing in the first place. And so even here, someone that I know commented on Instagram some months ago about a dress I really liked that she was wearing, and she's paring stuff down to get ready for a big trip, and she brought it for me. I'm going to wear it tonight at the closing party, and so I have a new dress and it's beautiful.

Carpe Diem Action Steps

- Observe how many times today you see an advertisement, commercial, or you're being sold to. If you have the ability, see how you can reduce your exposure to this consumerism pressure by 1% tomorrow.
- Write down your ideal family values and the rituals that pair with them.
- Share your family values and rituals with your spouse. Ask them to do the same with you. Discuss how you can support each other in making them come to life both financially and timewise.
- As a test to simplify your life, go one day without buying something. See how often you can fill your day with free enjoyable activities.
- The next time something comes up that you really want to or need to buy, test yourself to see if you can find an inexpensive alternative or a used alternative.
- When a friend or family member asks you do something that doesn't align with your family plan, suggest an alternate idea that does fit for you.

NOTES

1. BEA. (2025). *Gross domestic product* [Online]. Available at: https://www.bea.gov/data/gdp/gross-domestic-product
2. Griffin, M. (2016). *"No place for discontent": A history of the family dinner in America.* NPR. Available at: https://www.npr.org/sections/thesalt/2016/02/16/459693979/no-place-for-discontent-a-history-of-the-family-dinner-in-america
3. The Family Dinner Project. (n.d.). *Benefits of family dinners.* Available at: https://thefamilydinnerproject.org/about-us/benefits-of-family-dinners/
4. Kurczewski, N. (2021). The science of the new-car smell. *Car & Driver* [Online]. Available at: https://www.caranddriver.com/features/a36970626/science-new-car-smell/
5. Winters, M. (2025). A new car costs nearly $50,000 on average: Here's how much you'd pay per month. *CNBC*. Available at: https://www.cnbc.com/2025/03/08/a-new-car-costs-nearly-50000-heres-how-much-youd-pay-per-month.html
6. Car Edge. (2025). *Used car price trends for 2025 (updated weekly)* [Online]. Available at: https://caredge.com/guides/used-car-price-trends-for-2025 (accessed July 5, 2025).
7. Spending on experiences versus possessions advances more immediate happiness. (2020, March 9). *UT News* [Online]. Available at: https://news.utexas.edu/2020/03/09/spending-on-experiences-versus-possessions-advances-more-immediate-happiness/

CHAPTER NINE

USE YOUR 4 DAYS WISELY

"You exist on this planet to do more than just to create economic value."

– Simone Stolzoff

We spend so much time and energy focusing on retirement. Countless hours are dedicated to researching the perfect investment portfolio and the optimal withdrawal strategy so you can get the most out of your retirement years.

Retirement is put on a pedestal as the final destination of bliss, happiness, and endless hours of relaxation. We tell ourselves, "When I'm retired, I'll finally be happy."

While retirement may open up our calendars completely, happiness is not guaranteed. Depression can become an unfortunate side effect in retirement. One study found that self-reported depression goes up by 40% in the first few years of retirement.[1] Since work becomes such a core part of our identities, the loss of that identity can have a devastating effect on our mental health and well-being.

This is why diversifying our identities outside of work is so important. When we introduce ourselves using our job titles or center the majority of our conversations around our professional careers, it's no wonder that depression statistic exists. This is who we are. Work is our identity.

As we move into this world of working 3 days and living 4 days, this is our opportunity to test drive a "semi-retirement" life. We may find that the loss of our identity as a full-time worker is just too much to bear mentally. Or we take this challenge as an opportunity to invest in growing new identities and diversifying who we are. This way, we're finding contentment outside of work both today and in the future.

This is a mission worth fighting for.

INVEST IN YOUR HEALTH AND WELL-BEING

Part of being a family-first individual is knowing you can't pour from an empty cup. You need to feel healthy, vibrant, and alive before giving your time and energy to others.

The first area that we should focus on with our newfound time is our own personal health and well-being. If we're drained personally, then we can't pour into others.

Get Quality Sleep

Full-time jobs can extend 40–50 hours per week. What's not included in that time block are the hours thinking about work. If work stress persists into the evening hours, this can affect our sleep.

One study found that working longer hours (and the stress and worry that comes along with it) contributed to difficulty falling asleep, shorter sleeping hours overall, and waking up not feeling as refreshed.[2]

Sleep is incredibly important to your overall health and vitality. It supports a healthy heart and better weight management, reduces the risk of injury, and keeps your immune system strong.[3]

According to UC Davis Health, adults should aim for 7–8 hours of quality sleep each night. Without proper sleep, we're exposing ourselves to an increased risk of heart disease, cancer, and brain diseases like strokes or aneurysms.

With more time freedom, we can focus on getting quality sleep as well as the habits that lead to good sleep.

- *Recommendation: 56 hours per week (112 out of 168 hours remaining)*

Make and Eat Healthier Meals

When you're not sleeping well, working long hours, and overall pressed for time, your diet can suffer. We end up eating unhealthy fast food instead of healthy food that may take longer to prepare. As overworked corporate employees, we simply don't have the time we need to focus on eating well.

Consistently poor eating habits can lead to obesity, diabetes, and heart disease.[4] Even though the United States is one of the wealthiest nations in the world, it is not a leader in healthy living. Our overall calorie consumption outpaces other wealthy nations and leads to poorer overall health outcomes.

With more time, we can focus on creating healthy meals on a daily basis. Not only will this be better for our health, it will be better for our budgets. Making your own meals can help you focus on what ingredients to include in your meals, proper portion sizes, and showing our kids the importance of conscientious meal planning.

There is a cascading effect to eating properly as well. When we eat better, our sleep improves. Better sleep leads to the many health benefits we already discussed.

- *Recommendation: 12 hours per week (100 out of 168 hours remaining)*

Lock In an Exercise Routine

With a busy work life, we can often use that as an excuse for not exercising more. Eight hours emailing or sitting in meetings daily isn't quite the movement that experts recommend.

The US Department of Health and Human Services recommends adults get 150 minutes (2.5 hours) of physical activity per week.[5] This activity needs to get your heart pumping. If 150 minutes is too much time to dedicate in the beginning, "75 minutes per week of vigorous aerobic activity" works too.

Unfortunately, it is estimated that only one in five adults are getting this much exercise regularly.

This may have been you in the past, but not anymore. With more time in your schedule, you should lock in a disciplined exercise routine. Just 30 minutes a day for 5 days each week lowers your risk of heart disease, obesity, and depression.

Back to that cascading effect again, a regular exercise routine helps with getting better sleep.

Since reducing my overall working hours years ago, I've exercised more than I have in my entire adult life. I eat better and sleep better because of it. Before this lifestyle change, I was considered overweight by my doctor and in need of cholesterol medication. Today, my weight is healthy, and I have no need for cholesterol meds.

- *Recommendation: 3 hours per week (97 out of 168 hours remaining)*

Spend More Time Outdoors

Click-clacking away on laptops for a full workweek keeps us tied to our desks indoors. We miss out on the benefits of spending time outdoors when we work too much.

Harvard T.H. Chan School of Public Health found that time spent in nature reduces chronic diseases, improves sleep, and lowers blood pressure.[6] The American Psychological Association reports that time spent offline and outdoors reduces stress and promotes attention restoration.[7]

As far as how much time to spend in nature, a 2019 study found that just 2 hours per week can show increased mental and physical benefits.[8] Those benefits appeared to max out around 5 hours per week.

This outdoor time can come in the form of a nature walk, playing outdoor sports, or even cutting the lawn.

If your free time is starting to feel pinched with all these additions, consider some healthy living integration. Exercise outdoors instead of indoors. Enjoy a healthy lunch in a park with a friend instead of alone inside.

- *Recommendation: 3 hours per week (94 out of 168 hours remaining)*

Breath Work and Meditation

Deep breathing has been linked to several health benefits, including stress management, lower blood pressure, and sending more oxygen to your body's organs.[9]

One of my favorite ways to carve out time for deep breath work is through a daily guided meditation practice. Taking just 10 minutes per day for meditation and breath work helps me feel calmer. This practice helps me become a better husband and father because I become more rational in my thoughts and actions.

While there are several options out there, my favorite meditation app is Calm.

- *Recommendation: 1 hour per week (93 out of 168 hours remaining)*

Develop a Daily Gratitude Practice

Negative thinking can take over when we're overworking and underliving. Consistent negativity can lead to stress, anxiety, and depression.[10] That stress can cause the release of stress hormones and lead to physical health complications like increased blood pressure, heart rate, and blood sugar levels.[11]

If we continue that way of life for too long with too much work stress, those health complications have been linked to cancer.

One small daily practice that can support a healthier mind is developing a gratitude practice. Thinking of what we are grateful for in our lives helps to combat negative thinking and rumination on stressful thoughts. Both Berkley and Harvard have researched gratitude as a way to combat stress.[12] The participants in their studies found that it was easier to want to exercise and it helped promote a better night's sleep.

To put this into a simple daily practice, in the morning or evening, I simply write down three things I'm grateful for.

1. I'm grateful that I'm able to write a book.
2. I have a family that is encouraging and supporting me during this book writing process.
3. My body and mind are healthy enough to support the effort and time required to write this book.

As you can tell, book writing is top of mind for me lately.

If I'm dealing with a particularly stressful day or season in my life, it can be difficult to feel grateful. That's when I try to dig down deep and think about things that may not feel so apparent on a daily basis.

1. I'm grateful that I have two legs that can run.
2. There is clean water that comes out of a tap in my home.
3. I can walk outside of my home and breathe fresh air.

This habit is the quickest of all the ones we mentioned, and it may be the one with the most impact based on the time required.

- *Recommendation: <1 hour per week (92 out of 168 hours remaining)*

When we subtract the 20 hours spent on our fulfilling part-time work, we are left with 72 hours per week. This is more than half of your available time focused on yourself and the things you need to have a happy, healthy, and fulfilling life.

Let's explore some smart ways to spend the rest of your available time.

STRENGTHEN YOUR MARRIAGE

In the beginning of romantic relationships, a lot of time is spent together. We're learning from each other, laughing together, and making memories.

As marriage continues for many of us, the exciting sparks that once were ever present may start to fade after a few years.[13] Children and busy careers begin to dominate our time. We don't carve out the important hours for connection that spouses truly need to feel loved. This is unfortunately how marital problems, fights, and divorce occur so frequently in our country. With a 45% divorce rate, one major cause of divorce is a general lack of commitment.[14]

As you step into this newfound era of time freedom and leave 4 days to live your life fully, strengthening your marriage needs to be prioritized. If you truly love your spouse and you want to improve your connection together, time should be devoted to that commitment.

Morning Connection

Before the day begins, checking in with your spouse can go a long way. This is an opportunity to connect, review upcoming plans, and find ways to support each other with family or individual goals. When your spouse feels loved and supported, they are more likely to want to love and support you back.

For years, I missed this opportunity with my wife. I was too busy to sit down and ease into the day. It was go-go-go on work and parenting priorities from dawn to dusk. After I limited my work hours and our kids got older, we now take time in the morning to drink coffee and catch up in our favorite comfortable kitchen chairs. When the weather is nice, we'll sit outside on our back deck and listen to the birds sing.

And this doesn't need to be a long time either. Just dedicate enough time to enjoy a cup of coffee. This could be anywhere from 15 to 60 minutes. If you're not into coffee, consider hot tea or hot water with lemon. Hot beverages force you to slow down and wait for it to cool down. This encourages a slower pace and opportunity for more time together. This is something the English know very well with their tea rituals.[15]

- *Recommendation: 3 hours per week (69 out of 168 hours remaining)*

Date Night/Day

The ritual of date night or date day can help you get out of the house and out of your normal routine. Shaking things up in marriage can go a long way in keeping the romance alive.

When work and parenting dominate, they tend to take over the conversation too. Your dates could be a work-free and parenting-free conversation zone. Trying something new and experiencing it together creates an opportunity for new sparks in your relationship.

The following are some ideas:

- Going kayaking or paddle boarding
- Getting a couples massage
- Taking a dance lesson
- Exploring a new restaurant
- Trying rock climbing at an indoor gym

If money becomes an excuse not to go on dates together, we all need to think more creatively. Many date ideas don't require you to spend any money at all. Recently, my wife and I found a "paint your spouse's portrait" opportunity at our local library. It was completely free, and it was also completely hilarious. Let's just say I'm not an accomplished painter, but my attempt at it made my wife (and several other people in the library) cry with laughter. It was a great time, and we didn't spend a dime.

Here are some additional date ideas that don't cost anything:

- Go for a walk in a local park
- Cuddle around the fire pit
- Learn a new recipe together (with ingredients in your house)
- Give each other massages
- Volunteer for a local charity together

You get bonus points when you can combine activities that support a healthy lifestyle and time with your spouse. Going for a run with your spouse helps you exercise and dedicate time to your relationship.

Ditch the idea that date night needs to be some expensive dinner or evening out. If you have the money available in your budget, that's excellent. But don't let limited financial resources be an excuse for not spending quality time with your spouse.

Aim for a couple of date nights or date days per month to start and adjust according to your available time, budget, and how your spouse wants to be loved.

- *Recommendation: 2 hours per week (67 out of 168 hours remaining)— more likely every other week for a few hours*

Vacation Together

Work trips happen. Family vacations happen. What about a vacation with just the two of you?

With work and young kids, vacations together as a couple can become less and less frequent. But as time becomes more available in your overall schedule, consider increasing the frequency of trips with your spouse.

If you are able to get appropriate childcare, this can be ideal for anniversaries, birthdays, or other special occasions. Going on an extended European vacation when you have young children may be a fantasy, but stealing an evening at a local downtown hotel may be more feasible. If Grandma or Grandpa are local and able to support, experiencing a weekend getaway could go a long way in reigniting the passion in your relationship.

Marriage Counseling

Depending on the state of your marriage, you may need support from a third party. Marriage counselors can really make a difference if things are feeling rocky. According to the American Psychological Association, around 75% of couples who took advantage of marriage therapy said it improved their overall relationship.[16]

There can be a lot of stigma around marriage counseling. If you admit you're going to therapy, are you admitting that your relationship isn't healthy? I felt this way when my wife asked me to go to marriage therapy nearly a decade ago. We were having difficulty connecting, communicating, and finding joy in our relationship. I felt like I was drowning at work. My free time was mostly focused on parenting. My physical health and mental well-being were suffering. This was a time in my life when I was not showing up as the best husband I could be.

The 9 months we spent together in marriage counseling was an incredible investment in our marriage. We both learned so much from each other about how we can show up as better partners. Our counselor helped us communicate more effectively, become more empathetic toward each other, and learn the importance of dedicated time for connection.

If you've been trying to improve your relationship and it feels like there hasn't been progress lately, I would highly recommend seeking out a trusted marriage counselor. With their training and knowledge, they are able to provide tools and strategies to enhance your marriage. It was a blind spot for me personally. I keep thinking, "I just need to try harder." But what I didn't know is that I was trying harder in the wrong direction. The marriage counseling course corrected me as a husband, and our relationship is better because of it.

MAXIMIZE FAMILY EXPERIENCES

We started by discussing the importance of taking care of ourselves. After we're feeling our best, we then lean into enhancing our marriages. Now, let's discuss dedicating time to our kids, family rituals, and time with our extended family as well.

Become a More Present Parent

As parents, we all know our kids crave our time and attention. When they are babies, outside of sleeping, they need our near constant attention for survival. As the years pass on, our kids become more independent and are able to do some important things on their own. In their teen years, they need less of our time and attention until eventually, they don't really need us at all.

In the grand scheme of things, it's a relatively short time. When we're young parents though, the time required to care and support your child can feel overwhelming. This is especially true when demanding jobs take up too many hours of our week. Those demanding jobs keep us from investing in our health and overall well-being. The time stretched week also keeps us from dedicating time to our marriages as well.

If we're able to own 20 more hours of our week through the focused family financial independence moves that we've discussed in this book, we can use that time to invest in ourselves and our marriages. That way, when it comes time for parenting, we're ready to be the present, loving, and caring Moms and Dads we always wanted to be.

When we're less distracted by work, we can be fully present during the dance recitals, soccer games, art shows, musical performances, and much more. We're not as worried about checking our phones or "jumping back into email" when the pressure from the corporate world is decreased. And our kids appreciate this too.

Distracted parenting can have long-term effects on our younger children's development. One study found "consistent associations between parents' technology use and negative outcomes in children under 5. These include poorer cognitive development, increased behavioral and emotional problems, weaker attachment to parents, and higher screen time in children themselves."[17]

Outside of work obligations, parents can often be digitally distracted because they don't have the time to pour into themselves first. They need an outlet from the constant tug and pull of work and parenthood. Their phones or other digital devices can feel like a break. Scrolling on social media, watching a TV series, or texting with a friend can be enjoyable and relaxing, but when it takes over important time with your kids, that can be an issue. Like anything, find that middle ground that feels appropriate for you and your family.

Create Family Rituals

Family rituals are repeated activities that occur based on your family values. As you're figuring out the right rituals for your family, here are some to consider based on our experience and research.

Chore Time

In our family, we feel it is important for our children to contribute around the house (family value); therefore, our kids need to complete household chores during the week (family ritual). While our kids don't necessarily love chore time, we believe they realize that it's an important function in creating a happy home.

An 85-year Harvard study suggests that getting kids involved in household chores as early as 4 or 5 years old will have positive life-long effects.[18] Long term, the 700 "kids" (now older adults) in the study became more independent, less self-centered, and had a greater sense of self-worth.

Family Dinner

Carving out time for family dinner supports healthier eating habits and an overall strong family bond.[19] Children who have regular family dinners have better communication skills and lower rates of anxiety and depression than those children who don't eat regularly with family.

Similar to chore time, this is a ritual where your kids can get involved as well. Helping to place silverware, filling up water cups, setting out napkins, clearing dishes, and washing dishes are helpful activities your kids can do to make family dinner time a reality.

Showcasing an attitude of gratitude at the dinner table can be an excellent example for your children as well. Knowing the positive benefits of expressing gratitude, we often share what we're grateful for at the dinner table and then ask our children to share as well.

Family Vacations

With less work and more free time, creating lifelong family memories through vacations is money and time well spent. I know I'm more relaxed and present with my kids and my wife when I'm on vacation. I'm away from the demands of work and the daily duties of housework. This allows me to focus on family time above all else.

It appears our kids remember these positive vacation attributes as they grow older too. According to research conducted with 2,500 adults and 1,000 youth, childhood's most vivid memories of family life are of time spent on vacation.[20] While the actual details can be fuzzy, the good feelings remain.

These vacations don't have to be expensive budget busters either. Even just staying a night at a hotel with a pool can feel like a much-needed break from the daily routine. If we're able to put away our devices and focus on fun and take life a little less serious, we can show our kids how to live life to the fullest.

If you have multiple children, consider taking a variety of trips over their lifetimes.

- Full family vacations
- One-on-one solo trips (mother-daughter, mother-son, father-daughter, father-son)
- Vacations with extended family

These vacation memories will stay with your children for their entire lives and give them a guide on how to live a good family life as they grow into adulthood.

Spend Time with Your Parents

I had an incredible childhood. My parents showed me the importance of family time and enjoying the present moment. As I progressed in my career, got married, and raised our children with my wife, my quality time with my mom and dad has decreased significantly.

When my work hours decreased after dropping down to part-time work, I have made it a point to spend more time with them. We do Friday walks and Thursday evening golf in the summertime. A couple of times per year, we'll do extended family vacations in Northern Michigan or trips to Mexico in the winter. We even have Detroit Lions season tickets together.

These rituals help me schedule time for the two people who brought me into this world.

If you don't live close to your folks, consider using holiday time as a way to get together. And if you've fallen out of touch with your parents, remember they are just a phone call away. Depending on their age and overall health, you may not have many years left with your mom or dad. That average age of 78 years is something we've discussed for ourselves a lot in this book. *Memento mori* is also important to recognize for our parents too. Call them, thank them, and spend some time with them.

DIVERSIFY YOUR IDENTITY

When we get so focused on work, we can feel that's entirely who we are. Statements like these can be commonplace:

- "I'm a corporate marketer."
- "I'm an engineer."
- "My wife is a lawyer."
- "My husband is an accountant."

With so many hours dedicated to school, college, and ultimately our careers, it's no wonder we wear these titles as badges of who we are. A large bulk of our lives have been spent with our careers defining us.

Not anymore.

We're stepping back from work as our central identity. More of our time is being spent on ourselves outside of work, on our marriages, and with our families.

We may still be workers, but we're also athletes, cooks, nature walkers, runners, spouses, parents, and children. This identity diversification is healthy for our long-term well-being. Similar to investing in the stock market, we don't want to put all of our eggs in one basket. If we wear the badge of "engineer" and our engineering job goes away, then who are we? Personally, we'll feel a loss that may be too hard to bear. Instead, having a variety of life roles allows us to lean on another identity if one goes away or is in crisis.

Let's explore some other important identities as you craft your ideal life schedule.

Make Time for Friends

When you're young, your parents are your world. As you get older, friends become the center of your life. You spend most of your time with your friends in your teens and twenties. You laugh, make memories, and discover new things you never knew about before meeting your friends.

That is until you have a family of your own.

Suddenly, your friends who you used to spend so much time with get placed in the same time category as your parents. You love them and they are important to you, but during this season of life you can't allocate as many hours to your friendship.

But friends (outside of family and work) are crucial for a happy life. The Mayo Clinic highlights friendships as a key driver in improving self-confidence, supporting you during difficult times, and providing you with a sense of belonging and purpose.[21]

Friends can provide a certain type of support you may not get from your spouse, your kids or your coworkers. They can give you a second opinion, make you feel like you're "enough" by just showing up, and help you recall fond memories outside of work, marriage, and parenting.

There is also a loneliness epidemic that has been sweeping our globe lately. Half of US adults have reported measurable levels of loneliness.[22] The World Health Organization labeled loneliness a "global public concern" and reported loneliness can be as bad as smoking 15 cigarettes per day.[23] We're spending more time working and "socializing" online than ever before. This "faux socialization" presented through "social media" feels like time spent with friends, but it's truthfully nothing close to it. Likes, hearts, and emojis are no match for quality time talking with a friend.

Take time to schedule a lunch with a friend you haven't seen in a while. Host a friend over at your place to catch up over coffee. Try out a new experience and ask a friend to join you.

If you can integrate friend-time with other positive activities like exercise or giving back in your community, then you'll get a double win.

Volunteer in Your Community

Volunteering some of your free time to a cause you feel passionate about is a smart way to create connection and purpose in life. According to UC San Diego, benefits include stress reduction, skill development, and a boost to your overall health.[24]

Before I had kids, donating blood through the Red Cross was a simple, yet life-saving way to contribute to our community. If you're going for impact based on time spent, it's estimated that you are able to save three lives during a 1-hour blood donation session.[25]

After becoming a dad, I looked for ways to volunteer that supported my community and my children's lives. Over the years, I've been a soccer coach, soccer team manager, flag football coach, PTO treasurer, school mascot dressed in a banana costume, lunch time volunteer, and much more. This is a way for me to be involved in my kid's lives and support the type of community that I want to live in.

Getting kids involved in volunteer activities integrates quality family time as well. One tradition we recently started was picking up trash on or around Earth Day. After the ice and snow melts in our spring here in Michigan, there tends to be trash hiding underneath. Our family of four will walk up and down the road picking up trash. In our last session, we collected over four huge bags of trash in about an hour. This tradition keeps our neighborhood clean and shows our kids the importance of community pride.

There's a sweet spot to volunteering your time. Donate too much and you feel like you might be getting taken advantage of. Donate too little and you feel like you could be doing more to make your community a better place. Many sources suggest 50 hours per year is a good average to consider.[26] If you mix in other integrated life activities to your volunteering efforts (like family time, date nights, or time with friends), you could stretch this up to 100 hours per year.[27] At this point, the overall health benefits begin to plateau.

Discover New Hobbies and Interests

When we were younger, many of us had endless free time. We did things where we felt like time had no end. Activities like sports, drawing, painting, cooking, writing, singing, riding bikes, and making music filled our calendars.

When I was in middle school and high school, I enjoyed writing songs and crafting scripts for movies and making them come to life. Time would fly by as I used my creativity to play and have fun.

As we grow older and the structure of life begins to take hold, our ability to think creatively and play begins to fade. It's hard to think outside the box when the box is so set in stone.

With more available time in your schedule, find time to play for the sake of play. Draw because you enjoy it. Sing because it feels good. Write because it feels cathartic.

I feel like this is an area I'm still working on. It's not a coincidence that I've placed it as the last area to spend your newfound time. For me, I'm giving myself some grace as I'm still working on finding my groove with the areas we've already covered. Once I feel like I have a good routine in those areas, I'm going to learn an instrument. Playing the piano or guitar could be a lot of fun as I already love singing. If there's a karaoke bar nearby, you'll likely find me there.

To support you on finding your next hobby or interest, ask yourself some questions:

- What hobbies and interests did I have as a kid that really made me happy?
- Did I let those go when I became an adult?
- Could I find an hour to try one of those hobbies or interests this week?
- Was it fun? Or do I want to try something else next week?

Many of us use our hobby and interest time for watching TV, using social media, or playing games on our phones. There's nothing wrong with those things, but overuse can keep us away from other activities that might be more fulfilling. After all, there's quite a difference between consuming and creating. Consuming art does not feel as good as creating art. Listening to music is not as satisfying as creating your own music.

As we look for ways to utilize our 4 days wisely, a good mantra would be to create more than we consume.

FROM THE PODCAST

Family: Maggie and Greg Tucker, 44 and 46 years old from Georgia

Money Milestone: Left corporate America in their early forties (host *Inside Out Money* podcast)

Andy:	*How did you leave corporate America in your forties?*
Maggie:	My husband and I both worked for almost exactly 20 years in corporate America jobs, almost for the same companies. And I had always been pretty frugal, mindful of my money and avoided a lot of lifestyle inflation.

My husband had much more of a focus on his finances in the second half of his corporate career. And we met about 10 years into that 20-year career. We were both divorced, had young kids. And as a result, he was fixing his finances. I'll put it that way. Divorce can be expensive. We didn't really even have a goal of early retirement when we met. I was perhaps loosely aware of the concept, but in the last 3 to 5 years that we were working, really sort of started learning about it, understood the idea, and supercharged our savings goals.

I really heavily maxed out my company's Deferred Compensation Plan, which helped a lot. Around COVID, actually, is when we really started making some serious plans. And we would always toy with the idea.

But we made good money, which helped. We avoided lifestyle inflation. While we were making higher and higher salaries, we were not constantly inflating our lifestyles. I've lived in the same house for 15 plus years, and we just made a lot of smart decisions with our money. Not even all that smart, but decent decisions with our money and saved more than we spent at times.

Andy: *You've been utilizing your investments to live on? How has it been working?*

Maggie: I have a deferred compensation plan that is which gives me most of what I need to live off for the next 13 more years. That gets me to retirement age or when we get to use our 401(k), etc.

We also live off interest, dividends. Greg, my husband, has done a little bit of part-time work. You know, he's paying out child support, and so he likes the idea of having some extra, and he's got more time than I do. But I don't really earn any money. I do like a tiny bit of financial coaching. I'm talking like 20 hours a year. I think I made $2,300 last year.

Financial coaching and some resume career coaching. So, I don't really make any money in terms of traditional employment. And we have some rental properties, which I always forget about because they're a little hands off as of late, but they certainly ebb and flow. It's kind of like a little bit from here, a little bit from here, a lot from DCP. We haven't really started cashing in investments yet, though, but we will eventually.

Andy: *Was that a difficult transition from working full time?*

Maggie: In some ways it was really hard. I was scared about two things when I left. I was scared about money, like running out of it, and that I would regret the decision because so much of my identity was tied up in work. The easy part was the identity. Turns out I was fine. Both of us were fine. We were much happier on the other side in so many ways. It wasn't like the leaving work itself was hard per se. I had good friends and a lot of history and things like that there, but I thought that would be the hard part. The hard part was actually managing myself all of the sudden. I'm really good at working for someone else. When someone else is driving me every day, that works for me, and it keeps me going. When nobody is doing that and I'm the only one in charge, all of a sudden the wheels fall off productivity, which you could argue shouldn't be my focus anymore anyways. But we went through it. We couldn't put a word on it in the beginning. And it was cool because we were going through it together. But we couldn't put a word on it.

When the movie *Inside Out* 2 came out, way before that, we had named our feeling, which was "ennui." And then when the movie came out, I was like, "Oh my gosh, now everybody knows what this means." And it's a feeling of listlessness and dissatisfaction arising out of a lack of occupation or excitement. And we had a little bit of this listlessness.

We've got everybody's dream and ours. And like, what do we do with it now? You know, what are we doing? We got caught up on some TV, you know? I can only watch so much TV. There were pieces of it that were easier than I thought. And then things that were hard were not at all what I expected.

Andy: *What did you start to transition into that has made you feel like you've have a more fulfilled life?*

Maggie: One thing that I overlooked was we became stay-at-home parents. I've always had respect for stay-at-home parents to be clear, but I have way more respect for them now because I'm not sure, honestly, I'm like, where am I? How did I do all this before? Because I'm like barely doing it now. But we spend a lot of time just dealing with our life and driving kids to practice. And certainly we're more available and volunteering quickly to be the one driving. And so, we're over indexing on that more than we ever did when we had demanding jobs. But we spend a lot of time with our kids.

I see my mom way more often. She lives two miles away. I take her to all her doctor's appointments. I help her with a lot of stuff.

I play pickleball with a group of people a couple of times a week.

I have a lot of friends that are actually around during the day and new friends I've discovered are around during the day.

We travel more. We keep ourselves oddly quite busy actually. And more busy than I even want to be at times. You have the same problems you had when you were working. Like, "I don't know where all my time's going," and things like that.

Andy: *Can you imagine fitting 40 to 50 hours of work back in your life now?*

Maggie: No, I can't imagine how I used to do it. I remember when I was going to grad school, getting my MBA part time and working thinking, "What did I do before this?" But then it goes away. It's like activities fill the time allowed for them. There's some rule for that. I can't think of the name of it, but yeah, no, I could not imagine. I always say, "I'm not sure how I had the job I had." Because I wasn't even working 40 to 50 hours. I was working like 50 to 60 hours, and I was working nights and weekends at home, and I commuted. It was a lot, and I'm not there. I will say, it had me on a schedule. I was way more productive and on top of things then than I am now, which is probably good for someone like me to take a step back.

Sometimes I joke that I'm regressing in terms of my ability to deal with large amounts of complex things.

Andy: *What's one small step that somebody could take right now to move towards a position of owning more of their time like you have?*

Maggie: The reality is it's tons of tiny steps, but I think one of the biggest steps is probably getting your mindset right about what really matters in life. And that's something that I had done in my early 30s before I even knew about financial independence or early retirement. I was reading a lot around Buddhism, and I had a mentality of "I have so much to be thankful for."

And I always use the example of, you can drive by houses in your neighborhood, and you can see a house that's bigger than yours and think, "Why don't I have that? My house is smaller. I wish I had a big house." Or you can drive by people that don't own a home that are homeless. There's so many people who have less than you. And you can have that mentality of, "I'm so grateful and thankful for what I have." And "I don't really need more to be happy."

Be happy with less and get your mindset right around that.

One of my favorite books in the whole world is *The Art of Happiness* written by the Dalai Lama and somebody else who helped him write it. I forgot his name. And it really influenced me in my late 20s, early 30s around just being happy with less and being happy with what I already have and being thankful for what I already have. Not constantly wanting more. And I think that mentality quite honestly saved me a lot of money because I was avoiding lifestyle inflation. I was avoiding a lot of the things that people get trapped in in our modern consumeristic society.

Carpe Diem Action Steps

- Gauge how much time you are actually exercising each week. Compare it to the recommended amount and see how you can improve slightly this week.
- Analyze your overall eating habits. Plan a healthy family dinner into your routine and see how it could support your overall health, mental well-being, and family synergy.
- Schedule time to connect for a coffee or a date night with your spouse. Marriage requires action.
- Reach out to a friend you haven't seen in a while. Make a plan to get together and catch up. Lunch can be an easy thing to fit into most people's schedule.
- Think about some simple and enjoyable ways to volunteer in your community. You may not have time for them yet, but thinking about how you'd like to spend your time volunteering is a great start.
- Call your mom. Call your dad. Don't ask them for anything. Just let them know you're thinking about them, ask them what's going on in their lives, and be sure to thank them for all they have done in your life.

NOTES

1. Fifth Third. (n.d.). *Retirement and the risk of depression* [Online]. Available at: https://www.53.com/content/fifth-third/en/personal-banking/planning/retirement-university/retirement-risk-of-depression.html
2. Virtanen, M. et al. (2009). All work and no play makes jack lose sleep. *Sleep*, 32(6), pp. 737–745. Available at: https://pmc.ncbi.nlm.nih.gov/articles/PMC2690560/
3. Cultivating Health. (2023). *Better sleep: Why it's important for your health and tips to sleep soundly* [Online]. UC-Davis. Available at: https://health.ucdavis.edu/blog/cultivating-health/better-sleep-why-its-important-for-your-health-and-tips-to-sleep-soundly/2023/03

4. National Research Council, Institute of Medicine, and Woolf, S. H. (2013). *U.S. health in international perspective: Shorter lives, poorer health*. National Academies Press. Available at: https://www.ncbi.nlm.nih.gov/books/NBK154469/

5. American Heart Association. (n.d.). *American Heart Association recommendations for physical activity in adults and kids* [Online]. Available at: https://www.heart.org/en/healthy-living/fitness/fitness-basics/aha-recs-for-physical-activity-in-adults

6. Harvard. (2024). *Time spent in nature can boost physical and mental well-being*. Available at: https://hsph.harvard.edu/news/time-spent-in-nature-can-boost-physical-and-mental-well-being/

7. Weir, K. (2025). Nurtured by nature. *American Psychological Association*, 51(3), p. 50. https://www.apa.org/monitor/2020/04/nurtured-nature

8. Gritters, J. (2022). *Spending just 120 minutes a week has health benefits, research shows* [Online]. REI. Available at: https://www.rei.com/blog/news/this-is-the-optimal-amount-of-time-to-spend-outside-each-week

9. American Heart Association. (n.d.). *Breathing brings benefits infographic* [Online]. Available at: https://www.heart.org/en/healthy-living/healthy-lifestyle/stress-management/breathing-brings-benefits-infographic

10. Smith, A. J. (2023). *Gratitude – A mental health game changer* [Online]. Anxiety & Depression Association of America. Available at: https://adaa.org/learn-from-us/from-the-experts/blog-posts/consumer/gratitude-mental-health-game-changer

11. National Cancer Institute. (2022). *Stress and cancer* [Online]. Available at: https://www.cancer.gov/about-cancer/coping/feelings/stress-fact-sheet

12. NAMI. (n.d.). *The impact of gratitude on mental health* [Online]. Available at: https://namica.org/blog/the-impact-of-gratitude-on-mental-health/

13. Johns Hopkins Medicine. (n.d.). *Keep the spark alive in your marriage* [Online]. Available at: https://www.hopkinsmedicine.org/health/wellness-and-prevention/keep-the-spark-alive-in-your-marriage

14. Sember, B. (2024). *Causes of divorce: 19 of the most common reasons* [Online]. Divorce. Available at: https://divorce.com/blog/causes-of-divorce/

15. Pan, J. (2017). What Americans can learn from the soothing British ritual of tea time. *The Week*. Available at: https://theweek.com/articles/699010/what-americans-learn-from-soothing-british-ritual-tea-time

16. Stepko, B. (2020). *9 reasons you might need marriage counseling* [Online]. AARP. Available at: https://www.aarp.org/home-family/friends-family/info-2020/marriage-counseling.html

17. Gray, D. (2025). Parents' phone use may harm kids' health and development. *Newsweek*. Available at: https://www.newsweek.com/parents-phone-use-harm-kids-health-children-screen-2067235

18. Haden, J. (2024). Want to raise more successful (and happier) kids? Harvard research says give them more chores. *Inc*. Available at: https://www.inc.com/jeff-haden/want-to-raise-more-successful-and-happier-kids-harvard-research-says-give-them-more-chores.html

19. Anderson, J. (2020). *The benefit of family mealtime* [Online]. Harvard Graduate School of Education. Available at: https://www.gse.harvard.edu/ideas/edcast/20/04/benefit-family-mealtime

20. Pruett, K. D. (2019). Memorable vacations, despite limits of preschoolers' memory. *Psychology Today*. Available at: https://www.psychologytoday.com/us/blog/once-upon-child/201905/memorable-vacations-despite-limits-preschoolers-memory

21. Mayo Clinic. (2024). *Friendships: Enrich your life and improve your health* [Online]. Available at: https://www.mayoclinic.org/healthy-lifestyle/adult-health/in-depth/friendships/art-20044860

22. Summers, J., Acovino, V., and Intagliata, C. (2023). *America has a loneliness epidemic. Here are 6 steps to address it*. NPR. Available at: https://www.npr.org/2023/05/02/1173418268/loneliness-connection-mental-health-dementia-surgeon-general

23. Reed, B. (2023). WHO declares loneliness a "global public health concern." *The Guardian*. Available at: https://www.theguardian.com/global-development/2023/nov/16/who-declares-loneliness-a-global-public-health-concern

24. Center for Student Involvement. (n.d.). *Community service: Top 10 reasons to volunteer* [Online]. UC San Diego. Available at: https://getinvolved.ucsd.edu/service/resources/reasons.html

25. OSF Healthcare. (2022). *Donating blood: One easy trick to save three lives in an hour* [Online]. Available at: https://www.osfhealthcare.org/blog/donating-blood/

26. Burger, E. (2021). *Take a look at these 40 volunteer statistics … they will blow you away* [Online]. VolunteerHub. Available at: https://volunteerhub.com/blog/40-volunteer-statistics

27. Grassroots Volunteering. (2023). *How long should you volunteer to reap the full impact?* [Online]. Available at: https://grassrootsvolunteering.org/how-long-before-volunteering-benefits/

CHAPTER TEN

SHOW YOUR CHILDREN THE WAY

"It is not what you do for your children, but what you have taught them to do for themselves that will make them successful human beings."

– Ann Landers

After years of studying the ins and outs of owning your time, one thing continues to ring true: The earlier you start, the easier this all becomes.

Smart financial habits, confidence with money, and the pure math of investing are a whole lot easier when you've got time on your side. And what do our kids have in abundance?

Time.

Time to earn, save, and invest. Time to make mistakes and time to learn how to avoid them in the future.

And as parents, we always want the best for our kids. With every generation that passes, this is our opportunity to go from good to great. Money, and the way we use that money, has a big impact on the prospects of generational wealth, happiness, and time freedom.

Let's use our resources like time, money, energy, and knowledge to help our children thrive.

PUT ON YOUR OWN FINANCIAL OXYGEN MASK FIRST

You're sitting on the plane, and the flight attendants are going through their presentation on airline safety. After showing you how to properly fasten your seatbelt, inevitably they make their way around to the oxygen masks.

In an emergency situation, airline safety reminds us to put on our own oxygen masks before helping others (including children). They do this because adults need to be alert, conscious, and in control before attempting to help their kids. If it were to go in reverse, the kids trying to help adults with their masks could go very poorly.

Family financial planning isn't all that different.

Parents need to be on solid financial ground before even considering giving their kids a leg up in the future. To be specific, this means no saving and investing on behalf of your kids' future until you've eliminated your debt, secured your emergency fund, and created your Coast FIRE plan. This ensures your financial situation is secure today and in the future.

As new parents, this may not always be our first thought. We might be thinking, "Well, I want to give my kids a better life than I have." While that's admirable, I'd like to modify that sentence a bit to better course correct well-meaning parents out there: "By building a life I'm proud of, I will give my kids an example to follow."

Also, if we are so focused on investing for our kids' financial future and we neglect our own, we may find ourselves knocking on their doors when we run out of money in retirement. I'm sure our kids would take us in and support us, but is that really a choice we want them making as they are raising a family of their own?

When I interviewed financial coach and author, Dorethia Kelly, she said she's unfortunately seen this a lot in her community. She shared with me that she's come across parents who have emptied out their 401(k)s just to help their kids attend college. While this may feel like an investment in the future of your family, it could backfire in so many ways. The child could drop out of college or decide that the career path they chose isn't for them. All the while, the parent has no retirement plan. "We just have to be realistic about, as we get older, what our kids are going to be able to do for us financially," Dorethia Kelly explained.

Instead of trying to pour from an empty cup, let's give our kids the knowledge and strength to create their own cups full of potential.

INSPIRE YOUR KIDS TO BUILD WEALTH AND OWN THEIR TIME

As parents, our goal shouldn't be to simply give our children generational wealth. Instead, we should inspire generational wealth as well.

By showing our children how to build their wealth, they will gain the knowledge and skills to continue growing family wealth and happiness for generations. With that wealth and knowledge, they will know how to own their time too.

If we give our kids their wealth without the proper knowledge, they won't know how to effectively use, grow, and protect it. There are too many stories of lottery winners or professional athletes who get presented with a large sum of money and end up going bankrupt. Why? Because they didn't have the knowledge or experience on how to manage money.

The Third-Generation Challenge

There's a concept called the third-generation challenge. It focuses on research that shows generational wealth fades over time.

This is according to the William Group Wealth Consultancy, which surveyed 3,000 wealthy families, and they found that 70% of wealthy families lose their wealth by the second generation and 90% by the third.[1]

Many observations are refuting this study completely saying that wealthy families are at a huge advantage of keeping that wealth within their family, not only over generations but over centuries.[2]

Whether you believe the third-generation challenge or not, cultures around the world embrace this idea.

- The Chinese have a saying, "Wealth does not pass three generations."
- And the Japanese say, "Rice patties to rice patties in three generations."
- Scotland says, "The father buys, the son builds, and the grandchild begs."
- And even in the United States, they say, "Shirt sleeves to shirt sleeves in three generations."

Now, if this third-generation challenge has any truth to it, I believe that it comes down to communication.

We need to communicate with our kids about money early and often so they can become good stewards of it and have that wealth live on.

There's a great Benjamin Franklin quote that sums up this generational wealth situation well: "Tell me and I forget. Teach me and I may remember. Involve me and I learn."

It's important to involve our kids in the process so that they can learn, grow, and eventually become independent and keep this generational wealth journey going. You can crush those depressing statistics of 70% lost and 90% lost and wipe away these cultural fables, at least for your family.

The 60/40 Generational Wealth Plan

I've had the pleasure of interviewing hundreds of wealthy families about how they are inspiring generational wealth. And based on that knowledge, I've crafted something I like to call the 60/40 Generational Wealth Plan.

This theory of mine states that if we're able to live on 60% of our income and use the other 40% to give, invest, and save, we will build family wealth and happiness that lasts.

For those living paycheck to paycheck right now or at the start of their family financial independence journey, this might feel ridiculous to only spend 60% of our income. But if we teach this financial plan to our kids at an early age, and they get used to it, I believe that this will provide them with stability, independence, and a considerate heart in the future.

Spend (60%)

Most of the money in the 60/40 Generational Wealth Plan goes toward smart spending. We want our kids to enjoy the fruits of their labor and find joy in buying things they like.

This can be things like video games, candy, clothes, toys, or whatever your kid is into. Their interests obviously change from when they are little kids to when they become teenagers. As they make purchases, they'll make mistakes, and that's okay. This is how our kids learn.

Invest (20%)

The next biggest chunk goes toward investing for the future. This can be a difficult conversation, but if we develop the habits early, compound interest will do incredible things for your children's future.

Investing 20% of your child's allowance, family gifts, or chore money can help them graduate college student debt free, buy their first home, or even achieve Coast FIRE and start working part-time earlier than you did.

Save (10%)

Outside of goals that are decades away, our kids may have financial goals that are months or years away. That's where saving comes in.

Preferably, you're helping your child sock away 10% of their income into a high-yield savings account. With higher interest rates, your child can see how saving really pays.

Saving can be a smart way to prepare for a first bike, phone, laptop, or even a car.

Give (10%)

Generosity and service to others have been scientifically proven to help people lead happier lives.[3] And don't we want that for our kids?

With the last 10%, I recommend helping your kids find the joy in giving some of their money away. You can do this to charities and causes that call to their hearts, to family and friends on birthdays and holidays, and through random acts of kindness.

The 60/40 Generational Wealth Plan in Action

Where does this money come from to execute the 60/40 Generational Wealth Plan? Here are some examples:

- Birthday gifts
- Chore money
- Allowance
- Religious celebrations
- Money from Grandma or Grandpa
- Babysitting funds
- Pet sitting
- The lemonade stand
- Or any other way your kids make money

With that money, split it up so 60% goes to spending, 20% to investing, 10% to saving, and 10% to giving. Let's go over an example.

The "awesome Grandma" gives your daughter $50 for her birthday.

As much as you'd love to see your daughter buy $50 worth of slime or digital credits on her favorite video game, you as the parent are going to help her make some smart decisions with her newfound money.

Most of it will still go to some smart spending: $30 of the $50 will be allocated to spending. This money will be placed in a checking account (preferably with a debit card option) that your daughter can use for fun with your supervision.

Next, $10 of it will go toward investing. Depending on your situation, this could be investing for college (529 college savings plan). This could also be investing for a future home down payment for your daughter or even her eventual retirement (Roth IRA for kids if she has earned income).

Five dollars will go to savings in a separate high-yield savings account.

And then another $5 will go toward giving.

By allocating her income in this fashion, you will show your daughter why it's important not to spend every dollar she receives.

It's a tough sell in the beginning, speaking as a parent who has been doing this for a while. But if we're honest, what part of parenting isn't a tough sell? Convincing our kids to brush their teeth was a twice-daily drama over the years. Eventually, they brushed those teeth on their own, and eventually, my kids and your kids will learn the benefits of not spending every dollar they earn.

As parents, our job is to create smart, confident, and independent children. Not children who are waiting for us to die so that they can get their generational wealth, but children who have figured out with our example and our guidance how to build generational wealth for themselves.

Wealth comes from earning money and investing a whole bunch of it in stocks, real estate, and businesses for a long time. That's how it works. And I believe that happiness can come from serving and giving to others. And that's why that 10% giving is so important.

TEACH KIDS HOW TO CONTRIBUTE THROUGH CHORES

As parents, it is our job to teach our kids financial responsibility and independence. One excellent way to do this is with chores at home. For our family, this is something we've been doing for almost a decade now.

About 8 years ago, on a random Friday evening, I came home from a long day of work. To my surprise, I saw my 5-year-old daughter vacuuming our kitchen.

I asked my wife what our little one was up to, but she was just as perplexed as I was.

During the previous year, we'd been helping our daughter to do her chores every Saturday morning, but she never had taken the initiative to do them on her own.

After she finished vacuuming, she asked us to leave the kitchen while she put away the silverware. She told us that she wanted it to be a surprise.

We let this cleaning frenzy go on for another 15 minutes before we stopped her and asked, "Why are you doing your chores today?"

She said, "I love you. I want to help the family."

When those words came out of her mouth, my heart filled with such pride and love. Our little girl understood what it meant to be a part of our family.

We don't just express our love through words. We also express our love through action.

Now, were the spoons on top of the forks when she was done? Yes.

Did she vacuum every last Cheerio on the ground? No.

But at 5 years old, we're not looking for perfection. We're just looking for her to understand why it's important to help and how her effort means a lot to us.

Fast forward to today, my daughter is a teenager, and I'm happy to report that not only is she still doing her chores, but she's extremely helpful.

It's not just cute anymore. The chores she does actually make our lives more relaxing and peaceful.

She knows how to wash, dry, and fold her clothes. In addition, she empties the dishwasher, takes the recycling to the street, brushes our cat, vacuums the kitchen, and so much more.

We're raising a responsible, family-centric, independent woman. And I'm so proud of her.

And her younger brother is watching her, learning from her, and contributing in the same way.

There are so many benefits of kids doing chores at home.

- You are teaching your children that being a part of a family means everyone contributes.
- They learn the importance of teamwork and collaboration (crucial skills for life).
- Eventually, their chore skills get better and better, and before you know it, you're a lot less swamped as a parent.
- While chaos may seem to be the modus operandi for kids, structure is what they crave.

According to the Centers for Disease Control and Prevention, "Structure helps parents and their kids. Kids feel safe and secure because they know what to expect. Parents feel confident because they know how to respond, and they respond the same way each time. Routines and rules help structure the home and make life more predictable."[4]

Despite all the benefits associated with chores for kids, it appears to be falling out of favor in our society.

According to a recent survey by *BusyKid*, they found that while more than 90% of parents say they did chores as a child, only 66% of them regularly have their own children do chores.[5]

That honestly doesn't surprise me.

Again, that mindset from parents might be something like this, "Well, I want my kids to have it better than I did when I was a kid. And so, they don't need to do chores."

This is the wrong mindset. And there's research to back it up.

That 85-year Harvard Grant and Glueck study we mentioned in the last chapter followed two groups of people: 268 Harvard graduates from the classes of 1939 through 1944, and 465 men who grew up in poor inner-city neighborhoods in Boston.[6]

The study participants were observed over an 85-year period.

What did they find?

"The researchers found that those who were given chores, as adults ended up being more independent, better able to work in collaborative groups, and better able to understand that doing hard work means you're a valuable member of a community."

Those are the type of kids I want, and those are the types of community members I want as well. Chores are good for kids.

Helping your kids learn the importance of contributing to household responsibilities is a big deal. That's why it's important to be in lockstep with your spouse on the chore rules and schedule.

It takes teamwork and consistency from both parents to help make this life-changing tradition become a habit for your children.

Here are some of the things to discuss upfront with your spouse:

- What are the chores we feel are appropriate for our child?
- Which chores should we pay for, and which ones should we not pay for?
- When is the best time and day to complete these chores?

When we started this whole chore and reward program, my wife and I agreed that our kids would have both "Family Chores" and "Money Chores."

Determine Family Chores vs. Money Chores

Family Chores are activities that our kids do as members of the family.

Some of these chores include putting dirty clothes in the hamper, setting the table before dinner, clearing dishes after meals, and making the bed.

Money Chores are contributions that go above and beyond typical responsibilities.

When our daughter was a 5-year-old, she would receive $1 for each of her money chores.

Some of those activities where she got cash included putting away the silverware, emptying the trash receptacles around the house, and putting away her laundry (after Mom and Dad folded it).

Originally, we found that Saturday morning was the best time to complete the Money Chores with our kids.

In the years that followed, we all agreed that after school would be a better time so the weekends could be set for total relaxation. Do whatever works for your family.

We do our best to stay consistent with a schedule, so it becomes the normal way of life for our kids. When our kids get home from school, they know they have to complete their chores. They are used to it at this point.

My now teenage daughter doesn't require many reminders at all anymore. My preteen son requires some encouragement, but he's gotten so much more responsible over the last few years. Watching his older sister helps a lot.

Do we miss a couple of days here and there? Absolutely.

But overall, the regular schedule has helped our kids succeed and truly brings a sense of harmony to our home.

Age-appropriate Chores

A major key to household chore success is providing tasks that are simple enough to do but are also helpful. Here are some of the chores that fall into the simple yet helpful category. For each age that follows, know that the chores listed are in addition to the previous ones mentioned.

Ages 4–5
- Family Chores
  - Wiping up spills
  - Cleaning up toys
  - Setting napkins and silverware on the table for dinner
  - Putting dirty clothes in the hamper
  - Getting dressed without help
  - Making their bed
  - Putting pillows and blankets away after movie night

- Money Chores
  - Putting folded clothes in the drawers with help
  - Wiping off the counters
  - Vacuuming cars (with help from Mom and Dad)
  - Matching the socks from the laundry
  - Sorting silverware

Ages 6–7

- Family Chores
  - Clearing the dishes after dinner
  - Bringing in the mail from the mailbox
  - Feeding the cat or dog
  - Cleaning their room
- Money Chores
  - Moving clothes from the washer to the dryer
  - Emptying the small garbage receptacles from around the house (with help)
  - Raking leaves outside (with help)
  - Using the small vacuum to clean up the living room or the kitchen (something not too heavy)
  - Washing cars (with help from Mom and Dad)

Ages 8–9

- Family Chores
  - Helping prepare meals
  - Putting away groceries after shopping
  - Loading dishes in the dishwasher
- Money Chores
  - Taking the garbage and the recycling to the curb
  - Washing and drying their own laundry
  - Folding their own laundry (with some help)

Ages 10–11

- Family Chores
  - Bringing in the mail from mailbox
  - Feeding the cat or the dog
  - Washing their own dishes
  - Changing their own bedding
- Money Chores
  - Taking the garbage cans to the street
  - Folding their own laundry in addition to washing it and drying it
  - Emptying the dishwasher
  - Putting away the dishes
  - Putting away the silverware

Ages 12+

- Family Chores
  - Babysitting younger siblings
  - Walking the dog
  - Emptying the litter box for the cat
  - Washing, drying and folding their own laundry (We've moved them from being on the money chore side to the family chore side. After they get to a certain age, these are things that they can do without being paid for it. They are just a part of being in the family.)
- Money Chores
  - Washing the car
  - Cutting the lawn
  - Raking leaves
  - Clearing the snow from the sidewalk or driveway

These are some of the things that we've done with our kids. Everybody's family is unique, and maybe even their kids' abilities are unique.

As they grow older, the things you'd pay for on the Money Chore side can make their way over to the Family Chore side. For example, when your kids are teens, they can do their own laundry because it's something that promotes good hygiene planning and helps them to prepare to be an adult. Honestly, that's not something they should be paid for at that point in their lives.

How to Pay for Chores

Paying for chores varies from family to family. Here are three ways we've explored paying for chores:

- **Pay by Age:** Give a specific dollar amount for every year that they've lived. So, for example, if your son is 10, then he gets $10 per week if he completes all of his chores.
- **Pay by Chore:** With this route, you assign a dollar amount to each chore. Something might have a higher dollar amount or a lower dollar amount. For example, each chore is worth $1. And if they complete their three chores this week, then they get $3, or they can have different values. You can have $1 for the silverware or $2 for washing your own clothes.
- **Pay a Weekly Allowance:** This is when parents pay a set amount of money each week for a specific amount of chores. For example, your daughter receives $5 per week for completing her chores, regardless of her age and regardless of the difficulty of the chores.

I don't believe there is one right way to do this. We have tried them all. When they were young, we had the most success with paying them by their age. As my kids have grown, they have a lot of Family Chores, and they choose to earn money through Money Chores when they want.

Remember, if your kids are paid through their Money Chores, I suggest you use the 60/40 Generational Wealth Plan for distributing that money. That's 60% for smart spending, 20% for investing for the future, 10% for saving, and 10% for giving.

HELP KIDS MAKE MONEY OUTSIDE OF THE HOME

Learning how to contribute and make money at home is a life-changing financial literacy lesson for kids. But what about our kids making money outside of chores and allowance?

There comes a time when your kids may want more money than you are willing to shell out. We don't want to squash their interest in earning. That's when opportunities outside of the home come up.

For kids under 12 years old, working outside of the home needs to come with a warning label. We never ever want to put our kids in harm's way just for them to make some money and maybe learn some lessons from it. Their safety is most important.

They're going to need some parental supervision, but that extra time spent with them will go miles in their future financial independence.

For example, there's the timeless classic of the lemonade stand. Since my kids were 4 or 5 years old, we've done a lemonade stand together. When they were younger, I did most of the heavy lifting, but they helped by filling up cups for customers, greeting customers, and collecting money from customers.

As my kids got older, they did most of the preparation, and I helped with physically moving chairs and tables. Also, I was there when they were selling the lemonade and interacting with the customers that drive by. We want to give them independence and help them grow, but we also want to keep them safe. But the activity pays well. A few hours of doing a lemonade stand and our kids can pull in anywhere from $20 to $80.

One time a guy pulled over and gave our kids a $100 tip. It was absolutely insane. My kids were blown away, and I was blown away. We tried to give the money back to the guy and just say, "No, that's too much." He was very insistent. Our kids are always going to remember the generosity of that individual. The guy said, "We don't see enough lemonade stands anymore. I just wanted to support your kids' entrepreneurship."

Tips like that are very rare, but our kids have gotten $20 tips. They've gotten $5 tips. Most of the time they get few extra bucks, which is just fine for kids who are putting in the effort to earn and serve. Since doing lemonade stands, we now carry money in the glove compartment in our car so that we can always give at least a $5 tip to any lemonade stand we see out there. Our kids love giving and supporting other entrepreneurs in the same fashion.

Outside of lemonade stands, here are other ideas for kids under 12 to make money outside of home:

- Returning aluminum cans for money (We get $0.10 per can in Michigan; if you get no money where you live, this is not a good idea.)
- Selling stuff online with your kids (old video games, old toys, things they don't use anymore that have value)
- Selling things at a garage sale
- Having a bake sale (cookies, brownies, rice Krispy treats)
- Support with a family business (cleaning rental properties, shredding papers, organizing digital files, social media support, editing)
- Water plants for their neighbors

As our kids start to get older, they become more independent and more physically and emotionally mature. Here are some ways to make money outside of the home for teens.

- **Babysit:** As a teen, this was my top way for making money. I was able to find gigs through family, friends and sports teams. The hourly rates have increased significantly since I was a kid. This all depends on your state, but according to Zip Recruiter, the average hourly rate for a sitter nationally in the United States was $13–$20 per hour.[7] My great state of Michigan comes in around $16.76 per hour, which is not too bad. I was not paid that much when I was a kid.
- **Yard work:** Cutting lawns, raking leaves, and shoveling snow are all excellent physical activities that help your kids make money, stay healthy, and it even helps your neighborhood look nice.
- **Sports referee:** Being a referee is another healthy physical activity that helps your teens generate some excellent money as well. Kids in our neighborhood soccer league make $25–$35 per game as referees.
- **Pet sitting or dog walking:** The global pet care industry is expected to balloon to $427 billion by the year 2032.[8] If people are spending billions on their pets, you know they'll have some money for your teen to watch, feed, and walk them.
- **Freelance work:** If your teen has graphic design or video editing skills, they can offer their services as a freelancer. My teenage daughter has edited videos for me on my financial education platform, and I pay her for the work.
- **Become a tutor:** If your teen is really smart in math, English, Spanish, history, or any other subject, they can use those skills and teach others. They can offer their services through school, or they can connect with other kids who need tutoring.
- **Get a regular job:** When kids are of a legal age to work, they can be employed at places like a grocery store, a movie theater, the library, or a fast-food restaurant. Some of this work might be part-time or seasonal, but it can be an easy way to gain experience and learn what work they do or don't like to do.

With kids contributing through work, there's gonna be a desire for us to help as parents. When they're younger, we're going to have to help a lot more. We'd physically help by setting up the lemonade stand or holding the bag while they empty the trash cans around the house. And then we'd emotionally help by listening and helping them calm down when chores or jobs got frustrating. But as they get older, we need to slowly allow them to take on more responsibility.

We don't want to be helicopter parents that hang over their shoulders at every move and not allow them to own their own responsibilities. We want to be travel guides that help them understand the task at hand and then take ownership of it so they can experience the benefits of that responsibility. As parents, our instinct is to helicopter because we don't want our kids to make mistakes or experience hardship, but mistakes help our kids gain knowledge. Mistakes trigger memories that inform our future decisions.[9] As a parent, I would much rather my kids make money mistakes at age 10 with $20 than age 30 with $20,000. The same goes for work. As a parent, I would much rather my kid realize they hate a certain type of job in their teens than get a $200,000 college degree for that field of work and realize they hate it in their 20s and 30s.

Let's let our kids make mistakes. It's good for them.

ENSURE A STUDENT DEBT-FREE COLLEGE GRADUATION

The future cost of college is no joke. The average rate of inflation for college costs has been around 6% over the last 40 years.[10]

As an example, my alma mater, Michigan State University, in the 2025–2026 academic year costs $36,962 for an in-state student. This includes tuition, fees, room, and board. That's around $150,000 for 4 years of in-state tuition if my son or daughter were going to school today.

Fast forward to the year 2030 when my daughter starts her freshman year of college; 6% inflation on that $150,000 in 2030 comes to around $220,000! Add-in my son who will be attending college in 2032, and he'll need around $240,000.

That means I'm looking at around **$460,000** for my two children to eat, sleep, and learn during 4 years of college.

That number makes my head hurt. I want to throw my hands up in the air and quit.

But, I know how important college can be in this country. A study by Georgetown University found that college graduates earn $1 million more over their lifetime than high school graduates.[11] College leads to more education, connections, and money. I would not have the career and the privileges I have today if it weren't for my time in college.

How are we going to cover $460,000 to pay for college without student loans?

Here are some strategies we're going to try as a family and steps I'd suggest for you as parents if you want your child to avoid student debt and eventually own their time.

Start a 529 College Savings Plan Early

Since the cost of college is rising at 6% per year, we're going to need to chase that increase by investing in the stock market. That's where the *529 College Savings Plan* comes in.

This investment tool allows parents to invest in the stock market through a state-sponsored program. Depending on how you invest the money, your 529 college savings plan has the ability to massively outgrow the interest made with a traditional savings account.

We started investing for our daughter in a 529 plan when she was born with a $10,000 initial deposit. Thirteen years later with additional annual contributions, she now has around $70,000 in her account.

Fast forward 5 more years to when she starts school, the difference will become a lot bigger (depending on the market, of course). If our 529 account continues to grow at a conservative rate of 7% per year, she'll have around $100,000 at the start of college. Compound interest pays.

To combat the rising cost of college, we need the stock market on our side. Besides taking advantage of the stock market, 529 college savings plans have significant tax advantages as well.

Help Teens Apply for Scholarships

The easiest $2,000 I ever made was completing a college scholarship application when I was in my undergraduate at Michigan State University. Since I was making around $9 an hour folding sweaters at Eddie Bauer during that time, $2,000 for a few hours of work was well worth it.

Not everyone hits the $2,000 jackpot on the first application; that's why we're going to encourage our kids to do a lot of them. This is free money just waiting to be earned.

After interviewing Pam Andrews on how she helped her son earn $300,000 in private scholarships, I feel confident that my kids can score at least 1/10th of that to support their academic plans. Pam had her son fill out 147 applications, and he only received six awards, but those six netted him $300,000.

Try Community College First

There is absolutely nothing wrong with our kids attending a couple of years of community college. The average cost of community college tuition and fees (without room and board) in the 2022–2023 school year was around $3,800[12] while a 4-year public university came in at $9,750.[13] That's a huge difference.

For a lot of community colleges, your teens are able to take a lot of the prerequisite courses that can transfer over to the university level. This way, they would be taking care of the early coursework at a much cheaper amount.

There's something to "figuring it out" in community college first. Personally, I had no clue what career I wanted at 18 years old. Why spend top dollar when you're just "figuring it out"?

Encourage Part-time Work in College

It will be important for our kids to work during their time in college. They don't need a full-time job. A part-time job and internships will give them a perspective on the real working world that college just won't provide.

Also, by the time they are in their late teens and early twenties, we're going to start transferring over some of the financial responsibility of college. We may have enough to cover their tuition, fees, and books, but if they want to rent a house with some friends during college, that part-time job will definitely come in handy as the "Mom and Dad Bank" starts to run dry.

This will not only help us financially, but it might just help our kids' grades. According to data by the Bureau of Labor Statistics, students who work part-time (20 hours or less) receive better grades.[14] It's a win-win for everyone.

If we're semi-successful in each of these areas, I think that'll add up to a debt-free future for both of our kids. This plan will show our kids that living a debt-free life overall takes effort and sacrifice, but it's worth it in the long run.

As we've discussed earlier, starting off with a debt-free life can lead to a future of time ownership. That's definitely what I want for my kids.

INVEST FOR YOUR CHILD'S FUTURE TIME FREEDOM

When we began our investing journey 15 years ago, we didn't realize the impact of starting early. We thought, "A few thousand dollars wasn't going to get us to a comfortable retirement, right?"

Today, we're amazed at how our balances have grown substantially. Compound interest, patience, and practicing buy and hold passive investing has helped our retirement balances soar to over $850,000 by our mid-forties.

If we didn't contribute another dime for the next 15 years, our retirement accounts could grow to well above $2 million. This assumes a 7% real rate of return. That is the power of compound growth.

Recently, I started thinking about how this same process could be applied to our kids.

With around 50 years before their retirement, time is truly on their side. Outside of investing for their future college expenses, here's how we're saving and investing for our kids' future with compound interest, patience, and buy and hold investing in mind.

Custodial Brokerage Account

To get our kids to understand the power of compound interest and investing, we started a custodial brokerage account for each of them 5 years ago.

This was initially funded as a $1,000 gift from their late grandmother who wanted them to have something special later on in their lives. Our kids have also contributed to their investment accounts through their chore and reward program at home as well as work outside of the home. Although their balances in this investment account are relatively small, these accounts could be perfect for a down payment for their first home or buying their first car in cash in the future.

Custodial Roth IRA

Since my small business is all about my family, I wanted to include my kids in on the fun as well. My son and daughter have been co-hosts on my podcast, supported as video and photography talent on my financial education content, and even shot and edited videos for my social media accounts. For this type of work, I can pay them a fair hourly wage for their time.

This has allowed me to contribute their earnings to a Roth IRA in each of their names. It's been an excellent way to kick start their retirement savings. Over the years, their Roth IRA balances have grown to around $8,000.

Since my net worth was around −$50,000 at 28 years old, I feel proud knowing my kids are light years ahead of where I was at this time.

By the time they reach retirement age, I'm hoping they will thank their parents for getting them on track toward a comfortable retirement.

Our goal is to help them learn the importance of starting early with investing, saving for the important things in the future, and how money is a tool to help you own your time.

Only time will tell if our tactics work. We're amazed at how they've worked for our lives so far. So, we're excited to give it a shot for our kids. That way, we're strengthening our family tree for generations to come.

FROM THE PODCAST

Family: Andrew and Irene Giancola, 35 years old from Florida

Money Milestone: Millionaire couple focused on making millionaire kids

(Host of *The Personal Finance* podcast)

Andy:	*You have a $1.5 million net worth. What is that made up of?*
Andrew:	A big portion of my net worth and what I really want the largest portion of my net worth to be is in my investments. So, getting as many dollars as possible into my investments. And for me, that is index funds and ETFs. And then in the future, I'm interested in investing in real estate as well.
	So, for me, about $750,000 now is in index funds and ETFs. And then the second portion is how much equity I have in my home. So, you can take what your home's value is and then subtract how much you owe on that home. And whatever equity you have available there is how much equity is available that you can add to your net worth. So, for me right now, my home has about $750,000 in equity as well.
	I would much rather have a much higher portion of my net worth in my investments than in my personal residence, because I don't love a personal residence as an investment long term. I think it gets an average of like 3% historically, but I would much rather have it in my index funds and ETFs. So, for me, I would like to increase that net worth on the investment side so that my personal residence isn't so large and isn't such a large portion of my net worth currently.

283

I don't count cars and things like that. We could add those in there. Business assets are kind of hard to evaluate as well. So, for right now, that's kind of where we're standing is between the two. It's kind of a 50–50 right now.

Andy: *I love what you and your wife have done to build wealth for your young family. One big conversation that's come up for a lot of young parents is college. Do you find college to be worth it? And if you do, what are you guys doing to prepare for that higher education expense?*

Andrew: I do think college is worth it in a lot of situations. And when I went to college, I didn't really learn as much on the textbook side or in my classes. What I really learned is how to take care of myself in life and how to finish things. And so, when I went to college, that was a big portion for me.

I think I learned a lot more on the other side by reading books after I left college. But we are preparing for college for our kids. And I think it's a big factor for a lot of people to think through, well, what do you do? Because there's so many different options that you can do when you start to save for college.

I like to use a flexible 529 plan and that is what we put our dollars in. I think it is one where it gives you a lot of flexibility. It gives you a lot of options when you use this and it gives you a lot of tax breaks. And those are the three things that I love about it. So that 529 plan is absolutely incredible.

Andy: *What ways are you teaching your kids about money?*

Andrew: My favorite party trick is to have my 4-year-old tell everybody what an asset and a liability is every time we go to a party. If you're gonna live in my house, you're gonna know how money actually works. And that's one big thing that I'm trying to start as early as possible.

We're starting to have money conversations, real money conversations, because he's processing this information. Maybe we'll go by a house, and I'll say, "You can buy a house like this, and it can make you more money," and explain the process of a rental property. Or I'll show him Disney Plus, for example, if we watch a Disney movie and say, "You can actually buy a piece of Mickey Mouse's company." And this is something where you can own a piece of this company. It's really cool.

There are a lot of studies that have been done where your money psychology is actually set by the age of 7. So how you actually talk about some of this stuff is really important, especially very early on. I want to make sure that we are having positive money conversations and talking about how money can be abundant. And it's something that you can really go out and earn and truly build wealth over time. And so, I love having these conversations with my kid. And I try to start as early as possible.

Andy: *What's advice somebody could take to build wealth for themselves and their children?*

Andrew: One of the biggest things that you can do very early on is understand the levels of wealth. And one big thing that a lot of people will talk about is growing the gap. The gap is one of the most important things that you can do. This is the difference between your income and your expenses. Look at your expenses and say, "Do I need to cut back somewhere?" And sometimes you can't, if you don't make enough money, sometimes you can't cut back. And so, what you have to do is look at the other side of the equation, say, "How can I increase my income?" This is what I had to do when I first started is I had to increase my income because I really couldn't cut back much more without really feeling deprived and not enjoying life whatsoever.

Looking at the two sides of the coin to increase your income, you can negotiate your salary. You can start to have some side hustles as well and increase that income on that side. And then as you grow this gap, the most powerful thing that you can do is take these dollars and put them towards your freedom because most people want to have freedom in life. So, taking these dollars, put them towards your priorities and put them towards your freedom.

You can invest these dollars into some of these areas that we've talked about today. I like index funds and ETFs. You may like a different category, but that is one of the best things that you can do for yourself and for your family is invest those dollars towards your financial freedom.

And what you're gonna see is this is going to start to compound over time. It may feel like it's starting slow. It may feel like it's taking forever. But once you start to get to the point where maybe you have $100,000 invested, for example, then it starts to take off. And you could see compound interest starting to change. This is how you can really have that freedom in place and really see your path to wealth start to accelerate. And this is one of the most powerful things I ever did.

Carpe Diem Action Steps

- Ask yourself if you are "putting your financial oxygen mask on first" before supporting your children's financial future. Are you debt free? Do you have your emergency fund secured? Are you on the path to Coast FIRE? If not, shift your focus back to your financial security and prosperity.

- Start a chore and reward program for your kids at home. Help them learn the importance of contribution around the house and in life. It may be difficult to implement at first, but you are setting them up for a better future.
- Open a bank account for your children where they can spend wisely (with 60% of their earnings), invest (with 20%), give (10%), and save (10%). Use that 60/40 framework throughout their childhood, and hopefully it'll stick when they become adults.
- Research 529 college savings plans to support your children's future career and earning abilities. Start contributing as early as possible only if you and your spouse have your family finances set first.
- When your children have earned income (outside of chores at home), consider a Custodial Roth IRA (aka Roth IRA for kids). Get compound interest working in their favor early. That way, they can achieve Coast FIRE earlier than you. This opens up opportunities for them to work less and live more.

NOTES

1. Williams, R. O. (n.d.). *Celebrating more than 60 years of preparing heirs* [Online]. Williams Group. Available at: https://www.thewilliamsgroup. org/our-story/
2. Baron, J. and Lachenauer, R. (2021, July 19). Do most family businesses really fail by the third generation? *Harvard Business Review.* Available at: https://hbr. org/2021/07/do-most-family-businesses-really-fail-by-the-third-generation
3. Onque, R. (2024). An act of generosity is one of the "quickest and easiest ways to get happier"—here's why. *CNBC.* Available at: https://www.cnbc.com/ 2024/02/28/heres-the-science-behind-why-you-feel-happier-after-being-generous.html
4. CDC. (2024). *Tips for building structure* [Online]. Available at: https://www. cdc.gov/parenting-toddlers/structure-rules/structure.html
5. Miller, K. (2019). Should your kids do chores? we asked the experts and TBH, their answer might surprise you. *Parade.* Available at: https://parade.com/ 923850/korinmiller/should-kids-do-chores/

6. Harvard. (2015). *Study of adult development* [Online]. Available at: https://www.adultdevelopmentstudy.org/grantandglueckstudy

7. Port, D. R. and Srinivasan, H. (2024). The average hourly rate for a babysitter in every state. *Parents*. Available at: https://www.parents.com/parenting/money/hourly-babysitting-rate-states/

8. Fortune Business Insights. (2025). *Pet care market size, share & industry analysis* [Online]. Available at: https://www.fortunebusinessinsights.com/pet-care-market-104749

9. Einhorn, C. S. (2024, September 25). How to learn from your mistakes and make better decisions. *Harvard Business Review*. Available at: https://hbr.org/2024/09/how-to-learn-from-your-mistakes-and-make-better-decisions

10. JP Morgan. (2024). *Tuition inflation* [Online]. Available at: https://am.jpmorgan.com/us/en/asset-management/adv/investment-strategies/college-planning-essentials/viewer/college-costs/cpe-ccinflation/

11. High school graduates earn $1MILLION less over a lifetime than college grads (and picking the wrong major could cost $3.4m). (2015, May 9). *Daily Mail*. Available at: https://www.dailymail.co.uk/news/article-3075189/High-school-graduates-earn-1-million-lifetime-graduate-college-new-report-finds.html

12. Hanson, M. (2024). *Average cost of community college* [Online]. Education Data Initiative. Available at: https://educationdata.org/average-cost-of-community-college

13. Hanson, M. (2025). *Average cost of college & tuition* [Online]. Education Data Initiative. Available at: https://educationdata.org/average-cost-of-college

14. Schneider, M. (2022). *Full-time college students who work part-time reap better grades and graduate with less debt* [Online]. McPherson College. Available at: https://www.mcpherson.edu/2022/02/full-time-college-students-who-work-part-time-reap-better-grades-and-graduate-with-less-debt/

CONCLUSION

Pursuing life goals that are outside of the norm of general society is difficult. By definition, you are choosing to be someone that doesn't fit in with the majority.

When we make positive financial choices that will help us own more of our time in the future, it can feel awkward and difficult when we spend time with people who don't do the same.

But if living and working like the majority of people do doesn't feel right, it's time to choose.

Grin and bear the corporate path you're not enjoying until you reach traditional retirement age? Or spend most of your money in accordance with your family values and invest some of it so you can ditch the corporate grind and enjoy more time freedom earlier?

In this book, we've outlined the 10 steps you can take to make the latter a reality in your life. It has worked for my family and hundreds of other families I've interviewed. We're using our newfound time freedom to live healthier, well-rounded lives, invest in our marriages, and give our children a better tomorrow.

While we are not in the majority today, I'm hopeful over time that this simple solution to family time deprivation will become a path out of the cubicle and back into life. Carpe diem!

ACKNOWLEDGMENTS

'm honored to share our family story. Of course, it would not be possible without my family. Ever since I started my podcast a decade ago, my wife and kids have been incredibly supportive. They have worked alongside me as podcast co-hosts, video editors, and social media assistants. I'm grateful for their love and patience as I've ventured into this world of solopreneurship.

My mom and dad, who demonstrated the importance of "family first" as I was growing up, have been some of my biggest supporters during the last decade as well. Mom, thank you for being my first subscriber and sharing it with your friend's children. Dad, thank you for listening to the show and calling me to chat about the topics and guests. Your love and support have shown me that love is a verb, not a noun.

To my entrepreneurial siblings and brother-in-law, thank you for demonstrating how to create something of your own. Watching you pursue what you wanted and winning inspired me to win too.

To the Marriage Kids and Money Community, I'm forever grateful for your trust and support over the last decade. The fact that this simple message of family wealth and happiness has impacted thousands of you across the world fills me with so much pride. If you watched a video, listened to a podcast, read an article, or laughed at a ridiculous social media post of ours, I thank you and I hope you're ready for more.

To my friends who have stuck with me and my family as our lives have evolved over the years, I cherish your friendship. I know it's not easy when people change. Our family goal has been to move in a direction that gives us more time freedom. That long-term goal has led to some short-term sacrifice. You've been there to support us, evolve with us, and understand when we've had to say, "No thanks, but how about this idea instead?"

To my book agent Elaine Spencer from the Knight Agency, thank you for making this book come to life. I'm excited to hold it in my hands and see other families doing the same.

To Judith Newlin and Stacey Rivera from Wiley for keeping me on task and on-time. I hope this newbie author has been a good partner to work with.

To my local library, your internet connection was reliable, your staff was friendly, and your workspaces were plentiful. Thank you for being my writing sanctuary for the last 6 months.

To the hundreds of families that I had the pleasure of interviewing over the last decade, your transparency, vulnerability, and willingness to serve is a true gift to the world. I hope your positive action-based words inspire millions of families in the years to come.

And I have a special last note to my wife, Nicole. You are the best thing that has ever happened to me. I would not be the man I am today without your love. Thank you for trusting me when things got tough. Thank you for putting up with my "And-And-Andy" nature. Thank you for sharing your story and your light to thousands of people you don't know. You are a shining light in this world, and I'm grateful to be the man that walks alongside you.

ABOUT THE AUTHOR

Andy Hill, AFC®, is the award-winning family finance coach behind Marriage Kids and Money—a platform dedicated to helping families build wealth and happiness.

Andy's advice and personal finance experience have been featured in major media outlets like CNBC, Forbes, MarketWatch, Kiplinger's Personal Finance, and NBC News. With more than 10 million podcast downloads and video views, Andy's message of family financial empowerment has resonated with listeners, readers, and viewers across the world.

When he's not "talking money," Andy enjoys being a soccer dad, singing karaoke with his wife, and relaxing on his hammock.

INDEX